VOCABULARY
for
ADVANCED READING
COMPREHENSION
the keyword approach

VOCABULARY for ADVANCED READING COMPREHENSION

the keyword approach

JOHN T. CROW

North Texas State University

Prentice Hall Regents, Englewood Cliffs, NJ 07632

Library of Congress Cataloging-in-Publication Data

Crow, John T.
  Vocabulary for advanced reading comprehension.

  Includes index.
  1. Vocabulary. 2. College readers. 3. English
language—Textbooks for foreign speakers. I. Title.
PE1449.C68 1986   428.1   85–19253
ISBN 0–13–942988–3

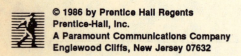

© 1986 by Prentice Hall Regents
Prentice-Hall, Inc.
A Paramount Communications Company
Englewood Cliffs, New Jersey 07632

Printed in the United States of America

11

ISBN 0-13-942988-3

Prentice-Hall International (UK) Limited, *London*
Prentice-Hall of Australia Pty. Limited, *Sydney*
Prentice-Hall Canada Inc., *Toronto*
Prentice-Hall Hispanoamericana, S.A., *Mexico*
Prentice-Hall of India Private Limited, *New Delhi*
Prentice-Hall of Japan, Inc., *Tokyo*
Simon & Schuster Asia Pte. Ltd., *Singapore*
Editora Prentice-Hall do Brasil, Ltda., *Rio de Janeiro*

Contents

Acknowledgments

Tradition requires that an author place his or her name in conspicuous places at the front of a book and that people who "only assisted" be relegated to a page that few people bother to read. The simple truth is that this project would never have come to fruition without the assistance of several people, and I wish there were some way to have their names displayed more prominently. I express my sincerest gratitude:

To Nancy Strickland for giving me the initial idea upon which this text was constructed.

To Tom Hoemeke for writing the computer programs that allowed me to keep accurate records of the words. The index of this book I owe to his programming ability. The fact that I rarely (and only consciously) used the same word more than one time is also due to his computer expertise.

To Jean Zupanchich Crow for her constant encouragement and innumerable contributions. Whenever I experienced difficulties, I turned to her. Some of these sentences, then, are hers, and many of the keyword groups were formed after consultation with her. In addition to collaborating throughout the preparation, she also painstakingly proofread the entire manuscript, correcting my errors and improving upon my style.

To Lisa Marie and John Emory Crow for assisting in some of the more tedious aspects of preparing this text, for putting together several of the crossword puzzles, and for helping me proof the exercises.

To June Quigley for carrying out experimental procedures to determine the effectiveness of the approach. She also provided innumerable suggestions, corrections, and revisions based on her classroom experience with the manuscript. Without her input the text would have suffered noticeably.

To Kim Jindra and Gaye Childress for coming up with the games that are described in the Directions for the Teacher.

To the entire teaching staff of the North Texas State University Intensive English Language Institute for trying various versions of the manuscript in the classroom. They provided me with invaluable pedagogical suggestions and typographical corrections.

To Terry Tehan for assisting with some of the initial typing and for providing logistical and spiritual support from start to finish.

To the administrative staff of the Intensive English Language Institute for occasionally taking on additional duties so as to give me more time to devote to this project.

To all of these people I owe an incalculable debt. I bear sole responsibility for any inaccuracies that this text may contain; any success that it may enjoy, however, is due largely to my family and to my colleagues.

*To my parents, Emory S. and Georgia Reeves Crow,
for their patient, kind, and unselfish support throughout the years*

Directions for the Student

Before you begin to use this book, it is very important that you understand its purpose clearly. This book will teach you to recognize words while you are reading. It is *not* designed to teach you how to use words when you are speaking or writing. Let's look at what this means, why it is important, and what you should do with the material covered in this book.

Active and Passive Vocabulary

Words that we use when we speak or write are called **active.** Words that we recognize when we hear them or read them are called **passive.** We normally do not use passive vocabulary when we speak or write. Maybe we do not know what grammar to use with such words. Maybe we do not know *exactly* what they mean. Whatever the reason, these passive words are *not* part of our language when we produce sentences. They do not, however, cause a problem for us when we see them or hear them: we know what they mean well enough to understand them when someone else uses them.

A native speaker of any language has a much larger passive vocabulary than active vocabulary. As a result, he or she can read difficult material without stopping to use a dictionary all the time. In contrast, a person who studies a foreign language, even at the advanced level, quite often has a passive vocabulary that is only a little larger than his or her active vocabulary. Therefore, the biggest single problem for the advanced student when reading is a poor *passive* vocabulary.

Statistical Information

Statistical analyses of spoken English show that an active vocabulary of 2,000 words is enough for everyday conversations. Of course the average native speaker of English has an active vocabulary that is much larger than 2,000 words and can, therefore, discuss a wide range of topics. Nevertheless, you, the advanced student of English, already have an active vocabulary that is large enough to allow you to be understood in most social situations.

On the other hand, an average American university freshman has a passive vocabulary of 60,000 to 100,000 words in English. If you, using word lists, could learn 25 words a day, *and* never forget them (which is impossible, of course), you would need more than 6 and a half *years* to learn 60,000 words—studying seven days a week, 365 days a year!

What Can You Do?

If you want to learn to read advanced English quickly and efficiently, you must *stop* trying to learn every word actively. You must learn to accept the idea that, in order to read, you do *not* have to understand exactly what every word means. You do *not* have to be able to translate every word into your native language. You *cannot* try to learn to use every word. You need to work on building a large recognition (passive) vocabulary so that you do not have to stop after every few words to use a dictionary.

The Purpose of This Book

This book will help you develop your passive vocabulary. You will learn to substitute easier words for more difficult ones as you read. Always remember, however, that you *cannot* freely substitute one of the related words for another as you speak or write. Look at the following sentence:

A1. He flew into a rage.

If you learn that **rage** means something like **anger,** a word you already know, you can understand what the above sentence means. You cannot put **anger** in the sentence because **to fly into a rage** is an idiom. However, knowledge of how this idiom works is not important in reading. You *can* understand that the sentence means, "He became angry." Thus you understand the sentence *passively,* even if you cannot produce it *actively,* and you can continue to read.

One of the reasons, then, for *not* substituting related words involves idioms. There are at least two other reasons: exact meaning and grammatical structure. For example, you will learn that **veer** and **deflect** both mean **change direction (of).** However, their exact meanings differ, and so do the grammatical structures that they require. Look at the following sentences:

B1. The road veers to the right.
C1. Water deflects rays of light.

Exact Meaning: The subject of **veer** is what changes direction. It can be a thing that moves or a thing that does not move. However, the direct object of **deflect** is usually the thing that changes directions, and this thing is usually moving in a straight line. It almost always changes directions because it hits something else.

Grammatical Structure: In grammatical terms, **veer** is intransitive. It cannot take a direct object. In contrast, **deflect** can be transitive (see C1 above) or intransitive.

The keyword can be mentally substituted for meaning in both sentences. The style is not as good, but you can understand the idea:

B2. The road changes directions to the right.
C2. Water changes the direction of rays of light.

However, you cannot exchange **veer** and **deflect.** The grammar and the meaning would be wrong. But, again, you will never be required to choose proper words when reading—the author has done that. Your job is to understand; so the keyword substititution works.

As you are studying this book, remember the following:

1. You are developing your passive vocabulary, not your active vocabulary.
2. You will *not* be able to use all of the words in this book in your writing or speaking: you will not understand them well enough to utilize them actively.
3. Although you will learn that five difficult words have more or less the same basic idea, you cannot freely substitute any one of the words for another.
4. The final product of this book is that, when reading, you will be able to substitute in your mind an easier word for a more difficult word. This will often give you enough information to allow you to continue reading without stopping to look up the word in your dictionary.

How This Book Works

Each chapter begins by introducing **keywords** and **related words.** You will then do exercises designed to help you remember which keyword goes with which related words. The final exercises are reading passages that use the related words, many of which you probably did not know. If you can read the words, substitute the proper keyword in your mind, and continue reading with good understanding, you have successfully learned the material in that chapter.

If, by the way, you find a related word in a group that is easier to you as a keyword, make that word the keyword and put the keyword in the list of related words. The important thing is that you have *one thought* in your mind with a meaning that you understand clearly and that you can substitute it for the related words when you read.

As you do the exercises in this book, you will see that you can acquire an increased passive vocabulary quickly and easily. The words that you have learned in this manner will allow you to understand countless other related words. The final exercise in Chapters 2 through 9 will show you some of the ways that words change by adding or changing beginnings and endings. Words from previous chapters will be used so that you can review their meanings.

Just remember that, as an advanced student of English, the biggest single problem for you in reading is vocabulary. Complex grammatical structures bother you only occasionally; usually it is the number of unknown words that interferes. Since you cannot learn all of the words actively, and since you do not *need* to have active knowledge of all the words in order to read them, you must build your passive vocabulary as quickly and as efficiently as possible. That is exactly what this book will help you do!

After This Book

No method for learning passive vocabulary works unless you *read.* You will begin to forget the words you have learned if you do not continue to read after completing the exercises. Read anything that interests you. Read as much as possible. Whenever you see a word that you studied in this text, but whose keyword you have forgotten, look it up in the index of this text rather than in a dictionary. The next time you see it, you will have a much better chance of remembering its keyword than its dictionary definition.

Words often have more than one meaning. The keywords in this book usually represent the most common meaning of related words. However, you may occasionally find that substitution of the keyword does not work. If the meaning of the word is important for the understanding of the reading, you might need to look it up in a dictionary to see its other meanings.

As you continue to read, these words and their derivations will become your friends. You will begin to acquire more active knowledge of the more useful words. Then, and only then, should you try using them in conversation or in writing.

Conclusion

This book is *not* magic. You must study, do the exercises, and read. The approach *does* work, however. You will find yourself learning words more quickly than ever before. Like all things in life, though, the results you get from using this text depend directly upon how hard you try.

Directions for the Teacher*

Nonnative English speakers who are bound for the university or whose jobs require that they read various professional publications often experience difficulties with the reading task. Although they are able to communicate effectively, they lack the skills required to do the reading quickly and accurately. The largest single obstruction to their reading is an inadequate **passive** vocabulary. This text for advanced students is designed to build a large recognition vocabulary in a short time.

Each chapter contains 36 groups of words. Each group consists of a word or phrase that the student should already know, which is called the **keyword,** and five words that are similar in meaning, which are called **related words.** All of the exercises are designed to reinforce the association between the keyword and its related words. The ultimate goal is increased reading comprehension; achievement of the goal relies on the following procedure: when the student encounters one of the related words in a reading passage, he or she can mentally substitute the keyword—that is, the concept—and continue to read without stopping to look up a new word. Obviously, the five related words and their keyword cannot always be exactly interchanged; however, substituting the keyword for a related word will give the student enough information to allow the reading comprehension process to continue.

Each chapter is divided into three main parts:

1. Three groups of 12 keywords, each keyword having five related words. The students begin to familiarize themselves with each keyword group by completing introductory exercises at the discourse, word, and sentence level. Many of the sentence-level exercises are contextualized. Each keyword group is numbered, and the numbers are given in parentheses in the exercises to facilitate looking back as necessary.
2. Exercises utilizing all 36 keyword groups. The objective continues to be the reinforcement of the connection between the related words and their keywords.
3. Reading passages incorporating many of the related words in context. There are two parts:
   a. Reading passages with related words in boldface type to assist the student. The student should write keywords in blanks below the passages.

---

*If you have not read Directions for the Student, pp. ix–xii, please do so before reading Directions for the Teacher.

b. An advanced reading passage from a text or journal. Actually, this passage served as the basis for deriving the keyword groups in the first place, so at least one related word from each keyword group appears in the passage. These words are not, however, identified for the student. His or her task is to read the passage without a dictionary and to answer the comprehension questions given as part of the prereading introduction for each passage. A prereading passage is provided, and difficult vocabulary items that have not been dealt with previously are explained. The ultimate goal is reading comprehension, not vocabulary manipulation.

Beginning with Chapter 2, an additional section follows the final reading passage: an exercise on word derivations. Some common ways of deriving nouns from adjectives, adjectives from nouns, nouns from verbs, and the like are given, and the student practices substituting keywords for related word derivatives. Only words from preceding chapters are used, so that this exercise also serves as a review of previous material.

None of the exercises calls for **active** production from the students; the text is intended to instill **passive** vocabulary skills. The teacher should never, for example, require students to use any of the related words in a sentence. Sentence production is an active skill; the goal of this text is rapid *passive* vocabulary acquisition.

The reading selections upon which each chapter is based have been drawn from a variety of textbooks used mainly at the university freshman level. (See the Contents for the disciplines covered.) Technical terms that relate to a specific field are, by and large, not included as part of the keyword groups. The primary thrust is to familiarize students with the vocabulary that is used to describe phenomena or define terms.

Much of the material in this text can and should be done as homework. The teacher's main area of responsibility is, happily, the most enjoyable one. Working with the various keyword groups can be great fun if the teacher creates the proper environment. The material lends itself wonderfully to games. Adaptations of television games such as *Concentration, Password,* and *Family Feud,* for example, have been used successfully to enliven the process of learning keyword groups. Suggested rules for each game follow.

Concentration.   Select two related words from each of 12 keyword groups. Write each word on a 3-by-5-inch card, mix up the cards, and place them face down in a geometrical pattern. Divide the class into two teams. A player from one team selects any two cards and turns them over. If the player thinks that the words do not match, that is, that they do not come from the same keyword group, then he or she turns the cards face down in their original places and a player from the other team repeats the process. If they match, that is, if they are from the same keyword group, the player must name the keyword *or* another related word. If successful, the player's team is awarded the two cards. If unsuccessful, the cards are turned face down in their original places and the next team takes its turn. The game ends when all of the cards have been awarded. The team having the most cards is, of course, the winner.

Password.   Write each of the keywords on a separate slip of paper. Divide the class into pairs. Select two pairs to play against each other so there are two teams, Team A and Team B, each with two members: A1/A2 and B1/B2. Show the *same* keyword to A1 and B1. A1 says a related word to A2. If A2 is able to give the correct keyword, Team A is awarded a point. If not, B1 then says another related word to B2, and this team tries to give the correct keyword. Each round can go between the pairs twice. Teams take turns going first. The first team to accumulate five points wins. However, a team must win by at least *two* points, and play continues until one team is two points ahead. It is also possible to have three pairs competing simultaneously. *Note:* There should be no penalty for pronunciation, and the teacher should help with pronunciation when necessary.

Keyword Feud.   Divide the class into two teams. Have the students face each other. The teacher gives a keyword to the first member of one team. He or she has to give a related word. The team then has the option of playing in the category or passing it to the other team. If a team decides to play, each member of the team, in turn, must supply one related word. If one team member cannot provide a previously unstated related word, the opposing team is allowed to confer in an attempt to come up with one. If they are successful, they are awarded a point; if not, the first team is awarded a point. Of course, if the original team comes up with all five related words, it receives the point. The process is then repeated, giving a member of the other team the first opportunity. Remember that team members are not allowed to confer unless they are attempting to steal a point from the opposing team. Again, the teacher should willingly help with pronunciation.

In addition to providing an atmosphere of friendly cooperation and competition, teachers should use class time to:

1. Assign material in a timely manner. The text is designed to be completed in one semester.
2. Discuss concepts that the keyword groups embody. While some students may need little assistance in understanding the semantic field involved, others will need some elaboration by the teacher to refine and reinforce their comprehension and retention.
3. Provide mechanisms to insure that students are doing the work. Spot check exercises, give quizzes (on recognition skills only!), and so on.
4. Discuss the reading selections at the end of each chapter, both before and after the students have read them.
5. Ensure that students have a healthy diet of additional reading assignments both while they are using and after they have completed this text.

During class, however, the teacher should *not:*

1. Go over each question of each exercise.
2. Spend time discussing differences in meaning or grammatical environment of the words in a keyword group. You will not have time in a semester to do that adequately, and your students will not remember most of what you say.
3. Spend much time on pronunciation. Pronouncing the words or having the students pronounce them after you provides an additional source of sensory input for the students. However, the ultimate goal is recognition in a reading environment, which does not require that students know how to pronounce these words.
4. Require students to use the words actively. Never, for example, ask the stu-

dents to use any related words in original sentences. Also be careful to test only for recognition skills, primarily in fully specified contexts.

Always remember that the related words are *not* intended to be synonyms. They are included with a keyword because, in at least one meaning of the word, the keyword or phrase can be substituted for comprehension.

If, as you are using this text, you find errors or have suggestions for improving the approach, please write to a very grateful

John T. Crow
Department of English
North Texas State University
Denton, Texas 76203

1 Scientific Experimentation

Very important: *Please read the proper introduction (see page ix or page xiii) before beginning to use this text.*

EXERCISE 1

In the following paragraph one word in each sentence is in heavy type. Find the keyword from the list below that is closest in meaning to each of these words, and write the keyword in the proper blank underneath the paragraph. Check your answers by looking at Exercise 2.

KEYWORDS

smart	method	to show where	to choose
crazy	doubt	usual	to invent
to twist	only	to persuade	very

What if there had been an **ingenious** man 50 years ago who could see into the future? Although this man would have been unable to **create** a computer-like machine himself, he could have told people what the machine would do in the 1990s. Everyone would have thought that he was **insane.** Today, however, it is not necessary to **urge** people to believe in the power of computers. Computers have become as **ordinary** as telephones in our daily lives. They are **immensely** powerful machines that can be used in many areas of life. Every day, scientists are finding new **processes** that depend upon the speed and accuracy of computers. However, even though everybody today can appreciate the power of computers, many people have serious **misgivings** about their effect on humanity. These people are afraid that computer technology will somehow **contort** human beings of the future. They fear that future humans will **pick** a direction away from thinking and toward automation. Such people would use their minds **merely** to decide which button to push. Are they right? It is, of course, hundreds of years too early to know, but early signs **indicate** that they are wrong.

ingenious	_____	create	_____
insane	_____	urge	_____
ordinary	_____	immensely	_____
processes	_____	misgivings	_____
contort	_____	pick	_____
merely	_____	indicate	_____

EXERCISE 2

The first word in each group below is the keyword. All the words under each keyword (the related words) have similar meaning. Read each group and try to remember which related words go with each keyword.

1. **crazy**
   insane
   mad
   maniacal
   lunatic
   deranged

2. **very**
   extremely
   intensely
   considerably
   immensely
   exceedingly

3. **doubt**
   hesitation
   qualm
   uncertainty
   suspicion
   misgiving

4. **to invent**
   contrive
   create
   forge
   think up
   devise

5. **to twist**
   disfigure
   contort
   bend
   warp
   distort

6. **method**
   process
   way
   manner
   system
   procedure

7. **to choose**
   select
   pick
   elect
   single out
   opt

8. **only**
   just
   simply
   merely
   exclusively
   solely

9. **to show where**
   indicate
   point to
   designate
   disclose
   denote

10. **usual**
   ordinary
   everyday
   customary
   normal
   commonplace

11. **smart**
   ingenious
   cunning
   clever
   intelligent
   shrewd

12. **to persuade**
   convince
   urge
   convert
   talk into
   coax

EXERCISE 3

A. The 12 groups of related words are written below without keywords. Write the correct keyword over each keyword group.

B. Each group of related words has *one* word that does not belong in the group.

Find that word, cross it out, and write it under the group to which it belongs. The first one is done for you as an example.

KEYWORDS

smart	**method**	**to show where**	**to choose**
crazy	doubt	usual	to invent
to twist	only	to persuade	very

1. ~~crazy~~

insane
mad
~~shrewd~~
maniacal
lunatic
deranged

2. _very_

extremely
intensely
considerably
~~solely~~
immensely
exceedingly

3. _doubt_

hesitation
~~procedure~~
qualm
uncertainty
suspicion
misgiving

4. _invent_

contrive
create
forge
~~denote~~
think up
devise

5. _to twist_

disfigure
devise
contort
bend
warp

6. _method_

process
way
manner
misgiving
system
procedure

7. _to choose_

select
pick
elect
coax
single out
opt

8. _only_

~~exceedingly~~
just
simply
exclusively
merely
solely

9. _to show where_

indicate
point to
opt
designate
disclose
denote

10. _usual_

ordinary
deranged
everyday
customary
normal
commonplace

11. _smart_

ingenious
cunning
clever
intelligent
commonplace
shrewd

12. _persuade_

convince
urge
convert
distort
talk into
coax

═══════════════════════════════

EXERCISE 4

═══════════════════════════════

Each sentence below contains one keyword, which is in heavy type.

A. Find the word below each sentence that is *not* a related word for the keyword. Circle that word. (The keyword numbers from Exercise 2 are in parentheses. These will help you if you need to look back.)

B. After completing instruction A, write each circled word under the keyword in the sentence to which it belongs.

1. Scientists have found new **methods** for getting oil out of the ground.

   a. ways   b. systems   c. processes   d. suspicion (6)

              (9)

2. Her view of life was **twisted** after the accident.

    a. contorted   b. singled out   c. distorted (5)

3. Because of the robbery, the storekeeper was **persuaded** to buy new locks.

    a. denoted   b. urged   c. coaxed (into buying) (12)

4. The statue **showed** the spot **where** the king had been killed.

    a. designated   b. indicated   c. forged   d. pointed to (9)

5. Necessity has forced mankind to **invent** a truly remarkable number of tools.

    a. create   b. warp   c. devise (4)

6. In order to succeed in business, a person must be **smart** as well as hard-working.

    a. cunning   b. intelligent   c. clever   d. lunatic (11)

7. The teacher **chose** a student to represent the school in the speech contest.

    a. talked into   b. picked   c. selected (7)

8. His **crazy** actions got him into a lot of trouble.

    a. maniacal   b. mad   c. customary   d. deranged (1)

9. The new information only increased my **doubts** about the success of the missions.

    a. qualms   b. uncertainties   c. misgivings   d. procedures (3)

10. The lawyer was **very** pleased about the results of the election.

    a. exceedingly   b. simply   c. extremely (2)

11. The teacher did not seem to be in his **usual** good mood that day.

    a. normal   b. ordinary   c. shrewd (10)

12. I attended the lecture **only** for the purpose of seeing who was there.

    a. just   b. merely   c. solely   d. immensely (8)

EXERCISE 5

In the following paragraph one word in each sentence is in heavy type. Find the keyword from the list below that is closest in meaning to each of these words, and write the keyword in the proper blank underneath the paragraph. Check your answers by looking at Exercise 6.

KEYWORDS

obvious	**bit**	**choice**	**agreement**
to mystify	**safe**	**change**	**to control**
serious	**to explain**	**co-worker**	**to get**

It is an **apparent** fact that computers are an important part of life today. However, many people wonder whether humans of the future will **direct** the computer or whether the opposite will be true. Perhaps we can **account for** this fear as follows. It is human nature to dislike anything that causes **alteration** in one's life-style. Since there is **unanimity** of opinion that computers have made and will continue to make our lives different, this is one reason for fear. A second reason is that, since many people do not understand the limits of computers, they are **perplexed** by them and afraid of them. However, as computers become cheaper to buy and easier to use, more people are **procuring** their own personal computers for use at home. As a result, the public is learning that, while computers may be good "**collaborators**," they can only do exactly what humans tell them to do. In addition, the smallest **speck** of dust in the wrong place can cause the machines to break down. These limitations, and others, are **grave** ones. So, although people know that they will never be able to have an **option** of a life free from computers in the future, they are becoming less afraid of them. They are learning that computers can be both **innocuous** and helpful machines for improving the quality of life.

apparent	_ovious_	direct	_to control_
account for	_to explain_	alteration	_CHANGE_
unanimity	_agreement_	perplexed	_to mystify_
procuring	_to get_	collaborators	_co-worker_
speck	_bit_	grave	_serious_
option	_CHOICE_	innocuous	_safe_

EXERCISE 6

The first word in each group below is the keyword. All the words under each keyword (the related words) have similar meaning. Read each group and try to remember which related words go with each keyword.

13. **safe**
    innocuous
    innocent
    harmless
    secure
    inoffensive

14. **change**
    modification
    alteration
    variation
    diversity
    variety

15. **agreement**
    accord
    unanimity
    concordance
    unity
    congruence

16. **to explain**
    clarify
    shed light on
    elucidate
    account for
    clear up

17. **obvious**
    evident
    apparent
    conspicuous
    glaring
    distinct

18. **choice**
    preference
    determination
    pick
    selection
    option

19. **serious**
    profound
    weighty
    critical
    grave
    important

20. **to mystify**
    puzzle
    bewilder
    perplex
    baffle
    confound

21. **to control**	22. **bit**	23. **co-worker**	24. **to get**
manage	trace	associate	attain
manipulate	speck	collaborator	gather
operate	trifle	colleague	secure
govern	shade	partner	procure
direct	particle	comrade	obtain

EXERCISE 7

A. The 12 groups of related words are written below without keywords. Write the correct keyword over each keyword group.

B. Each group of related words has *one* word that does not belong in the group. Find that word, cross it out, and write it under the group to which it belongs. The first one is done for you as an example.

KEYWORDS

obvious	bit	choice	agreement
to mystify	safe	change	to control
serious	to explain	co-worker	to get

13. _____ safe _____	14. _____ change _____	15. _____ AGREEMENT _____	16. _____ TO EXPLAIN _____
innocuous	modification	accord	clarify
innocent	alteration	unanimity	shed light on
harmless	variation	(option)	elucidate
secure	(particle)	unity	account for
~~profound~~	variety	congruence	manipulate
Inoffensive	_diversity_	_Concordance_	_to clear up_

17. _____ OVIOUS _____	18. _____ choice _____	19. _____ serious _____	20. _____ to mystify _____
evident	preference	(conspicuous)	puzzle
apparent	determination	weighty	bewilder
(inoffensive)	pick	critical	procure
glaring	selection	grave	baffle
distinct	(colleague)	important	confound
Conspicuous	_option_	**profound**	_perplex_

21. _____ to control _____	22. _____ bit _____	23. _____ co-worker _____	24. _____ to get _____
manage	trace	associate	attain
clear up	speck	collaborator	gather
operate	trifle	(diversity)	secure
govern	shade	partner	(perplex)
direct	(concordance)	comrade	obtain
manipulate	_particle_	_colegga_	_procure_

EXERCISE 8

Each sentence below contains one keyword, which is in heavy type.

A. Find the word below each sentence that is *not* a related word for the keyword. Circle that word. (The keyword numbers from Exercise 6 are in parentheses. These will help you if you need to look back.)

B. After completing instruction A, write each circled word under the keyword in the sentence to which it belongs.

1. He was **mystified** by her sudden change in behavior.

   a. perplexed   b. baffled   c. bewildered   d. gathered (20)

2. The **agreement** of the group was threatened by the important issue that faced the members.

   a. concordance   b. accord   c. unanimity   d. partner (15)

3. His **co-worker** suddenly felt a strong desire to go into business by himself.

   a. associate   b. speck   c. colleague   d. collaborator (23)

4. The detective **got** his information slowly and carefully.

   a. shed light on   b. obtained   c. secured   d. procured (24)

5. The powerful dictator **controlled** every aspect of the citizens' lives.

   a. manipulated   b. governed   c. puzzled   d. directed (21)

6. A **bit** of dust in the wrong place can interfere with the delicate machinery.

   a. trace   b. variation   c. particle (22)

7. It was not a question of **choice;** all members were forced to attend the meeting.

   a. unity   b. determination   c. option (18)

8. The police were hoping that the new information would **explain** what had happened.

   a. clarify   b. clear up   c. account for   d. manage (16)

9. I awoke to the **obvious** sound of the front door closing.

   a. conspicuous   b. apparent   c. weighty (17)

10. Life is full of **serious** decisions.

   a. critical   b. innocent   c. important (19)

11. What she said seemed **safe** enough at the time, but later on, it got her into a lot of trouble.

   a. inoffensive   b. harmless   c. distinct   d. innocuous (13)

12. In the desert there is very little **change** in the weather.

   a. diversity   b. preference   c. variety (14)

EXERCISE 9

In the following paragraph one word in each sentence is in heavy type. Find the keyword from the list below that is closest in meaning to each of these words, and write the keyword in the proper blank underneath the paragraph. Check your answers by looking at Exercise 10.

KEYWORDS

huge	**hard**	**to guess**	**observable**
real	**large**	**short-lived**	**to declare**
to scare	**danger**	**to cause**	**lie**

True scientists never **speculate.** If they want to know what **brought** something **about,** they must find out through careful experiments. Their control over the experimental environment must be **exacting.** They look for **valid** information that comes from their experiments. They must always remember the **risk** they take if they make a decision too quickly. Sometimes **considerable** differences appear suddenly. These may seem to have a **massive** effect on people's lives, either positive or negative. If scientists publicize these results immediately, they may **alarm** the general public. However, further experimentation and analysis may show that these differences are **temporary.** So, although **striking** differences may appear quickly, good scientists are careful and patient. When good scientists **avow** that something is true, they must be certain, basing their conclusions on a complete analysis. Neither mistakes nor **distortion** has a place in the scientific world.

speculate	_____		brought about	_____
exacting	_____		valid	_____
risk	_____		considerable	_____
massive	_____		alarm	_____
temporary	_____		striking	_____
avow	_____		distortion	_____

EXERCISE 10

The first word in each group below is the keyword. All the words under each keyword (the related words) have similar meaning. Read each group and try to remember which related words go with each keyword.

25. **observable**
noticeable
clear
prominent
striking
pronounced

26. **to cause**
impel
induce
bring about
effect
incite

27. **to scare**
frighten
panic
horrify
terrify
alarm

28. **large**
considerable
sizable
respectable
noteworthy
substantial

29. **danger**
risk
menace
jeopardy
peril
hazard

30. **huge**
massive
enormous
gigantic
vast
immense

31. **to declare**
claim
avow
assert
state
affirm

32. **lie**
deception
falsehood
distortion
misrepresentation
fabrication

33. **real**
genuine
valid
authentic
true
actual

34. **hard**
stern
rigorous
severe
harsh
exacting

35. **to guess**
speculate
surmise
conjecture
suppose
reckon

36. **short-lived**
transient
temporary
ephemeral
momentary
fleeting

EXERCISE 11

A. The 12 groups of related words are written below without keywords. Write the correct keyword over each keyword group.

B. Each group of related words has *one* word that does not belong in the group. Find that word, cross it out, and write it under the group to which it belongs. The first one is done for you as an example.

KEYWORDS

huge	**hard**	**to guess**	**observable**
real	**large**	**short-lived**	**to declare**
to scare	**danger**	**to cause**	**lie**

25. _____
noticeable
clear
~~massive~~
striking
pronounced

_____

26. _____
impel
induce
bring about
effect
assert

_____

27. _____
frighten
surmise
horrify
terrify
alarm

_____

28. _____
considerable
sizable
respectable
harsh
noteworthy

_____

29. _____   30. _____   31. _____   32. _____

risk	authentic	claim	deception
menace	enormous	avow	falsehood
jeopardy	gigantic	panic	distortion
peril	vast	state	misrepresentation
fabrication	immense	affirm	hazard
_____	*massive*	_____	_____

33. _____   34. _____   35. _____   36. _____

genuine	stern	speculate	transient
valid	rigorous	incite	temporary
prominent	severe	conjecture	ephemeral
true	fleeting	suppose	momentary
actual	exacting	reckon	substantial
_____	_____	_____	_____

EXERCISE 12

Each sentence below contains one keyword, which is in heavy type.

A. Find the word below each sentence that is *not* a related word for the keyword. Circle that word. (The keyword numbers from Exercise 10 are in parentheses. These will help you if you need to look back.)

B. After completing instruction A, write each circled word under the keyword in the sentence to which it belongs.

1. The politician **declared** that crime was on the rise.

    a. claimed   b. asserted   c. impelled   d. stated   (31)

2. Scientists have discovered that many of the old beliefs are **lies.**

    a. fabrications   b. misrepresentations   c. deceptions
    d. menaces   (32)

3. The **huge** wave hit the shore and caused extensive damage.

    a. actual   b. immense   c. enormous   d. massive   (30)

4. We can only **guess** about how languages first developed.

    a. speculate   b. state   c. conjecture   (35)

5. The patient made **observable** progress after beginning the medication.

    a. striking   b. pronounced   c. gigantic   (25)

6. His loss of faith in the revolution **caused** him to perform personal acts of terrorism.

    a. terrified   b. induced   c. incited   (26)

7. It is difficult to tell the difference between a **real** diamond and a man-made one.

    a. genuine   b. true   c. (an) authentic   d. (an) emphemeral (33)

8. The **hard** exercise program benefited his health as well as his appearance.

    a. exacting   b. noticeable   c. harsh   d. severe (34)

9. The possibility of war **scared** the politicians.

    a. frightened   b. alarmed   c. panicked   d. supposed (27)

10. Because he had been poor all his life, 200 dollars was a **large** amount of money to him.

    a. considerable   b. sizable   c. rigorous   d. substantial (28)

11. The use of certain chemicals to control insects was found to be a **danger** to other animals.

    a. falsehood   b. risk   c. hazard (29)

12. Mary's joy was **short-lived;** by the following week she was sad again.

    a. fleeting   b. temporary   c. momentary   d. respectable (36)

EXERCISE 13

In each blank write the keyword that corresponds to the word(s) in heavy type in the sentence. The number in parentheses can be used to check your answer.

1. It is an **everyday** occurrence today to eat food that contains chemicals.

    _____ (10)

2. Are there any **risks** involved with eating this kind of food?

    _____ (29)

3. A doctor in California **claimed** that these chemicals were bad for children.

    _____ (31)

4. He said that a child's actions can be **distorted** by them.

    _____ (5)

5. Some children are so active that they appear to be almost **mad.**

    _____ (1)

6. These children had **baffled** scientists and **frightened** parents for years and years. _____ (20) _____ (27)

7. In 1973, this doctor said that the overactivity in children might be **brought about** by the chemicals that were added to food. _____ (26)

8. If this doctor was correct, it was of **critical** importance to thousands of parents. _____ (19)

9. If he was wrong, it meant that **harmless** chemicals would no longer be used to keep food fresh. _____ (13)

10. Scientists began to look for **genuine** evidence from scientific experiments. _____ (33)

11. How could this evidence be **secured?** _____ (24)

12. A decision could not be made by **conjecturing.** _____ (35)

13. It was necessary to conduct research in an **extremely** scientific **manner.** _____ (2) _____ (6)

14. Two **sizable** groups of overactive children had to be established. _____ (28)

15. One group would eat natural foods **exclusively,** without the smallest **trace** of chemical additive. _____ (8) _____ (22)

16. The other group would be able to **opt for** any kind of food—natural or prepared. _____ (7)

17. Scientists would then look for **modification** of actions in both groups. _____ (14)

18. If the natural food group stopped being overactive, the scientists could say without a **qualm** that the presence or absence of chemicals in food **governed** children's actions. _____ (3) _____ (21)

19. If neither group changed, this would **point to** some other cause of the problem. _____ (9)

20. Many such experiments with **exacting** controls have been carried out over the years. _____ (34)

21. Any **noticeable** differences in actions between the groups have been **momentary.** _____ (25) _____ (36)

22. There have been no **glaring** differences between the groups over a longer period of time. _____ (17)

23. Even so, the California doctor and his **associates** have continued their work and believe in their solution to overactivity. _____ (23)

24. They have **talked** many parents **into** trying the special diet which they **thought up.** _____ (12) _____ (4)

25. Many of the parents who tried the diets are in **accord.** _____ (15)

26. They say there is an **enormous** difference in their children after a few months on the diet. _____ (30)

27. Scientists are unable to **shed light on** how this is possible. _____ (16)

28. Nobody believes that the parents or the doctor was in any way involved in **misrepresentation** of the facts. _____ (32)

29. Perhaps some **clever** scientist will make the right kind of experiment that will give answers to this question some day. _____ (11)

30. Meanwhile, every parent has a **determination** to make: whether to listen to the scientists or to the doctor and the many parents who believe in the special diet as a cure for overactivity in children. _____ (18)

EXERCISE 14

Solve the puzzle by writing the correct keyword for each of the words given below. The numbers in parentheses can be used to check your answers, but try to complete the puzzle without using them.

ACROSS

3. unanimity (15)
4. authentic (33)
7. temporary (36)
8. exceedingly (2)
12. enormous (30)
13. effect (26)
16. prominent (25)
17. menace (29)
20. manipulate (21)
24. bewilder (20)
26. profound (19)
27. deranged (1)

28. customary (10)
29. designate (9)
31. opt (7)
33. fabrication (32)
34. clarify (16)
35. trifle (22)

DOWN

1. rigorous (34)
2. coax (12)
5. considerable (28)
6. procedure (6)
9. horrify (27)

10. selection (18)
11. devise (4)
14. harmless (13)
15. glaring (17)
18. reckon (35)
19. hesitation (3)
21. distort (5)
22. colleague (23)
23. affirm (31)
25. shrewd (11)
30. solely (8)
31. modification (14)
32. attain (24)

EXERCISE 15

Some of the words in the following reading passages are in heavy type. Read the passages and write the keywords for these words in the blank below.

THE PRESSURE COOKER

Cooking food under pressure has been common for a long time. Have you ever thought how it works?

Water boils at 212°F, or 100°C. The temperature of the water rarely rises higher because steam carries heat away with it. However, sealing a pot full of boiling water to allow you to **manipulate** the escape of the steam **brings about** a **modification.** The heat that the steam carries is trapped inside the pot, and the pressure of the steam begins to push down on the surface of the water. This force, which can be **sizable,** prevents water molecules from breaking apart into steam. As a result, more heat is kept in the pot, and the temperature of the water becomes **exceedingly** high, cooking the food inside the pot much more quickly.

The speed of pressure cooking **converted** many people to this **manner** of food preparation. However, working with this kind of controlled pressure is not without its **hazards.** Explosions have happened, the results of which were sometimes **horrifying.** With the invention of the microwave oven, a comparatively **harmless** and **extremely** convenient **way** of cooking foods, pressure cookers have become less common.

1. _____   4. _____   7. _____   10. _____

2. _____   5. _____   8. _____   11. _____

3. _____   6. _____   9. _____   12. _____

VIEWING INSIDE THE BODY

A group of scientists has **devised** an **ingenious procedure** for **obtaining** information about the internal processes of the body without having to do surgery.

This technique is being used by Lionel Lieberman and his **colleagues** at the University of Wisconsin to locate infections. After taking a blood sample from a patient, they isolate the white blood cells and mix them with a radioactive element, indium-III. This element begins to release energy immediately. The white blood cells are injected back into the body, and a special camera is used to pick up signals from the indium-III. Since white blood cells fight infection, they will travel to the infected area, producing a **conspicuous** signal from the region. The location of the signal **discloses** to the doctor where the infection is and how **critical** it is. They can then **select** a treatment without the **hesitation** of years past when physicians were **bewildered** by their inability to find the infected area.

This technique has **enormous** potential. Knowing where the problem is gives doctors the **distinct** advantage of not relying upon **conjecture.** And, since the life of indium-III is **fleeting,** the **risk** to the patient is small.

1. _____   5. _____   9. _____   13. _____

2. _____   6. _____   10. _____   14. _____

3. _____   7. _____   11. _____   15. _____
4. _____   8. _____   12. _____   16. _____

EARTHLY LIGHTS

It is late at night. Suddenly a ball of light is seen moving around the New Jersey sky. Many people in the area **affirm** its existence and **assert** that it is an **authentic** UFO (unidentified flying object). Given the **unanimity** of opinion, it is not the imagination of a few **deranged** individuals. What causes the lights?

A group started investigating the light in 1976 in an attempt to **clarify** what was happening. They found that similar lights had been reported in more than 100 locations throughout the United States. They learned through **rigorous** investigation that the light always appeared over or near geological fault zones.

Quartz, a common mineral, gives off an electrical charge when **distorted** under pressure. The group theorized that the quartz in the fault zones was under enough pressure to **induce** a glow in the air resulting from the electricity produced.

To prove the theory, the group set up cameras and sensors in New Jersey and waited for the light to appear. When it did, the instruments measured an increase in voltage and radiation at the location. Thus the light was not **merely** the **fabrication** of a group of people, nor was it visitors from outer space: it was a **genuine** phenomenon of nature.

There is **considerable** evidence to support the possibility that the **temporary** appearance of the light may be connected to **normal** movements within the earth. If a relationship between these two phenomena can be established, who knows what scientists will be able to predict?

1. _____   5. _____   9. _____   13. _____
2. _____   6. _____   10. _____   14. _____
3. _____   7. _____   11. _____   15. _____
4. _____   8. _____   12. _____

EXERCISE 16

Read the following article. Do *not* use a dictionary. At least one related word from each of the keyword groups is in this article. Try to remember the proper keywords as you read.

Prereading Introduction

The people who are around you can have a very great influence on your judgments and decisions. How strong is this influence? What effect does group pressure have on a person? Scientists have only recently begun to understand the power that a group of people can have over an individual.

The following article describes a few of the experiments that have been done to explore this area of human psychology. This type of research helps us to understand the way that opinions, judgments, and decisions are formed and how they can be changed.

After reading the article, you should answer the following questions:

1. What kind of people were chosen for this experiment?
2. What do the subjects think the psychologists are studying? What are they actually studying?
3. Why do the subjects choose the wrong lines?
4. What does unanimity of a group do to a person's judgments?
5. Is strong pressure needed in order to make people choose the wrong answer? Why or why not?
6. Why is the "majority effect" important in our daily lives?
7. What happens to the "majority effect" when people are allowed to keep their choices secret?
8. A good politician in the United States always tries to make the people believe that he or she is *the* leading candidate for the particular office in question. After reading this article, can you see why it is important to do so?

THE PRESSURE TO CONFORM*

Suppose that you saw somebody being shown a pair of cards. On one of them there is a line, and on the other, three lines. Of these three, one is obviously longer than the line on the other card, one is shorter, and one the same length. The person to whom these cards are being shown is asked to point to the line on the second card which is the same length as the one on the first. To your surprise, he makes one of the obviously wrong choices. You might suppose that he, or she, perhaps suffers from distorted vision, or is insane, or perhaps merely cussed.[a] But you might be wrong in all these suggestions; you might be observing a sane, ordinary citizen, just like yourself. Because, by fairly simple processes, sane and ordinary citizens can be induced to deny the plain evidence of their senses— not always, but often. In recent years psychologists have carried out some exceedingly interesting experiments in which this sort of thing is done.

The general procedure was first devised by Dr Asch in the United States. What happens is this: Someone is asked to join a group who are helping to study the discrimination of length. The victim,[b] having agreed to this seemingly innocent request, goes to a room where a number of people— about half a dozen—and the experimenter are seated. Unbeknown to our victim, none

of the other people in the room is a volunteer like himself; they are all in league with[c] the experimenter. A pair of cards, like those I have described, is produced; and everyone in turn is asked which of the three lines on the second card is equal to the line on the first. They all, without hesitation, pick—as they have been told to pick—the same wrong line. Last of all comes the turn of our volunteer. In many cases the volunteer, faced with this unanimity, denies the plain evidence of his senses, and agrees.

An ingenious variation of this experiment was devised by Stanley Milgram of Harvard. He used sounds instead of lines, and the subjects were merely asked to state which of two successive sounds lasted longer. The volunteer would come into a room where there was a row of five cubicles[d] with their doors shut, and coats hanging outside, and one open cubicle for him. He would sit in it and don[e] earphones provided. He would hear the occupants of the other cubicles tested in turn, and each would give a wrong answer. But the other cubicles were, in fact, empty, and what he heard were tape-recordings manipulated by the experimenter. Milgram conducted a whole series of experiments in this way, in which he varied considerably the pressure put upon the subjects. As expected, their

---

*Max Hammerton, "The Pressure to Conform," *English Study Series 2*, ed. M. J. Clarke (Oxford University Press, 1966), pp. 51–53. Excerpt from an article originally published in *The Listener*, October 18, 1962.

conformity varied with the pressure, but, over all, he clearly showed that, faced with the unanimous opinion of the group they were in, people could be made to deny the obvious facts of the case in anything up to 75 per cent of the trials.

The victim of brainwashing can be induced to assert falsehoods, as we well know. But he is subjected to terrible and continuous stress: to hunger, sleeplessness, cold, and fear. The people we have been discussing were free of all these things, and subjected to nothing more than the complete agreement of the group in which they found themselves. Nevertheless, they too could be made to assert manifest falsehoods. I find this more than a trifle alarming—and very thought-provoking.[f]

You may reply that there is no cause for alarm, because in real situations the total unanimity of a group is rare. The more usual case concerns the effects of what we might call a 'pressure group'. This has been examined, at least partially, by W. M. and H. H. Kassarjian, in California. They used the 'group in a room' and 'lines on cards' situation; and I imagine that they must be kindly people, because they made things much easier for their volunteers. In the first place, the genuine volunteers were in a majority: twenty out of thirty. Secondly, the volunteers never had to make their selections out loud, but always enjoyed the anonymity[g] of paper and pencil. The experimenter explained that some people would be asked to declare their choices publicly, and asked only his primed collaborators.[h] Thus each volunteer heard the views of only a third of the group he was in. This third was unanimous, and the volunteers prob-

ably concluded that they expressed a majority view, but they were not put in a glaring minority of one, and their choice was secret. Nevertheless, a substantial distortion was still produced: almost, though not quite, as large as in the harsher situations we looked at first. So there is only small comfort here.

I am aware that there is grave danger in taking results obtained in the special and carefully simplified situation of the laboratory, or of the clinic, and applying them directly to the immensely complicated affairs of normal life. But these results seem to me so interesting and so suggestive that, in spite of the obvious risks, it may be worth while to see where they may shed a little light. In speculating thus, I am stepping outside the proper bounds of scientific rigour;[i] so, if I only make myself a laughing-stock, it is my own fault.

Whether one line is or is not the same length as another is a matter fairly easy to judge as a rule. But many things—and many more important things—are by no means so clear cut.[j] If we are asked which of two cars or two schools is the better, or which of two 'pop' songs or two politicians is the worse, we may be genuinely perplexed to answer. We may guess that in such doubtful cases the 'majority effect' or the 'pressure group effect' would be even more pronounced. Recent experiments by A. E. M. Seaborne suggest that they would not always be, but it seems generally likely. Can we observe such effects taking place around us now, or having taken place in the past? I think we can, and that they help us a little to understand the massive inertia[k] of commonly held ideas, and the fantastic standing of some more ephemeral ones.

Notes

[a]merely cussed: difficult to get along with, uncooperative, disagreeable.
[b]the victim: the person on whom the experiment is performed.
[c]in league with: working together with.
[d]cubicle: small room.
[e]don: put on.
[f]very thought-provoking: causes one to think a lot.
[g]anonymity: no one knowing who you are.

[h]his primed collaborators: the helpers to whom the experimenters had already given instructions about how to respond.
[i]I am stepping outside the proper bounds of scientific rigour: I am not following correct scientific procedure; I am saying more than I should from a scientific point of view.
[j]so clear cut: so easy to define.
[k]inertia: resistance to motion or change.

2 History

EXERCISE 1

In the following paragraph one word in each sentence is in heavy type. Find the keyword from the list below that is closest in meaning to each of these words, and write the keyword in the proper blank underneath the paragraph. Check your answers by looking at Exercise 2.

KEYWORDS

product	**people**	**to repair**	**interruption**
to keep	**to worsen**	**wealth**	**to trouble**
piece	**trade**	**to delay**	**work**

At first, energy production came only as a result of human or animal **toil.** This requirement for living sources of energy **hampered** the development of society. However, it was discovered that the **opulence** of a person or a country could be increased by finding nonliving sources of energy: water, wind, steam, electricity, and so on. **Merchandise** could be made more quickly and more cheaply with this type of energy. **Exchanges** could also be handled more easily when nonliving energy was used for transportation. History shows that the life-style in any area depended upon the amount of nonliving energy the **inhabitants** had available to them. Areas that continued to depend on living sources of energy have not improved—they have been able only to **preserve** the same life-style. Areas that developed or received a bigger **share** of the energy produced by nonliving sources have improved. Life in these "developed" societies could certainly **decline** quickly, however. If anything should **afflict** the sources of nonliving energy, those societies that depend on this type of energy would have serious problems. Any long **disruption** in the supply of this energy would create a very grave situation. If the societies could not **fix** the problems, they would be required to change their way of living completely.

toil	_____	hampered	_____
opulence	_____	merchandise	_____
exchanges	_____	inhabitants	_____
preserve	_____	share	_____

decline	_____	afflict	_____
disruption	_____	fix	_____

EXERCISE 2

The first word in each group below is the keyword. All the words under each keyword (the related words) have similar meaning. Read each group and try to remember which related words go with each keyword.

1. **interruption**	2. **piece**	3. **trade**	4. **to worsen**
gap	share	intercourse	slump
disjunction	portion	barter	decline
disruption	allotment	dealings	deteriorate
interval	appropriation	exchange	degenerate
disconnection	proportion	commerce	regress

5. **product**	6. **to repair**	7. **work**	8. **to delay**
ware	fix	labor	hinder
commodity	renovate	toil	hamper
goods	refurbish	effort	obstruct
merchandise	restore	exertion	impede
produce	mend	drudgery	retard

9. **to keep**	10. **people**	11. **to trouble**	12. **wealth**
preserve	colonists	beset	opulence
sustain	settlers	perturb	means
uphold	inhabitants	afflict	resources
maintain	residents	distress	affluence
conserve	dwellers	harass	prosperity

EXERCISE 3

A. The 12 groups of related words are written below without keywords. Write the correct keyword over each keyword group.

B. Each group of related words has *one* word that does not belong in the group. Find that word, cross it out, and write it under the group to which it belongs.

KEYWORDS

product	**people**	**to repair**	**interruption**
to keep	**to worsen**	**wealth**	**to trouble**
piece	**trade**	**to delay**	**work**

1. _____
   gap
   affluence
   disruption
   interval
   disconnection
   _____

2. _____
   share
   portion
   allotment
   exertion
   proportion
   _____

3. _____
   intercourse
   barter
   dealings
   exchange
   dwellers
   _____

4. _____
   slump
   decline
   uphold
   degenerate
   regress
   _____

5. _____
   ware
   disjunction
   goods
   merchandise
   produce
   _____

6. _____
   fix
   renovate
   refurbish
   restore
   perturb
   _____

7. _____
   labor
   toil
   effort
   commerce
   drudgery
   _____

8. _____
   deteriorate
   hamper
   obstruct
   impede
   retard
   _____

9. _____
   preserve
   sustain
   hinder
   maintain
   conserve
   _____

10. _____
    colonists
    settlers
    inhabitants
    commodity
    residents
    _____

11. _____
    beset
    mend
    afflict
    harass
    distress
    _____

12. _____
    opulence
    means
    resources
    prosperity
    appropriation
    _____

EXERCISE 4

Each sentence below contains one keyword, which is in heavy type.

A. Find the word below each sentence that is *not* a related word for the keyword. Circle that word. (The keyword numbers from Exercise 2 are in parentheses. These will help you if you need to look back.)

B. After completing instruction A, write each circled word under the keyword in the sentence to which it belongs.

1. Payment for the **products** must be made upon receipt.

   a. merchandise   b. goods   c. labor   d. commodities   (5)

2. The discovery of oil resulted in **wealth** for the entire area.

   a. affluence   b. barter   c. opulence   (12)

3. When the police listened to the tape of the conversation, they found an eight-minute **interruption.**

   a. disruption   b. disconnection   c. prosperity   (1)

4. The possibility of war alarmed the **people.**

    a. settlers   b. dwellers   c. inhabitants   d. portions (10)

5. A **piece** of our taxes goes to support public education.

    a. (An) allotment   b. gap   c. share (2)

6. The **work** involved in completing the project was enormous.

    a. residents   b. effort   c. toil (7)

7. The economy of the country was based on **trade.**

    a. exchange   b. wares   c. commerce (3)

8. From the time she was small she was **troubled** by a series of illnesses.

    a. harassed   b. beset   c. obstructed (11)

9. The situation quickly **worsened,** and war was declared.

    a. deteriorated   b. regressed   c. declined   d. renovated (4)

10. No one thought that the house could ever be **repaired.**

    a. sustained   b. restored   c. fixed   d. refurbished (6)

11. The rulers of the two countries tried to find a way to **keep** peace.

    a. preserve   b. degenerate   c. uphold   d. maintain (9)

12. Traffic was **delayed** by the accident on the highway.

    a. afflicted   b. impeded   c. hampered   d. hindered (8)

EXERCISE 5

In the following paragraph one word in each sentence is in heavy type. Find the keyword from the list below that is closest in meaning to each of these words, and write the keyword in the proper blank underneath the paragraph. Check your answers by looking at Exercise 6.

KEYWORDS

plentiful	to agree	geographical limit	lonely
poor	difficulty	to think about	destruction
false	to happen	mystery	to live

    World War I ended in 1918, and another world war began only 21 years later. How could this **take place?** After seeing the **desolation** caused by one world war, we might think that governments would do anything to stop another one from happening. However, those very people who had **endured** through World War I acted in such a way as to cause World War II. One problem was that some governments were not satisfied living within the **boundaries** of their countries. Another fact we must **bear in mind** is that no country would reduce its military strength.

Even those countries whose people were **impoverished** felt the need to spend a lot of money on their armies. There is no great **enigma** about why this was true. No country **was willing** to weaken itself. Each country thought that the other countries were making **deceptive** promises or proposals. So, while discussion was **bountiful,** results were minimal. Rather than cooperate, each country acted as if it were a small, **isolated** island that could not believe its neighbors. History repeated itself so quickly because the people involved learned very little from the **hardships** they had experienced in World War I.

take place	_____	desolation	_____
endured	_____	boundaries	_____
bear in mind	_____	impoverished	_____
enigma	_____	was willing	_____
deceptive	_____	bountiful	_____
isolated	_____	hardships	_____

EXERCISE 6

The first word in each group below is the keyword. All the words under each keyword (the related words) have similar meaning. Read each group and try to remember which related words go with each keyword.

13. **plentiful**	14. **to think about**	15. **lonely**	16. **poor**
copious	take into	out of the way	penniless
ample	account	secluded	needy
abundant	contemplate	isolated	destitute
profuse	ponder	solitary	impoverished
bountiful	weigh	reclusive	indigent
	bear in mind		

17. **to happen**	18. **geographical limit**	19. **mystery**	20. **destruction**
befall	boundary	perplexity	ruin
come about	frontier	paradox	desolation
occur	confines	puzzle	annihilation
transpire	edge	enigma	ravage
take place	border	bewilderment	demolition

21. **to agree**	22. **difficulty**	23. **to live**	24. **false**
consent	adversity	endure	deceptive
be willing to	privation	subsist	deceiving

acquiesce	hardship	persevere	misleading
concur	tribulation	survive	fraudulent
assent	burden	exist	deceitful

EXERCISE 7

A. The 12 groups of related words are written below without keywords. Write the correct keyword over each keyword group.

B. Each group of related words has *one* word that does not belong in the group. Find that word, cross it out, and write it under the group to which it belongs.

KEYWORDS

plentiful	to agree	geographical	lonely
poor	difficulty	limit	destruction
false	to happen	to think about	to live
		mystery	

13. _____
copious
ample
abundant
deceitful
bountiful
_____

14. _____
take into account
contemplate
come about
weigh
bear in mind
_____

15. _____
out of the way
profuse
isolated
solitary
reclusive
_____

16. _____
penniless
needy
destitute
impoverished
secluded
_____

17. _____
befall
acquiesce
occur
transpire
take place
_____

18. _____
boundary
frontier
confines
edge
perplexity
_____

19. _____
tribulation
paradox
puzzle
enigma
bewilderment
_____

20. _____
ruin
desolation
annihilation
ravage
border
_____

21. _____
consent
be willing to
endure
concur
assent
_____

22. _____
adversity
privation
hardship
demolition
burden
_____

23. _____
ponder
subsist
persevere
survive
exist
_____

24. _____
deceptive
deceiving
misleading
fraudulent
indigent
_____

EXERCISE 8

Each sentence below contains one keyword, which is in heavy type.

A. Find the word below each sentence that is *not* a related word for the keyword. Circle that word. (The keyword numbers from Exercise 6 are in parentheses. These will help you if you need to look back.)

B. After completing instruction A, write each circled word under the keyword in the sentence to which it belongs.

1. Thirty years later one could still see the **destruction** caused by the war.

    a. ravage   b. desolation   c. bewilderment   (20)

2. The soldiers pushed the invaders back to the **geographical limit** of their homeland.

    a. frontier   b. burden   c. boundary   d. confines   (18)

3. It was not a great **difficulty** for him to work 12 hours a day.

    a. ruin   b. hardship   c. privation   (22)

4. His attempts to investigate the situation resulted in even greater **mystery.**

    a. perplexity   b. enigma   c. paradox   d. edge   (19)

5. Only three of the five mountain climbers **lived through** the expedition.

    a. endured   b. took into account   c. persevered through   (23)

6. Today every president must **think about** the international significance of his or her actions.

    a. weigh   b. bear in mind   c. contemplate   d. survive   (14)

7. The secretary of state **agreed with** the decision of the president.

    a. acquiesced to   b. transpired   c. assented to   (21)

8. After the accident, it was quite some time before they knew what had **happened.**

    a. taken place   b. come about   c. occurred   d. concurred   (17)

9. The twisted buildings provided **plentiful** evidence of the strength of the storm.

    a. abundant   b. deceiving   c. bountiful   (13)

10. Many families were **poor** after the stock market crashed in 1929.

    a. indigent   b. penniless   c. impoverished   d. solitary   (16)

11. He was buried in a **lonely** grave on a hillside.

    a. secluded   b. destitute   c. isolated   d. out of the way   (15)

12. One should always remember that appearances can be **false.**

    a. misleading   b. ample   c. deceptive   d. deceitful   (24)

EXERCISE 9

In the following paragraph one word in each sentence is in heavy type. Find the keyword from the list below that is closest in meaning to each of these words, and write the keyword in the proper blank underneath the paragraph. Check your answers by looking at Exercise 10.

KEYWORDS

to divide	hardworking	more than necessary amount	world
problem	seller	to say no to	wealthy
good (noun)	to surprise	to force upon	skillful

In earlier times, almost every businessman on this **globe** worked for himself. In those days, if a person was **diligent,** he or she was economically safe. The money one made or the food one produced was **allotted** to one's family and friends. There was nobody to **reject** one's ideas or plans. However, as communication and trade developed, **merchants** needed more and more products to satisfy their buyers. Manufacturers had to become more **resourceful** in order to produce enough material to meet the demand. New ways of doing business were **imposed upon** people by changes that developed in the marketplace. Factories, stores, agencies, and the like appeared, allowing the owners or bosses to become **affluent** while the working person became poorer and poorer. Nobody was worried about the **welfare** of the everyday person. Job security disappeared: if there was a **glut** of a certain type of worker or product, people suddenly lost their jobs. This approach to business hit a **snag** in the Western world in 1929 when the system of doing business and giving credit fell apart. Although most people were **astounded** when this happened, many historians and economists expected it.

globe	_____	diligent	_____
allotted	_____	reject	_____
merchants	_____	resourceful	_____
imposed upon	_____	affluent	_____
welfare	_____	glut	_____
snag	_____	astounded	_____

EXERCISE 10

The first word in each group below is the keyword. All the words under each keyword (the related words) have similar meaning. Read each group and try to remember which related words go with each keyword.

25. **problem**	26. **more than necessary amount**	27. **to surprise**	28. **wealthy**
obstacle	glut	amaze	well-to-do
barrier	excess	astound	opulent
hindrance	surplus	startle	thriving
snag	overage	astonish	affluent
obstruction	oversupply	stun	prosperous

29. **to say no to**	30. **to divide**	31. **skillful**	32. **seller**
renounce	allot	dexterous	retailer
reject	distribute	resourceful	vendor
refuse	apportion	versatile	merchant
deny	disperse	adroit	peddler
decline	mete	inventive	salesman

33. **to force upon**	34. **hardworking**	35. **world**	36. **good (noun)**
impel	diligent	planet	welfare
compel	assiduous	orb	merit
impose	indefatigable	sphere	avail
inflict	zealous	globe	benefit
levy	industrious	earth	benevolence

EXERCISE 11

A. The 12 groups of related words are written below without keywords. Write the correct keyword over each keyword group.

B. Each group of related words has *one* word that does not belong in the group. Find that word, cross it out, and write it under the group to which it belongs.

KEYWORDS

to divide	hardworking	more than	world
problem	seller	necessary	wealthy
good (noun)	to surprise	amount	skillful
		to say no to	
		to force upon	

25. _____	26. _____	27. _____	28. _____
obstacle	glut	amaze	well-to-do
barrier	excess	astound	opulent
surplus	vendor	startle	thriving
snag	overage	astonish	zealous
obstruction	oversupply	mete	prosperous

_____

29. _____   30. _____   31. _____   32. _____

stun	allot	dexterous	retailer
reject	distribute	resourceful	sphere
refuse	apportion	versatile	merchant
deny	disperse	affluent	peddler
decline	levy	inventive	salesman

_____   _____   _____   _____

33. _____   34. _____   35. _____   36. _____

impel	diligent	planet	welfare
compel	assiduous	orb	hindrance
impose	indefatigable	merit	avail
inflict	adroit	globe	benefit
renounce	industrious	earth	benevolence

_____   _____   _____   _____

EXERCISE 12

Each sentence below contains one keyword, which is in heavy type.

A. Find the word below each sentence that is *not* a related word for the keyword. Circle that word. (The keyword numbers from Exercise 10 are in parentheses. These will help you if you need to look back.)

B. After completing instruction A, write each circled word under the keyword in the sentence to which it belongs.

1. Scientists know very little about the origin of this **world.**

   a. planet   b. benefit   c. globe   d. sphere (35)

2. His poor education was a serious **problem** for him in his career.

   a. hindrance   b. obstruction   c. overage (25)

3. **Sellers** from all over the world went to the fashion show.

   a. vendors   b. merchants   c. salesmen   d. barriers (32)

4. A **more than necessary amount** of sugar made the prices go down sharply.

   a. surplus   b. (An) excess   c. glut   d. retailer (26)

5. The magician's tricks **surprised** the people.

   a. allotted   b. astonished   c. amazed   d. astounded (27)

6. The lawyers had a difficult time trying to **divide** the money according to the dead man's wishes.

   a. apportion   b. distribute   c. impel (30)

7. The heavy taxes **forced upon** the people caused the new government to fail.

   a. levied   b. denied   c. inflicted   d. imposed (33)

8. The lawyer was certain that the judge would **say no to** the appeal.

   a. refuse   b. decline   c. reject   d. startle (29)

9. Some people are **hardworking;** others are simply lazy.

   a. assiduous   b. indefatigable   c. diligent   d. well-to-do (34)

10. **Skillful** scientists are always exploring solutions to problems with nature.

   a. Resourceful   b. Industrious   c. Versatile (31)

11. Doctors in the United States are almost always **wealthy.**

   a. affluent   b. inventive   c. prosperous (28)

12. The politician promised to work for the **good** of the poor.

   a. earth   b. welfare   c. benevolence (36)

EXERCISE 13

In each blank write the keyword that corresponds to the word(s) in heavy type in the sentence. The number in parentheses can be used to check your answer.

1. Did you ever **contemplate** the difficulty of writing a peace treaty after a long war? _____ (14)

2. After World War I, three men **consented** to write the Treaty of Versailles. _____ (21)

3. Today historians are **astonished** that only three people were given such an immense responsibility. _____ (27)

4. Almost the entire **planet** was involved in some way in the war. _____ (35)

5. The **ravages** of war were spread out over many countries. _____ (20)

6. Many governments were almost **penniless** as a result of the war. _____ (16)

7. The **borders** of several countries had to be reestablished. _____ (18)

8. **Commerce** had to be controlled. _____ (3)

9. The "winners" of the war were not to become **prosperous** at the expense of the "losers." _____ (28)

10. And yet the victorious countries certainly wanted to receive some type of an **allotment** from the defeated countries. _____ (2)

11. At the same time, the treaty had to insure that the defeated countries had the **means** to recover from the war. _____ (12)

12. It would be to no **avail** to make these countries remain poor and unable to operate. _____ (36)

13. After barely **subsisting** for so many years, the **residents** of these countries needed to have a better future. _____ (23) _____ (10)

14. Given all of the **obstacles** that had to be overcome, why only three men were chosen to write the treaty is an **enigma.** _____ (25) _____ (19)

15. No three humans, no matter how **assiduous** and **resourceful** they were, could hope to be very successful. _____ (34) _____ (31)

16. As they began their **efforts,** these men knew the **adversities** they would have to overcome. _____ (7) _____ (22)

17. They were **hampered** by disagreements and misrepresentations. _____ (8)

18. One man would suggest one idea and another would **refuse** to accept it. _____ (29)

19. After a four-month **interval,** they began to be **distressed** by time pressure. _____ (1) _____ (11)

20. The final document was, of course, supposed to **mend** the damage **inflicted** upon the world by the war. _____ (6) _____ (33)

21. However, rather than **maintaining** peace after World War I, the Treaty of Versailles caused world politics to **regress.** _____ (9) _____ (4)

22. Many people feel that there is **abundant** evidence to show that this treaty helped cause World War II, which **occurred** just 21 years later. _____ (13) _____ (17)

23. This was not because the treaty contained **misleading** statements. _____ (24)

24. It happened partly because there was an **oversupply** of selfish interests in the final treaty. _____ (26)

25. Countries were interested in how to **distribute** land, how to allow **vendors** to receive and sell their **merchandise,** and so on.

_____ (30) _____ (32) _____ (5)

26. While the Treaty of Versailles was supposed to be between the major countries involved in World War I, its future impact would be felt in even the most **out of the way** areas of the world. _____ (15)

EXERCISE 14

Solve the puzzle by writing the correct keyword for each of the words given below. The numbers in parentheses can be used to check your answers, but try to complete the puzzle without using them.

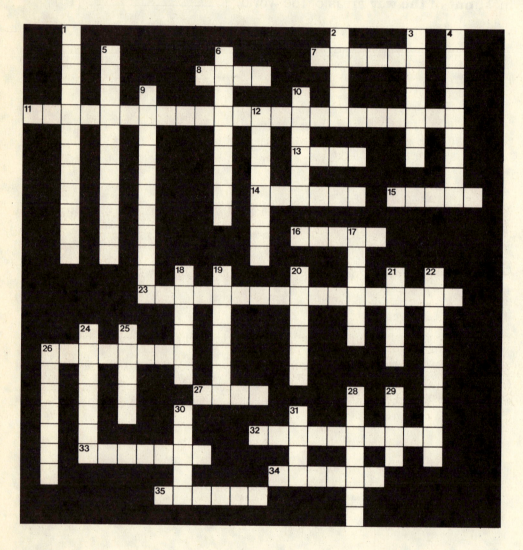

ACROSS

7. refurbish (6)
8. drudgery (7)
11. glut (26)
13. needy (16)
14. secluded (15)
15. sphere (35)
16. deceitful (24)
23. confines (18)
26. stun (27)
27. preserve (9)
32. weigh (14)
33. perplexity (19)
34. opulence (12)
35. settlers (10)

DOWN

1. disjunction (1)
2. retard (8)
3. goods (5)
4. bountiful (13)
5. annihilation (20)
6. impel (33)
9. diligent (34)
10. take place (17)
12. adroit (31)

17. peddler (32)
18. slump (4)
19. harass (11)
20. disperse (30)
21. portion (2)
22. adversity (22)
24. obstruction (25)
25. dealings (3)
26. renounce (29)
28. well-to-do (28)
29. merit (36)
30. acquiesce (21)
31. subsist (23)

EXERCISE 15

Some of the words in the following reading passages are in heavy type. Read the passages and write the keywords for these words in the blanks below.

THE GROWTH OF EUROPE

Historians **concur** that Europe **maintained** a central position in the world during the 19th century. It is impossible to understand the **obstacles** that face the **inhabitants** of the **planet** today without **bearing in mind** what allowed this to **take place.** There were three factors that were primarily responsible.

The first was the fact that there was, within the the **boundaries** of Europe, an exceptionally large **portion** of the world's farmland. As a result, European countries could feed their people without serious **adversity** and developed a **thriving** trade.

The second factor was control of the seas. The Europeans, with their superior arms and ships, could attack any other continent while defending themselves from **annihilation** at home. Dealings in **commodities** by sea brought **affluence** to the European continent while many other areas of the world **deteriorated.** No one can **deny** that many problems that **beset** other continents during the 19th century were not present in Europe because of its control over the oceans.

The third advantage that the Europeans enjoyed was their **astounding** development in science and technology. With the development of steam power and electricity came a **bountiful** supply of energy, allowing the **diligent** workers to produce **goods** for the **merchants** more cheaply and quickly, speeding up transportation, and improving communication.

1. _____   7. _____   13. _____   19. _____
2. _____   8. _____   14. _____   20. _____
3. _____   9. _____   15. _____   21. _____
4. _____   10. _____   16. _____   22. _____
5. _____   11. _____   17. _____
6. _____   12. _____   18. _____

POSTWAR BRITAIN

The British people found it difficult after 1918 to **restore** their prewar **prosperity.** The **disjunction** of trade, the **decline** of industry, the increase of foreign competition, and the heavy taxation **levied** upon the people to improve the economy **hindered** recovery. Another factor that **impeded** restoration was that Britain was geographically **isolated** from the rest of Europe, so the country was dependent upon **commerce** to **survive.**

Although the people were **versatile** and made great efforts to work for the common **welfare** of the country, the postwar debts of the country, as well as the continuing costs of defense, threatened to leave the country **destitute.** Attempts to **apportion** the debts through taxation caused the market to **slump** and threw the country into a postwar depression that provided a further **hindrance** to recovery. Suddenly there was an **oversupply** of workers for the jobs that were available.

The **perplexities** that **perturbed** Britain after World War I were, therefore, serious and complex. It remained to be seen whether the country had the talent and the **means** to **persevere** in the 20th century.

1. _____   7. _____   13. _____   19. _____
2. _____   8. _____   14. _____   20. _____
3. _____   9. _____   15. _____   21. _____
4. _____   10. _____   16. _____
5. _____   11. _____   17. _____
6. _____   12. _____   18. _____

EXERCISE 16

Read the following article. Do *not* use a dictionary. At least one related word from each of the keyword groups is in this article. Try to remember the proper keywords as you read.

Prereading Introduction

In the past 200 years, societies have changed very much. Each family, town, and nation used to be very *in*dependent, growing and producing what the people of the area needed. Today, however, most of the world is *inter*dependent; that is, people depend on international trade to supply the products that they need or want.

The following article examines the development of interdependence and how it affected various parts of the world. It offers some explanation for why certain areas of the world had faster economic development than others and why it is so difficult for other parts of the world to catch up today.

After reading this article, you should answer the following questions:

1. Were all primitive societies truly self-sufficient?
2. What role did the Age of Discovery play in increasing the economic interdependence of the modern world? The Industrial Revolution?
3. Why did Henry George say that civilization is cooperation?
4. Why was the prosperity created by world trade *not* distributed equally?
5. Discuss the role that World War I played in determining the share of world trade that Europe controlled.
6. This article states that "the peoples whose need is greatest buy the least." Why is that true?
7. Why does the United States, for example, refuse to buy cotton and rice from Asia?
8. How do governments regulate their trade?

9. What is the most important advantage in protecting the production of a commodity within a nation's frontiers?
10. What is the paradox created by international trade?

ECONOMIC INTERDEPENDENCE OF THE MODERN WORLD*

In modern times the methods by which civilized peoples obtain food and goods and services have grown more involved and more complex with each passing year. In a primitive society a tribe or even a single family may manage to support itself with little or no outside aid. During the Middle Ages the inhabitants of many European hamlets[a] raised their own food, made and mended their own tools, tanned their own leather, fashioned their own shoes and harness, and wove their own cloth. People who meet their own simple needs from their own limited local resources are said to be economically self-sufficient.[b] Even in the Middle Ages, however, dwellers in remote isolated villages obtained a few articles they could not produce themselves by buying them from travelling merchants. Or they might journey to a town a few miles away and purchase goods at a fair. Thus they were not exclusively dependent on their own labor.

The Age of Discovery, at the close of the Middle Ages, opened the oceans of the world to European ships and made it possible for Europe to obtain goods from distant continents. Later, with the Industrial Revolution, the Europeans learned to produce quantities of manufactured goods cheaply, and to sell what they did not need in exchange for raw materials, tropical products, and additional food. During the nineteenth century *international* trade—trade between countries and between continents—increased at a rapid rate. By 1900 the total value of such commerce was ten times as great as it had been in 1800. By 1913 it was twenty times as great; and by 1929 (despite the disruption of World War I) it was over thirty times as valuable as it had been in 1800. In other words, almost all nations in the nineteenth and twentieth centuries became increasingly dependent on *foreign* markets, on selling goods to and buying goods from countries in other parts of the world.

As the value of this international trade increased the peoples of the world became more dependent on one another. Countries that possessed a surplus of some commodities sought to exchange that surplus for goods they wanted but lacked the means to produce for themselves. International trade brought the nations of the world into closer contact. It made them more dependent on one another, and made it more important that they *cooperate* in supplying one another's needs for the benefit of all. The American economist, Henry George, summed up this situation very simply in three words. He said: *civilization is cooperation.*

The fact that, by the twentieth century, the world had come to resemble one vast market helps to explain its rapid progress and development. It helps to explain why goods were produced more abundantly and distributed more widely than ever before, why standards of living rose, and the global population increased at an astonishing rate. Unfortunately, however, the increase in food and manufactured goods, the increase in wealth and prosperity, was not equally distributed. Some nations, that possessed or achieved unusual advantages, that developed more effective machines and techniques, grew wealthy. Other nations, less favored by nature, less efficient, less resourceful or less industrious, remained poor. Just as in individual countries, a small minority of the inhabitants might be exceptionally wealthy and might preserve and enlarge their family fortunes, while the majority remained relatively poor, so among the nations of the world a few achieved a high standard of wealth while the majority subsisted on very much lower incomes.

---

*Geoffrey Bruun and Victor S. Mamatey, *The World in the Twentieth Century*, Fourth Edition, pp. 391–94. Copyright © 1962 by D. C. Heath and Company. Reprinted by permission.

Some countries and continents enjoyed a much larger share of world trade than others, and the countries with a large foreign trade were the wealthy countries where income and living standards were high. Before World War I, for example, Europe, with about one-fourth of the world's people, monopolized[c] nearly 60 per cent of the world's international trade. This was more than twice as much as the Europeans would have controlled if the international trade of each continent had been proportional to its population. After World War I the European share declined to less than half the world total while that of North America (the United States and Canada) rose. By 1926 the North Americans claimed one-fifth of the international trade of the globe, nearly three times as much as their numbers would have entitled them to if this trade had been divided in proportion to population. But their good luck was due in part to the destruction and dislocation Europe had suffered during the war. After 1926 the Europeans recovered some of the trade they had lost, while the share the North Americans had obtained declined.

These facts suggest several points concerning international trade which it is important to remember. In *theory* the universal exchange of goods seems deceptively simple. If every people produced those goods which their resources and skills best fitted them to produce, and all nations were willing and able to exchange goods freely, the whole world would benefit and its peoples would become more and more cooperative and interdependent. To some extent this is what has come about in modern times. But the growth of international trade has been slowed and hampered by three difficulties that proved very hard to overcome. It is impossible to understand the strains and tensions of the modern world unless these obstacles to trade, and their causes, are taken into account.

The first difficulty is that the peoples whose need is greatest buy the least. For trade is an *exchange* and very poor people with low incomes have little surplus to offer for things they lack. In 1926, for instance, Asia, Africa, and South America together held over three-quarters of the world population but enjoyed only one-quarter of its international trade. A second

difficulty is that a rich nation that could afford to buy the surplus a poor nation offers frequently refuses to do so. Some Asian countries that need and want to buy machines or medicines from the United States may have cotton or rice to offer in exchange. But American farmers also raise cotton and rice. To protect them, the United States may refuse to buy cotton or rice from Asia although it is cheaper than their own. This may mean that American consumers pay higher prices for their home-grown rice or cotton than they need to do, and the Asian people, who want to buy goods from the United States, are unable to buy them. Tariff[d] barriers and other obstacles that nations impose on the free exchange of goods obstruct international trade. Governments do not regulate their trade in the way that will be best for humanity as a whole. They do not always regulate it in the way that would be most advantageous for their own people as a whole. Sometimes they impose import duties[e] on a commodity in a way that inflicts a hardship on foreigners and on most of their own people, but enables a small number of their own people to obtain a higher price for their products. It must be kept in mind, however, that by producing a commodity within its own frontiers, even if it could buy an ample supply more cheaply abroad, a nation preserves one important advantage. Its supply of that commodity cannot be cut off by a blockade[f] or a war.

In a world of competing states every nation seeks to protect itself. It wants other countries to become dependent on it but it does not want to become dependent on them. This situation creates a paradox. For while international trade makes nations more *interdependent*, they try to regulate their imports and exports in such a way that they will be more *independent*. The basic wish of every nation is to be secure and prosperous but these selfish goals are unattainable. In the world of the twentieth century no country is secure from attack and prosperous countries excite the envy[g] of the impoverished majority. This is one reason why the modern age has been called "the Age of Anxiety," but there are other reasons also for the strains and tensions that afflict modern society.

Notes

^ahamlets: small towns or villages.
^bself-sufficient: able to take care of one's own needs.
^cmonopolize: control entirely.
^dtariff: tax on imported goods.

^eimport duties: tax on imported goods.
^fblockade: the closing off of an area, usually by military force.
^gexcite the envy: create a strong wish to have similar possessions or wealth.

Note to Students

With this book, you are learning to recognize a lot of new words very quickly. You can increase your recognition vocabulary easily if you take the time to learn how words are *derived* in English. For example, let's say you learned the adjective form of a word. In your reading, you see the same word, but this time it is in its noun form. It is probably not necessary to look up the word in your dictionary—it is very likely that it has the same meaning. If you become familiar with the more common ways that words are derived, you can still substitute the keyword in the proper form and continue to read.

Beginning with this chapter, the final exercise will work on derivations of some of the words studied in the previous chapters. This will be a review of some of the earlier words as well as an opportunity for you to study word endings.

Remember that this book is to help you with *reading.* Do *not* try to learn which words take which endings. This is very difficult in English and *absolutely unnecessary* in the reading process—the words are already formed for you. Your job is to understand the meaning.

EXERCISE 17

The following exercises show how different word forms are derived in English. Try to remember the endings and what parts of speech they indicate.

A. Words that end in *-(i)ty* are usually nouns:

Examples: real → reality
safe → safety

Put the letter of the correct keyword in the blank after each derived noun. Some keywords are used more than one time.

a. real   b. crazy   c. hard   d. safe   e. smart   f. serious
g. huge

1. valid → validity ____

2. severe → severity ____

3. enormous → enormity ____

4. The **insanity** of the new king soon became obvious to all. ____

5. In **actuality,** the situation was much worse than we thought. ____

6. I put the money into the bank for **security.** ____

7. The **ingenuity** of the young child allowed her to solve the problem. ____

8. One was immediately impressed by the **immensity** of the land. ____

B. Words that end in *-ness* are usually nouns.

> **Examples:** hard → hardness
> crazy → craziness
> serious → seriousness

a. crazy   b. hard   c. safe   d. smart   e. serious   f. obvious
g. huge

1. vast → vastness ____

2. mad → madness ____

3. The audience enjoyed the **cleverness** of the movie. ____

4. The parent talked to the child with a **sternness** that indicated that the child had gotten into trouble. ____

5. The **conspicuousness** of the manner in which he showed his wealth angered people around him. ____

6. The **inoffensiveness** of her actions made the child trust her. ____

7. The **graveness** of my wife's tone of voice frightened me. ____

8. The **shrewdness** of the politician was evident as he made his speech. ____

9. The policeman reacted with a **harshness** that surprised everyone. ____

C. Words that end in *-ive* are usually adjectives.

> **Examples:** deception → deceptive
> perception → perceptive

a. lie   b. to show   c. choice   d. to guess

1. speculate → speculative ____

2. selection → selective ____

3. In the case of many snakes, their frightening appearance is **deceptive.** ____

4. The high fever and pain in the stomach were **indicative** that the person needed to see a doctor quickly. ____

5. A **misrepresentative** sampling of public opinion caused the analyst to make the wrong prediction. ____

D. Words that end in *-(i)ous* are usually adjectives.

Examples: danger → dangerous
suspicion → suspicious

a. danger   b. doubt   c. change   d. agreement

1. hazards → hazardous ____
2. unanimity → unanimous ____
3. The man's actions looked very **suspicious** to the policeman. ____
4. The **various** types of birds in the area were a pleasant sight for the tourists. ____
5. The explorer began his **perilous** journey through the jungles of Africa. ____

In summary:

Words that end in *-ive* are _____.

Words that end in *-(i)ty* are _____.

Words that end in *-(i)ous* are _____.

Words that end in *-ness* are _____.

3 Psychology

EXERCISE 1

In the following paragraph some of the words are in heavy type. Find the keyword from the list below that is closest in meaning to each of these words, and write the keyword in the proper blank underneath the paragraph. Check your answers by looking at Exercise 2.

KEYWORDS

fright	**kind**	**characteristic**	**cruelty**
basic	**complicated**	**environment**	**laughter**
action	**fight**	**difficult**	**anger**

Hundreds of years ago, people attempted to gain a **rudimentary** understanding of the **atmosphere** in which they lived. These people thought that things around them had minds of their own. Therefore they believed that natural phenomena had human **traits.** They thought, for example, that when the sea was rough, it was due to its **wrath.** The sun, on the other hand, was considered **benevolent.** Today we talk about the **savagery** of these early people. However, we must remember that their life was very **arduous.** Their usual reaction to natural events was **horror;** they could not afford to see **jocularity** reflected in nature. Their lives were nothing more than an endless **struggle** for survival. Only through physical **accomplishments** could they deal with the **complex** elements of nature, which they considered to be psychological forces.

rudimentary	_____	atmosphere	_____
traits	_____	wrath	_____
benevolent	_____	savagery	_____
arduous	_____	horror	_____
jocularity	_____	struggle	_____
accomplishments	_____	complex	_____

EXERCISE 2

The first word in each group below is the keyword. All the words under each keyword (the related words) have similar meaning. Read each group and try to remember which related words go with each keyword.

1. **basic**
   primary
   intrinsic
   fundamental
   rudimentary
   inherent

2. **difficult**
   laborious
   burdensome
   arduous
   toilsome
   tough

3. **kind**
   considerate
   benevolent
   solicitous
   thoughtful
   magnanimous

4. **cruelty**
   savagery
   barbarity
   brutality
   inhumanity
   sadism

5. **characteristic**
   trait
   attribute
   quality
   property
   feature

6. **environment**
   surroundings
   setting
   atmosphere
   context
   framework

7. **fight**
   strife
   struggle
   combat
   conflict
   battle

8. **action**
   feat
   accomplishment
   deed
   achievement
   exploit

9. **laughter**
   mirth
   hilarity
   levity
   humor
   jocularity

10. **anger**
    wrath
    animosity
    fury
    rage
    resentment

11. **fright**
    dread
    fear
    awe
    terror
    horror

12. **complicated**
    complex
    involved
    entangled
    intricate
    elaborate

EXERCISE 3

A. The 12 groups of related words are written below without keywords. Write the correct keyword over each keyword group.

B. Each group of related words has *one* word that does not belong in the group. Find that word, cross it out, and write it under the group to which it belongs.

KEYWORDS

fright	**kind**	**characteristic**	**cruelty**
basic	**complicated**	**environment**	**laughter**
action	**fight**	**difficult**	**anger**

1. _____
   primary
   intrinsic

2. _____
   laborious
   burdensome

3. _____
   considerate
   benevolent

4. _____
   savagery
   levity

intricate	arduous	solicitous	brutality
rudimentary	fundamental	toilsome	sadism
inherent	tough	thoughtful	inhumanity
_____	_____	_____	_____

5. _____   6. _____   7. _____   8. _____

trait	surroundings	achievement	feat
resentment	setting	struggle	accomplishment
quality	atmosphere	combat	deed
property	context	conflict	dread
feature	barbarity	battle	exploit
_____	_____	_____	_____

9. _____   10. _____   11. _____   12. _____

mirth	wrath	attribute	complex
hilarity	animosity	fear	involved
strife	fury	awe	entangled
humor	rage	terror	magnanimous
jocularity	framework	horror	elaborate
_____	_____	_____	_____

EXERCISE 4

Each sentence below contains one keyword, which is in heavy type.

A. Find the word below each sentence that is *not* a related word for the keyword. Circle that word. (The keyword numbers from Exercise 2 are in parentheses. These will help you if you need to look back.)

B. After completing instruction A, write each circled word under the keyword in the sentence to which it belongs.

1. The description of what happened is very **complicated.**

   a. entangled   b. complex   c. burdensome   d. intricate   (12)

2. The **fight** for control over the road was very costly.

   a. struggle   b. combat   c. rage   (7)

3. The **fright** caused by the last scene in the movie stayed with me for several days.

   a. terror   b. hilarity   c. horror   (11)

4. An understanding of trigonometry is **basic** in most types of engineering.

   a. rudimentary   b. primary   c. fundamental   d. involved   (1)

5. It was very **kind** of you to send me the flowers.

   a. considerate   b. magnanimous   c. inherent (3)

6. The very pleasant **environment** helped the composer to write his music.

   a. deed   b. setting   c. atmosphere (6)

7. Stalin's **cruelty** is well-known today.

   a. savagery   b. barbarity   c. brutality   d. battle (4)

8. When the referee made a mistake, the **anger** of the crowd increased.

   a. inhumanity   b. animosity   c. fury   d. resentment (10)

9. Taking care of the neighbor's house proved to be a **difficult** job.

   a. tough   b. arduous   c. thoughtful   d. toilsome (2)

10. The **actions** of famous people live after them.

   a. exploits   b. achievements   c. feats   d. features (8)

11. The distinctive **characteristics** of the elephant make it easy to recognize.

   a. traits   b. surroundings   c. attributes (5)

12. He was not known for his **laughter;** he very rarely even smiled.

   a. levity   b. fear   c. humor   d. jocularity (9)

EXERCISE 5

In the following paragraph one word in each sentence is in heavy type. Find the keyword from the list below that is closest in meaning to each of these words, and write the keyword in the proper blank underneath the paragraph. Check your answers by looking at Exercise 6.

KEYWORDS

to use	**numberless**	**exact**	**likelihood**
to name	**unclear**	**worry**	**to hide**
respect	**knowledge**	**reason**	**to lessen**

   Sigmund Freud developed a method in psychology that is still widely **utilized** today. This method is **identified as** psychoanalysis. According to Freud, the **rationale** for a person's behavior cannot be understood unless we examine his or her past experiences. One's **awareness,** both conscious and unconscious, of what happened in the past has a very strong influence on one's behavior. For example, perhaps someone had a very unpleasant experience which his or her mind tries to **cover up.** Even though this person cannot remember the experience, certain **tendencies** exist that are the result of what happened earlier. The person may have tremendous **anxieties** and have no idea why. Psychoanalysis attempts to find and make conscious the **precise** experience or experiences that are causing one's behavior. According to Freud, one cannot change one's behavior as long as the early experiences that cause it remain unknown or **vague** to one's conscious thinking processes. It is impossible to **diminish** one's reactions, then, until conscious recall of these experiences is possible. Since Freud's time there have been **countless** examples to support many of his theories. While many psychologists disagree with some of his ideas, **regard** for Freud as the father of psychoanalysis is virtually universal.

utilized	_____	identified as	_____
rationale	_____	awareness	_____
cover up	_____	tendencies	_____
anxieties	_____	precise	_____
vague	_____	diminish	_____
countless	_____	regard	_____

EXERCISE 6

The first word in each group below is the keyword. All the words under each keyword (the related words) have similar meaning. Read each group and try to remember which related words go with each keyword.

13. **exact**
   precise
   unequivocal
   specific
   absolute
   verbatim

14. **unclear**
   blurry
   indistinct
   vague
   amorphous
   obscure

15. **knowledge**
   cognition
   awareness
   consciousness
   cognizance
   realization

16. **respect**
   consideration
   regard
   reverence
   deference
   esteem

17. **to name**
   label
   designate
   identify
   term
   entitle

18. **to hide**
   conceal
   eclipse
   camouflage
   cover up
   disguise

19. **numberless**
   infinite
   myriad
   countless
   innumerable
   incalculable

20. **to lessen**
   diminish
   curtail
   allay
   reduce
   alleviate

21. **worry**
   concern
   anguish
   apprehension
   uneasiness
   anxiety

22. **to use**
   resort to
   apply
   employ
   wield
   utilize

23. **reason**
   ground
   incentive
   motive
   inspiration
   rationale

24. **likelihood**
   tendency
   penchant
   predisposition
   inclination
   propensity

EXERCISE 7

A. The 12 groups of related words are written below without keywords. Write the correct keyword over each keyword group.

B. Each group of related words has *one* word that does not belong in the group. Find that word, cross it out, and write it under the group to which it belongs.

KEYWORDS

to use	numberless	exact	likelihood
to name	unclear	worry	to hide
respect	knowledge	reason	to lessen

13. _____

precise
unequivocal
specific
absolute
indistinct

_____

14. _____

blurry
myriad
vague
amorphous
obscure

_____

15. _____

cognition
awareness
consciousness
apprehension
realization

_____

16. _____

consideration
regard
reverence
deference
motive

_____

17. _____

wield
designate
term
identify
entitle

_____

18. _____

conceal
eclipse
alleviate
cover up
disguise

_____

19. _____

infinite
verbatim
countless
innumerable
incalculable

_____

20. _____

diminish
curtail
allay
reduce
label

_____

21. _____

concern
anguish
cognizance
uneasiness
anxiety

_____

22. _____

resort to
apply
employ
camouflage
utilize

_____

23. _____

ground
incentive
penchant
inspiration
rationale

_____

24. _____

tendency
esteem
predisposition
inclination
propensity

_____

EXERCISE 8

Each sentence below contains one keyword, which is in heavy type.

A. Find the word below each sentence that is *not* a related word for the keyword. Circle that word. (The keyword numbers from Exercise 6 are in parentheses. These will help you if you need to look back.)

B. After completing instruction A, write each circled word under the keyword in the sentence to which it belongs.

1. Whenever a husband and a wife want to get divorced, the judge must decide whether or not the **reasons** they give are adequate.

   a. rationale   b. inclination   c. motive (23)

2. I want you to tell me the events in the **exact** order that they occurred.

   a. precise   b. specific   c. incalculable (13)

3. Even though the man said that he did not commit the crime, **worry** was written all over his face.

   a. realization   b. anxiety   c. apprehension   d. uneasiness (21)

4. **Respect** for his older brother was obvious as the boy continued to talk.

   a. Esteem   b. Reverence   c. Consideration   d. Uneasiness (16)

5. The times that my father helped me are **numberless.**

   a. infinite   b. amorphous   c. myriad   d. countless (19)

6. The **knowledge** that I had forgotten to bring money made my heart stop beating for a second.

   a. ground   b. consciousness   c. awareness   d. cognizance (15)

7. Even though public support was minimal, the political group refused to **lessen** its activities.

   a. diminish   b. reduce   c. employ (20)

8. Memories of events that took place at a very early age are usually **unclear** at best.

   a. indistinct   b. vague   c. blurry   d. absolute (14)

9. The woman wore clothes in a manner to **hide** the fact that she had gained a lot of weight.

   a. cover up   b. curtail   c. conceal   d. camouflage (18)

10. The engineer **used** several formulas to solve the problem.

    a. applied   b. designated   c. utilized (22)

11. We were unable to **name** a new representative for the group.

    a. disguise   b. identify (17)

12. Today some psychologists believe that the **likelihood** for criminal activity in an individual may be, to a certain extent, inherited.

    a. predisposition   b. tendency   c. penchant   d. consideration (24)

EXERCISE 9

In the following paragraph one word in each sentence is in heavy type. Find the keyword from the list below that is closest in meaning to each of these words, and write the keyword in the proper blank underneath the paragraph. Check your answers by looking at Exercise 10.

KEYWORDS

to omit	**unreality**	**angry**	**to hold back**
to meet	**to arrange**	**to represent**	**unending**
to stop	**to help**	**push**	**common**

Behaviorists believe that we learn as a result of our reactions to **constant** series of events in our environment. Positive results give us the **drive** that is necessary in order to remember and repeat behavior. Negative results **prohibit** the recurrence of behavior. So, how we think and react depends on the experiences we have **encountered** in our past. This theory was **prevalent** in the mid-1900s. In contrast to the behaviorists, Gestaltists believe that mental life is not made of tiny units of associations that are **classified** into certain groups. Instead, one views the world as whole units of information, and these units **aid** in the learning process. How we remember someone's face is the example that is often used to **exemplify** a Gestalt point of view. We remember a face as a whole object, with many small pieces of information being **excluded.** So, according to Gestalt psychology, when we are unable to remember the small details of someone's face, our mind is not **restricting** this information from us—we never learned it as such in the first place. Therefore, unless a person has received special training, it is an **illusion** for one to think that one can remember exactly what a face looked like. Trying to force a witness, for example, to recall details may actually make him or her **hostile** because the person is incapable of such accuracy.

constant	_____	drive	_____
prohibit	_____	encountered	_____
prevalent	_____	classified	_____
aid	_____	exemplify	_____
excluded	_____	restricting	_____
illusion	_____	hostile	_____

EXERCISE 10

The first word in each group below is the keyword. All the words under each keyword (the related words) have similar meaning. Read each group and try to remember which related words go with each keyword.

25. **to stop**	26. **angry**	27. **to help**	28. **to hold back**
prohibit	belligerent	aid	restrain
cease	bitter	lend a hand	curb
preclude	spiteful	do a service	suppress
prevent	antagonistic	cooperate	restrict
halt	hostile	assist	inhibit

29. **to arrange**	30. **common**	31. **unreality**	32. **push**
categorize	prevalent	illusion	impulse
classify	ubiquitous	hallucination	momentum
sort	rife	fantasy	stimulus
rank	pervasive	mirage	drive
catalog	widespread	delusion	impetus

33. **to represent**	34. **to omit**	35. **unending**	36. **to meet**
depict	bar	constant	encounter
embody	exclude	persistent	be faced with
typify	disregard	eternal	be confronted with
exemplify	leave out	permanent	come across
symbolize	overlook	perpetual	run into

EXERCISE 11

A. The 12 groups of related words are written below without keywords. Write the correct keyword over each keyword group.

B. Each group of related words has *one* word that does not belong in the group. Find that word, cross it out, and write it under the group to which it belongs.

KEYWORDS

to omit	unreality	angry	to hold back
to meet	to arrange	to represent	unending
to stop	to help	push	common

25. _____	26. _____	27. _____	28. _____
prohibit	belligerent	aid	restrain
cease	bitter	lend a hand	curb
preclude	rife	disregard	suppress
prevent	antagonistic	cooperate	restrict
depict	hostile	assist	be faced with
_____	_____	_____	_____

29. _____	30. _____	31. _____	32. _____
do a service	prevalent	illusion	impulse
classify	ubiquitous	impetus	momentum

sort	perpetual	fantasy	stimulus
rank	pervasive	mirage	drive
catalog	widespread	delusion	hallucination
_____	_____	_____	_____

33. _____   34. _____   35. _____   36. _____

exemplify	bar	constant	encounter
embody	exclude	persistent	halt
typify	categorize	permanent	come across
inhibit	leave out	eternal	to be confronted
symbolize	overlook	spiteful	with
			run into
_____	_____	_____	_____

EXERCISE 12

Each sentence below contains one keyword, which is in heavy type.

A. Find the word below each sentence that is *not* a related word for the keyword. Circle that word. (The keyword numbers from Exercise 10 are in parentheses. These will help you if you need to look back.)

B. After completing instruction A, write each circled word under the keyword in the sentence to which it belongs.

1. Understanding one's past does not, of course, **stop** the possibility of having problems in the future because of it.

   a. prohibit   b. overlook   c. preclude   (25)

2. The desire to improve one's position in life usually provides the **push** to make one work or study.

   a. impulse   b. momentum   c. drive   d. delusion   (32)

3. The nurse **helped** the patient as she walked down the hall.

   a. lent a hand to   b. restrained   c. aided   (27)

4. The characters in this story **represent** the kind of people who live in Boston.

   a. depict   b. embody   c. exemplify   d. assist   (33)

5. That he might become president was an **unreality.**

   a. (a) fantasy   b. (a) stimulus   c. illusion   (31)

6. This book **arranges** stamps according to their current value.

   a. catalogs   b. classifies   c. categorizes   d. typifies   (29)

7. Be careful not to **omit** any of the steps involved in the experiment.

   a. be confronted with   b. disregard   c. leave out   d. exclude   (34)

8. The injury was an **unending** source of trouble for the athlete.

    a. (a) permanent   b. (a) constant   c. (a) belligerent
    d. (a) persistent   (35)

9. Something that one learns while growing up is the ability to **hold back** one's anger in most situations.

    a. suppress   b. rank   c. curb   d. restrict (28)

10. The psychologists **met** a very serious problem in their research.

    a. came across   b. ran into   c. encountered   d. prevented (36)

11. Thunderstorms are **common** during the spring in that part of the country.

    a. prevalent   b. belligerent   c. widespread (30)

12. The student became **angry** when the teacher said that he had cheated.

    a. antagonistic   b. hostile   c. spiteful   d. pervasive (26)

EXERCISE 13

In each blank write the keyword that corresponds to the word(s) in heavy type in the sentence. The number in parentheses can be used to check your answer.

1. The general field of psychology is **sorted** into smaller fields called branches. _____ (29)

2. Although the lines between these fields are **indistinct,** let's examine a few of these branches. _____ (14)

3. There have been many experiments that show that certain methods of teaching **assist** learning. _____ (27)

4. Other methods may actually **inhibit** learning. _____ (28)

5. The **elaborate** process of human learning is studied in educational psychology. _____ (12)

6. If we **apply** the outcome of research in this field to our schools, we will be more effective educators. _____ (22)

7. The study of mental **attitudes** of preadult humans is called child psychology. _____ (5)

8. People in this branch show how growth and **surroundings,** both physical and psychological, affect behavior. _____ (6)

9. What **fundamental** tools do humans possess at birth? _____ (1)

10. How can we **reduce** the effects of negative events that occur during childhood? _____ (20)

11. For example, if a child is treated with **brutality** at home, how can we help him or her in school? _____ (4)

12. These are some of the seemingly **infinite** questions that child psychologists are attempting to answer. _____ (19)

13. Occasionally psychologists **come across** people who have serious problems with their mental processes. _____ (36)

14. Sometimes these people live in a world of **fantasy.** _____ (31)

15. Sometimes they are filled with **apprehension** for no reason. _____ (21)

16. At other times they react with **terror** when there is nothing to be afraid of. _____ (11)

17. Some of these people never develop the mental ability to perform even the simplest of **deeds.** _____ (8)

18. Abnormal psychology is the **specific** branch that studies these types of people. _____ (13)

19. The branch of psychology that studies how humans react to each other in groups is **termed** social psychology. _____ (17)

20. It examines the **constant** influence of social conditions on behavior. _____ (35)

21. Is a person's **cognizance** of his or her environment influenced by the social groups within it? _____ (15)

22. Can certain psychological **tendencies** be explained by sociological phenomena? _____ (24)

23. Or, more specifically, what makes a person sacrifice his or her life out of **deference** to a political belief? _____ (16)

24. These questions **exemplify** some of the areas that social psychologists examine. _____ (33)

25. Physiological psychology studies physical **grounds** for psychological phenomena. _____ (23)

26. For example, when we feel **animosity,** there are changes that occur in the nervous system. _____ (10)

27. These physiological changes can produce behavior that results in **conflict.** _____ (7)

28. Other changes might produce a reaction of **humor.** _____ (9)

29. Physiological psychology attempts to **prohibit** certain types of behavior through physiological control. _____ (25)

30. So, if a person becomes dangerously **belligerent,** for instance, he or she receives medical treatment to alter the chemical output of the nervous system. _____ (26)

31. This may result in behavior that is more **benevolent.** _____ (3)

32. Thus, while the causes of the behavior remain **concealed,** the behavioral reactions are temporarily altered. _____ (18)

33. Several psychological fields have been **left out of** this discussion because of space limitations. _____ (34)

34. However, it is obvious that, with so many areas to examine, the **impulses** that cause certain actions are not easy to isolate. _____ (32)

35. There is no **widespread** agreement regarding the relevance of particular kinds of information. _____ (30)

36. Thus, as the psychologist attempts to understand mental phenomena, he or she always faces the **laborious** task of separating meaningful information from unimportant information. _____ (2)

EXERCISE 14

Below each puzzle is a list of related words. Write the keyword for each related word in the appropriate squares. After you have written in all of the keywords for one puzzle, read the word in the circles going down. This will be a related word for the first keyword in the *next* puzzle. The numbers in parentheses can be used to check your answers, but try to complete the puzzle without using them.

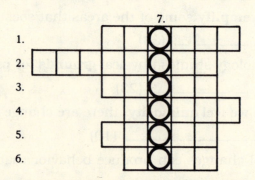

1. ubiquitous (30)	4. intrinsic (1)
2. permanent (35)	5. combat (7)
3. anguish (21)	6. cooperate (27)

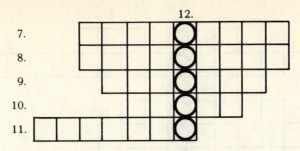

7. SEE PUZZLE ABOVE (31) 10. unequivocal (13)
8. cognition (15) 11. sadism (4)
9. obscure (14)

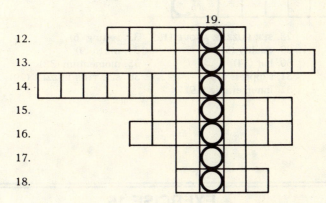

12. SEE PUZZLE ABOVE (20) 16. reverence (16)
13. exploit (8) 17. resort (to) (22)
14. tough (2) 18. run into (36)
15. terror (11)

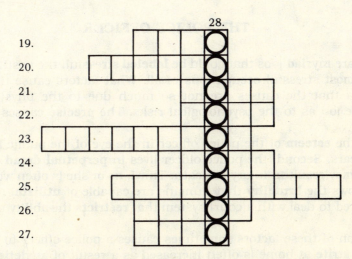

19. SEE PUZZLE ABOVE (18) 24. antagonistic (26)
20. inspiration (23) 25. predisposition (24)
21. preclude (25) 26. fury (10)
22. term (17) 27. solicitous (3)
23. embody (33)

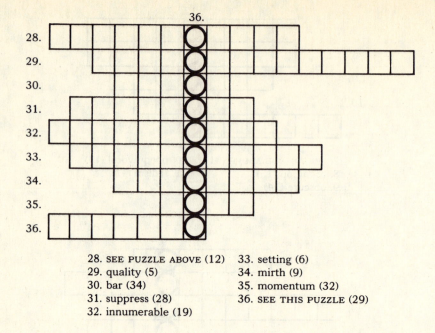

28. SEE PUZZLE ABOVE (12)   33. setting (6)
29. quality (5)   34. mirth (9)
30. bar (34)   35. momentum (32)
31. suppress (28)   36. SEE THIS PUZZLE (29)
32. innumerable (19)

EXERCISE 15

Some of the words in the following reading passages are in heavy type. Read the passages and write the keywords for these words in the blanks below.

THE POLICE OFFICER

While there are **myriad** jobs that could be **labeled** stressful, the position of police officer is one of the most stressful occupations of all. What factors cause this stress? Recent research shows that the causes are not so much due to the physical risks that are **inherent** in the job as to the psychological risks. The **precise** causes of these risks are rather complex.

First of all, the **esteem** of the police officer in the eye of the public has **diminished** in the past few years. Second, the police officer lives in **perpetual dread** of **encountering** a situation that may result in injury or death. Third, he or she is often working in a **setting** that clearly shows the **brutality** that humans are capable of **utilizing.** Finally, the police officer is required to deal with a court system that **restricts** the ability to function quickly and efficiently.

A combination of these factors sometimes causes a police officer to lose **impetus.** The **propensity** for **strife** at home is often increased as a result of **anxieties** on the job. The public should recognize the pressures of the police officer's **arduous** daily routine and do everything possible to **aid** him or her in the performance of duties.

1. _____   6. _____   11. _____   16. _____

2. _____   7. _____   12. _____   17. _____

3. _____	8. _____	13. _____	18. _____
4. _____	9. _____	14. _____	19. _____
5. _____	10. _____	15. _____	

SUICIDE

Suicide has been a cause of **concern** in most societies for a long time. The classical Greeks, for example, required people who wanted to kill themselves to get permission from the senate. While this law is not without **humor** by today's standards, it clearly shows an **awareness** of the problem in times gone by. In today's society, suicide is much more **prevalent** than we want to admit. Why do people try to take their own lives?

The **motives** for suicide can be **categorized** into areas such as failure, **wrath,** the need for attention, stress, and so on. However, the **qualities** of a person who wants to take his own life change from person to person, making it difficult to **depict** the typical victim. To make the problem even more **involved,** people will often **camouflage** their true feelings, thus causing their friends to **disregard** problems that should be viewed as serious.

In the United States, a network of centers has been created to attempt to **prevent** suicides. People who are **bitter,** worried, or depressed are encouraged to contact workers at these centers. These workers, often trained volunteers, offer **benevolent** advice to the callers, trying to help the callers to see that suicide as a solution to problems is an **illusion.** The **accomplishments** of these centers, insofar as their effectiveness to **reduce** suicide is concerned, are minimal. However, they have helped a lot of people with a wide variety of problems. So, in the somewhat **amorphous** area of man helping his fellow man, they are certainly a success.

1. _____	6. _____	11. _____	16. _____
2. _____	7. _____	12. _____	17. _____
3. _____	8. _____	13. _____	18. _____
4. _____	9. _____	14. _____	19. _____
5. _____	10. _____	15. _____	

EXERCISE 16

Read the following article. Do *not* use a dictionary. At least one related word from each of the keyword groups is in this article. Try to remember the proper keywords as you read.

Prereading Introduction

Every plant and animal in the world has certain ways of protecting itself from danger. These ways are called defense mechanisms. Color, taste, smell, and speed are but a few of the physical defense mechanisms that can be found in nature. The greatest defense mechanism that human beings have developed is their ability to think. However, the power of our minds represents a source of danger that no other living thing faces: our minds can play tricks on us, creating problems that can interfere with our ability to deal with our environment effectively. Therefore, human beings have developed a unique set of defense mechanisms designed to protect one from oneself. These mechanisms are not physical but rather psychological.

The following passage explains and exemplifies five types of psychological defense mechanisms: repression, reaction formation, projection, rationalization, and fantasy.

After reading the article, you should answer the following questions:

1. Why do people use defense mechanisms?
2. What is repression? How does it differ from suppression?
3. Give an example of repression.
4. What is reaction formation?
5. What is the main role of reaction formation as a defense mechanism?
6. What is projection?
7. When would a person employ projection as a defense mechanism?
8. What is rationalization?
9. How common a phenomenon is rationalization? When was the last time you used it?
10. How does fantasy differ from rationalization?
11. When is fantasy considered to be an unhealthy reaction to stress?

DEFENSE MECHANISMS*

There are many ways an individual may protect himself against conflict, anxiety, failure, and threatened loss of esteem. Since Freud originally described defensive adjustments, countless varieties have been identified. One useful distinction, which we shall employ here, is to recognize that Freud was concerned primarily with adjustments which occur without the organism's[a] conscious control or awareness. To these methods of avoiding anxiety-producing thoughts he gave the name ego-defensive mechanisms or simply *defense mechanisms.*

Persons using defense mechanisms often do not recognize any specific threat to the self or ego.[b] Instead, they experience vague feelings of fear or anxiety. Since anxiety is an unpleasant experience, it serves as a motive. The anxious person attempts to reduce his anxiety, sometimes through the use of defense mechanisms.

Repression. Repression is a complex concept with several different aspects, but here we refer only to its primary characteristic, the exclusion of unpleasant experiences from awareness. This process has been considered already in connection with memory. In that context we noted Freud's tendency to forget the names of patients who had not paid their bills, and an example was given of a frustrated suitor[c] who constantly forgot the name of his rival. Charles Darwin was so cognizant of the tendency to avoid or forget the unpleasant and so intellectually honest that he made a point of jotting down[d] immediately any observation which failed to support his views. Observations confirming them needed no special attention.

Freud regarded repression as the primary defense mechanism, not only because it appeared so widespread but also, as we shall see shortly, because it served as a

*Norman L. Munn, Dodge Fernald, Jr., and Peter S. Fernald, *Introduction to Psychology,* Second Edition (Boston: Houghton Mifflin Company, 1969), pp. 511–14.

basis for more elaborate mechanisms of defense. With regard to its pervasiveness, Freud viewed the repression of hostile and sexual impulses as virtually universal in nineteenth-century Western society.

The difference between repression and suppression also has been noted previously. Suppression involves consciously inhibiting a certain thought or activity, such as the desire to strike someone. Repression occurs when the individual is unaware of even the impulse to be aggressive. When little or no anxiety is experienced concerning the unwanted thought, it is assumed that repression is complete; the thwarting[e] or embarrassing thought is excluded from consciousness. When the individual experiences vague and uncomfortable feelings without knowing why, it appears that there is only partial repression.

The ego-defending nature of repression has been investigated in a variation of Zeigarnik's experiment, reported earlier. Two groups of college students were given different "sets" concerning the reason for performing the assigned task, a jigsaw puzzle. Members of one group, the *task-involved* group, were informed that the experimenter wanted to classify the puzzles for further use and that their reactions would assist him. Members of the other group, the *ego-involved* group, were told the puzzles were part of an intelligence test. Members of both groups were permitted to finish half the tasks[f] but were stopped midway through each of the remaining tasks. The hypothesis tested in this experiment was that the ego-involved group, since they presumably would experience considerable personal failure when prevented from completing tasks, would recall fewer unfinished tasks than the other group. The results supported this hypothesis. Of the thirty students in each group, eight from the ego-involved group and nineteen from the task-involved group recalled a preponderance[g] of unfinished tasks. It is hypothesized that repression occurred in these instances. Comparable results were obtained in two other experiments with different materials and different methods of producing ego involvement.

Reaction formation.   Sometimes behavior conceals fears or attitudes which are unknown even to the individual himself. For example, a bombardier[h] reported that he was eager to return to combat after a narrow escape from death during one of his missions, but he fainted[i] following each of his next two missions. During an interview he laughed at the interviewer's questions, stated he never experienced fear while flying, and declared that in fact he had never feared anything. Later, following administration of sodium pentothal, which releases the expression of unconscious material,[j] the bombardier's underlying feelings were revealed: " . . . the plane suddenly shook . . . . down we fell . . . . I was scared. Me scared! I didn't think I'd ever be scared—didn't think any man could scare me . . . ."[*]

It is suggested that in this case fears, particularly fears of flying, were repressed and that the opposite attitude was adopted by the flyer as a "second measure of defense." The flyer's bravado,[k] jocularity, and aggressiveness served to strengthen further his defense against the unwanted thought. In this mechanism, known as *reaction formation,* repression is accompanied or followed by conscious attitudes and behavior which are exactly opposite of those the individual has judged unacceptable. This reaction, it is hypothesized, increases the effectiveness of repression.

It is sometimes hypothesized that persons who crusade against the use of alcohol in any form and against any sexual expression may be struggling to control their own impulses toward engaging in such activities. Maternal overprotection may be a form of reaction formation. The mother usually wants to love her child, but inevitably she finds child rearing a difficult and burdensome task. Hence, she may try to conceal her resentment, even from herself, by being overly solicitous[l] of the child's welfare. In reaction formation, the individual adopts an attitude which is the opposite of his true feelings.

A college girl who was overly "sweet" and

---

[*]R. W. White, *The Abnormal Personality* (New York: Ronald Press, 1964), p. 64.

solicitous was asked whether she ever became angry. She replied in the negative. When asked what she would do if she ever did become angry, she replied, "I'd kill 'em with kindness!"

Projection.   In a general sense, whenever an individual inaccurately attributes[m] his own personal characteristics to others, he is projecting. We have discussed this term already in connection with the various projective tests. Children frequently project their thoughts and feelings, believing that others feel just as they feel. When a child is sad, for example, he may say that his friend is sad too.

In the present context, projection has a more restricted meaning. It refers to unknowingly attributing one's unwanted traits to others. Again, there are two aspects: repression of the unacceptable thoughts and ascribing them to others.

Projection also may involve an indirect wish fulfillment. In an extreme case, for example, a girl who becomes frustrated in attracting the interest of men may imagine that men have a special interest in her. A college girl known to one of the writers complained that men chased her through a park, but investigation revealed that no such events had occurred. A reaction of this type is dramatically depicted in Faulkner's short story *Dry September* (1950).

In a study of projection, fraternity brothers[n] rated themselves and each other on four socially undesirable traits: stinginess, obstinacy, disorderliness, and bashfulness. Some subjects demonstrated an awareness of their undesirable traits by giving themselves high ratings on traits for which they also received high ratings from their fraternity brothers. Others who were rated high gave themselves low ratings, showing little recognition of their undesirable traits. Of importance in the present discussion is that the latter subjects[o] showed a marked tendency to rate others in the group higher on their own unrecognized undesirable traits than did the rest of the group. Very simply, those lacking insight into their own undesirable traits were more likely to project these traits onto others.

Rationalization.   Aesop's fable, "The Fox and the Grapes," is a frequently quoted illustration of rationalization. When the fox couldn't obtain some delicious-looking grapes, he decided that they were sour anyway. In rationalization, "good" but false reasons are substituted for real reasons. Hence, we hear the expression "sour grapes" and also "sweet lemons." In the latter instances, one is forced to accept an undesirable outcome, and therefore overrates the object or event. A student forced to enroll in a course which he does not expect to like may say, "Well, it certainly will have to be better this term; it can't be any worse!" Not all such responses constitute rationalization, of course. There may be bona fide[p] reasons for expecting that the course will improve.

Rationalizing may begin at an early age. A three-year-old who did not want a neighborhood child of five to visit him because this child monopolized his toy fire engine was told he must invite the other child to come over and have a ride. He said that the other boy might be having his nap. When told that the other boy was up, he said the sky looked as if it might rain. When he was told that it would not rain, he said that the boy's mother might not want him to come. He made one excuse after another. The same boy, in conflict between his desire to take his teddy bear[q] to school, on the one hand, and being thought of as a "big boy," on the other, finally decided not to take the bear. His reason was that the bear might catch a cold.

Since our society places much value on rational behavior and thinking, people may go to great lengths to convince themselves and others that their behavior is based upon sound reasoning. As a result, frequently it is difficult to determine whether someone is giving true or false reasons. The distinction sometimes can be made by observing his willingness to examine his reasons. The individual may become upset when his reasons are questioned or when he is confronted with apparently more basic reasons. In these instances, it is hypothesized, the real reasons are not acknowledged and the individual becomes anxious because they are brought closer to his awareness.

Rationalization sometimes is excused on the grounds that it reduces the misgivings or qualms of conscience. Some assert that we all need little fictions[r] to make life easier. There is at least a grain of truth to such assertions, but even those statements *may* be rationalizations. As a rule, the most satisfactory outcomes occur when adjustment problems are dealt with directly.

Fantasy. While our actions generally must conform to the expectations of society, thoughts and dreams have no such limits. Without fear of failure, heroic deeds, brutality and unusual love affairs may be accomplished in wish-fulfilling thoughts, called fantasy. Hence, it is not surprising that personal problems frequently are "resolved" in fantasy. In Thurber's "The Secret Life of Walter Mitty" a frustrated henpecked[s] husband, generally treated with disdain, becomes a great lover, an outstanding surgeon, a skillful airplane pilot, and a courageous prisoner in his private world of fantasy.

Everyone, at one time or another, engages in some form of fantasy. Such activities are not necessarily deviant. Insofar as one uses fantasy to explore solutions to problems, fantasy is a constructive reaction. In fact, fantasy may be the father of invention. The Wright brothers had fantasies about flying . . . .

In contrast to these examples, fantasy is a sign of maladjustment when it becomes a persistent substitute for dealing with reality, rather than a creative use of imagination in solving unusual problems. The contribution of fantasy to any individual's adjustment is determined by the way in which it is used. In extreme cases, fantasy is usually a form of escape; reality is not represented at all. When one withdraws into unreality for extended periods, gradually the distinction between fantasy and reality becomes unclear. This use of fantasy typifies the thinking of many psychotic patients, who substitute an imaginary world for the real one, which is too threatening to be confronted.

Notes

[a]organism: any living thing.

[b]ego: that part of one's personality that is conscious and that most immediately controls one's actions.

[c]suitor: a man who is seeking a woman's hand in marriage.

[d]jotting down: writing down informally.

[e]thwarting: opposing, offending, or antagonizing.

[f]tasks: jobs to be done.

[g]a preponderance: the majority; most.

[h]bombardier: a person on a military plane who controls the machinery to drop bombs.

[i]fainted: passed out; fell to the floor because of a sudden weakness.

[j]following administration of sodium pentothal, which releases the expression of unconscious material: after being given a certain drug that allowed him to say thoughts that were not available to his conscious mind.

[k]bravado: false show of being brave.

[l]overly solicitous: too attentive, wanting to do too much.

[m]attributes: assigns, gives to someone.

[n]fraternity brothers: men belonging to a social organization, usually connected with a university.

[o]the latter subjects: the second of the previously mentioned two groups; that is, those who gave themselves low ratings.

[p]bona fide: real, genuine.

[q]teddy bear: a child's toy bear, stuffed with soft material.

[r]little fictions: small lies, unimportant untruths.

[s]henpecked: being completely controlled by one's wife.

EXERCISE 17

The following exercises show how different word forms are derived in English. Try to remember the endings and what parts of speech they indicate.

A. Words that end in *-tion* or *-sion* are usually nouns.

> **Examples:** deteriorate → deterioration
> regress → regression

Put the letter of the correct keyword in the blank after each derived word. Some keywords are used more than one time:

a. to worsen   b. to repair   c. to delay   d. to keep   e. to trouble
f. to think about   g. plentiful   h. lonely

1. seclude → seclusion ____
2. renovate → renovation ____
3. The child received a serious injury to the head which resulted in a **retardation** of mental development. ____
4. The sudden appearance of spring flowers created a **profusion** of color across the countryside. ____
5. A large tree fell across the river, creating an **obstruction** to boat traffic. ____
6. Inability to use the right arm for several months resulted in the **degeneration** of those muscles. ____
7. After World War II, many countries spent billions of dollars on the **restoration** of their buildings. ____
8. The man was unable to walk because of a childhood **affliction.** ____
9. The farmers were in danger of losing all of their land until strict laws of **conservation** were adopted. ____
10. I spent several hours in **contemplation** before beginning to write the composition. ____

B. Words that end in *-ment* are usually nouns.

> **Examples:** harass → harassment
> apportion → apportionment

a. to delay   b. to surprise   c. to divide   d. to say no to

1. renounce → renouncement ____
2. The child was sent to a clinic to receive special help with its speech **impediment.** ____

3. The people were lined up, waiting for their **allotment** of drinking water. ____

4. The best student in class failed the test, much to the **amazement** of the teacher. ____

5. The actors always enjoyed the **astonishment** of the audience at the end of the play. ____

C. Words that end in *-ance* or *-ence* are usually nouns.

> **Examples:** acquiesce → acquiescence
> maintain → maintenance

a. to happen   b. to agree   c. to live   d. wealth   e. hardworking

1. subsist → subsistence ____

2. The **occurrence** of major crime in the area is decreasing. ____

3. The **diligence** of the student earned her an A in the course. ____

4. The **affluence** of the neighborhood was obvious from the cars in the parking lot. ____

5. The university did not want to make any major changes in policy without the **concurrence** of the faculty and the students. ____

In summary: We have learned three endings that indicate that the word is a noun. What are they?

1. _____

2. _____

3. _____

4 Anthropology

EXERCISE 1

In the following paragraph some of the words are in heavy type. Find the keyword from the list below that is closest in meaning to each of these words, and write the keyword in the proper blank underneath the paragraph. Check your answers by looking at Exercise 2.

KEYWORDS

to cross	**unimportant**	**possible**	**open to question**
to further	**to lengthen**	**straight up**	**to consider true**
to change	**completely**	**finally**	**to become larger**

Anthropology is a science that **bridges** the centuries in an attempt to understand how human beings developed. Anthropologists gather information from every source **imaginable.** Through their findings, physical anthropologists often **alter** our understanding of prehistoric man. They examine pieces of rock, bone, wood, and the like that appear **trifling** to the average person, as they gather information from the time before humans walked in an **erect** position. These researchers **take** nothing **for granted.** Their approach to their work is **purely** scientific. However, since they are attempting to reconstruct such early times, their theories are often **equivocal.** Many of them believe that they will **eventually** have answers to most of the questions concerning the origin and development of humans. However, because of the difficulty of their task, this is probably **stretching** the truth a bit. Nevertheless, our knowledge in this area has certainly **swelled** in the past 50 years. The discoveries of anthropologists have **fostered** a better understanding not only of our past, but also of our present.

bridges	_____	imaginable	_____
alter	_____	trifling	_____
erect	_____	take for granted	_____
purely	_____	equivocal	_____
eventually	_____	stretching	_____
swelled	_____	fostered	_____

EXERCISE 2

The first word in each group below is the keyword. All the words under each keyword (the related words) have similar meaning. Read each group and try to remember which words belong to each keyword.

1. **unimportant**
   trivial
   frivolous
   petty
   trifling
   superficial

2. **finally**
   at last
   eventually
   ultimately
   in the long run
   lastly

3. **to lengthen**
   elongate
   prolong
   extend
   stretch
   draw out

4. **completely**
   absolutely
   utterly
   thoroughly
   entirely
   purely

5. **to further**
   promote
   foster
   encourage
   facilitate
   promulgate

6. **to cross**
   span
   traverse
   intersect
   ford
   bridge

7. **to change**
   modify
   alter
   vary
   fluctuate
   transform

8. **straight up**
   perpendicular
   vertical
   plumb
   upright
   erect

9. **possible**
   potential
   likely
   conceivable
   feasible
   imaginable

10. **to consider (as) true**
    presume
    posit
    presuppose
    take for granted
    assume

11. **to become larger**
    dilate
    expand
    swell
    enlarge
    increase

12. **open to question**
    controversial
    debatable
    equivocal
    contestable
    disputable

EXERCISE 3

A. The 12 groups of related words are written below without keywords. Write the correct keyword over each keyword group.

B. Each group of related words has *one* word that does not belong in the group. Find that word, cross it out, and write it under the group to which it belongs.

KEYWORDS

to cross	unimportant	possible	open to question
to further	to lengthen	straight up	to consider
to change	completely	finally	(as) true
			to become larger

1. _____   2. _____   3. _____   4. _____

superficial	lastly	draw out	absolutely
plumb	eventually	prolong	purely
frivolous	entirely	stretch	thoroughly
petty	ultimately	dilate	utterly
trivial	at last	elongate	in the long run

_____   _____   _____   _____

5. _____   6. _____   7. _____   8. _____

facilitate	traverse	vary	erect
promote	span	alter	perpendicular
posit	extend	intersect	equivocal
encourage	ford	fluctuate	upright
foster	bridge	modify	vertical

_____   _____   _____   _____

9. _____   10. _____   11. _____   12. _____

conceivable	presuppose	swell	controversial
imaginable	presume	expand	debatable
potential	take for granted	transform	disputable
trifling	assume	increase	contestable
likely	promulgate	enlarge	feasible

_____   _____   _____   _____

EXERCISE 4

Each sentence below contains one keyword, which is in heavy type.

A. Find the word below each sentence that is *not* a related word for the keyword. Circle that word. (The keyword numbers from Exercise 2 are in parentheses. These will help you if you need to look back.)

B. After completing instruction A, write each circled word under the keyword in the sentence to which it belongs.

1. I was **completely** lost by the time we arrived at his house.

   a. thoroughly   b. utterly   c. eventually   d. entirely   (4)

2. The amount of rainfall **furthered** the growth of vegetation in the area.

   a. promoted   b. forded   c. encouraged   d. fostered   (5)

3. One's education often **changes** one's thinking patterns.

   a. alters   b. modifies   c. varies   d. prolongs   (7)

4. As the need for oil **became larger,** the oil-producing countries became more powerful.

    a. assumed   b. increased   c. enlarged   d. swelled (11)

5. How modern man evolved is **open to question.**

    a. controversial   b. contestable   c. disputable   d. trivial (12)

6. Our system of justice **considers as true** that a man is innocent until proven guilty.

    a. presupposes   b. presumes   c. expands   d. takes for granted (10)

7. Is it **possible** that man will walk on Mars some day?

    a. vertical   b. conceivable   c. likely   d. imaginable (9)

8. We must **cross** a river in order to get to that canyon.

    a. traverse   b. transform   c. bridge (6)

9. **Finally,** he decided to change his major.

    a. At last   b. Ultimately   c. In the long run   d. Absolutely (2)

10. Through the years, the neck of the giraffe **lengthened** to allow the animal to reach higher sources of food.

    a. facilitated   b. extended   c. stretched   d. was drawn out (3)

11. The north side of the mountain was almost **straight up.**

    a. erect   b. plumb   c. feasible   d. perpendicular (8)

12. The things that my parents were worried about turned out to be **unimportant:** I graduated with honors.

    a. petty   b. frivolous   c. debatable   d. trifling (1)

EXERCISE 5

In the following paragraph at least one word in each sentence is in heavy type. Find the keyword from the list below that is closest in meaning to each of these words, and write the keyword in the proper blank underneath the paragraph. Check your answers by looking at Exercise 6.

KEYWORDS

result	equal	appearance	movement
place	child	to become smaller	forefather
size	to include	very important	nonprofessional

Man's **niche** in historical time is very small. Although the earth is at least 6 billion years old, our **forerunners** did not appear until about a million years ago. Thus the **rise** and development of mankind **encompasses** only a very small segment of the earth's history. However, the **magnitude** of the **effect** that man has had on the environment is huge, and there is no indication that it will soon **abate.** To help us better understand where we are going, it is **imperative** that we study how man developed. Anthropology, which is, comparatively speaking, a **fledgling** science, attempts to do exactly that. The **novice** might not appreciate the importance of this type of scientific investigation and might not consider anthropology to be **on a par with** chemistry, physics, and so on. However, there has been a **shifting** away from this type of thinking, so that today a course in anthropology is either an option or a requirement for many undergraduate degrees.

niche	_____	forerunner	_____
rise	_____	encompasses	_____
magnitude	_____	effect	_____
abate	_____	imperative	_____
fledgling	_____	novice	_____
on a par with	_____	shifting	_____

EXERCISE 6

The first word in each group below is the keyword. All the words under each keyword (the related words) have similar meaning. Read each group and try to remember which related words go with each keyword.

13. **size**	14. **place**	15. **to become smaller**	16. **forefather**
mass	niche	abate	predecessor
magnitude	locale	shrink	forebear
capacity	location	dwindle	precursor
stature	whereabouts	decrease	forerunner
volume	site	wane	ancestor

17. **appearance**	18. **movement**	19. **very important**	20. **result**
manifestation	motion	vital	outcome
emergence	locomotion	momentous	consequence
rise	mobility	major	effect
materialization	migration	imperative	upshot
advent	shifting	crucial	fruition

21. **child**	22. **nonprofessional**	23. **equal**	24. **to include**
fledgling	novice	corresponding	encompass
tot	layman	commensurate	subsume

offspring	neophyte	on a par with	incorporate
infant	apprentice	peer	entail
toddler	amateur	equitable	be comprised of

EXERCISE 7

A. The 12 groups of related words are written below without keywords. Write the correct keywords over each keyword group.

B. Each group of related words has *one* word that does not belong in the group. Find that word, cross it out, and write it under the group to which it belongs.

KEYWORDS

result	equal	appearance	movement
place	child	to become	forefather
size	to include	smaller	nonprofessional
		very important	

13. _____   14. _____   15. _____   16. _____

mass	niche	abate	predecessor
magnitude	precursor	shrink	forebear
capacity	location	dwindle	advent
motion	whereabouts	decrease	forerunner
volume	site	subsume	ancestor

_____   _____   _____   _____

17. _____   18. _____   19. _____   20. _____

manifestation	stature	vital	outcome
emergence	locomotion	peer	consequence
rise	mobility	major	effect
materialization	migration	imperative	upshot
fruition	shifting	crucial	toddler

_____   _____   _____   _____

21. _____   22. _____   23. _____   24. _____

fledgling	novice	corresponding	encompass
tot	layman	commensurate	wane
neophyte	locale	on a par with	incorporate
infant	apprentice	momentous	entail
offspring	amateur	equitable	be comprised of

_____   _____   _____   _____

EXERCISE 8

Each sentence below contains one keyword, which is in heavy type.

A. Find the word in the list below each sentence that is *not* a related word for the keyword. Circle that word. (The keyword numbers from Exercise 6 are in parentheses. These will help you if you need to look back.)

B. After completing instruction A, write each circled word under the keyword in the sentence to which it belongs.

1. The study of anthropology **includes** the study of culture and evolution.

    a. incorporates   b. entails   c. shrinks   d. subsumes (24)

2. The **place** where some of the earliest hominid fossils were found is in India.

    a. layman   b. site   c. locale (14)

3. The **size** of the head is a key to the intelligence of an animal.

    a. volume   b. consequence   c. mass   d. magnitude (13)

4. Darwin's theory of evolution had a **very important** effect on science.

    a. momentous   b. vital   c. crucial   d. commensurate (19)

5. People mistakenly thought that Darwin was saying that the monkey was the **forefather** of the human race.

    a. ancestor   b. precursor   c. predecessor   d. mobility (16)

6. How a monkey takes care of its **child** helps scientists understand its social organization.

    a. offspring   b. capacity   c. tot   d. fledgling (21)

7. Often the **nonprofessional** does not understand the importance of culture in human behavior.

    a. novice   b. amateur   c. infant   d. neophyte (22)

8. The amount of available oil **becomes smaller** as time passes.

    a. wanes   b. dwindles   c. abates   d. encompasses (15)

9. Man's social organization is a **result** of his ability to make and use tools.

    a. location   b. (an) outcome   c. (an) effect (20)

10. The money he received was **equal to** the effort he made in completing the job.

    a. on a par with   b. corresponding to   c. major
    d. equitable with (23)

11. The **appearance** of language allowed civilization to develop.

    a. materialization   b. forebear   c. rise   d. advent (17)

12. Survival of certain animals depends upon their ease of **movement.**

    a. migration   b. motion   c. locomotion   d. emergence (18)

EXERCISE 9

In the following paragraph one word in each sentence is in heavy type. Find the keyword from the list below that is closest in meaning to each of these words, and write the keyword in the proper blank underneath the paragraph. Check your answers by looking at Exercise 10.

KEYWORDS

automatic	together (with)	start	to hold on to
to care for	thought	to copy	to join
to sleep	small piece	tool	food

Social anthropology is a science of relatively recent **origin.** This new science involves the study of customs, habits, attitudes, and the like of groups of people **in conjunction with** their physical environment. What **unites** a group of people? How do they **watch over** each other? How do they cooperate to obtain **nourishment?** Why do some groups of people tend to **slumber** while others lean toward activity? What role do **utensils** play in their social organization? Which actions are **instinctive?** Which actions are learned by **imitating?** Why do people **cling to** certain beliefs and rituals? Social anthropologists gather every possible **splinter** of information in their attempts to answer these and many other questions. As in every other scientific field, careful **reflection** upon the smallest detail sometimes reveals very important information.

origin	_____	in conjunction with	_____
unites	_____	watch over	_____
nourishment	_____	slumber	_____
utensils	_____	instinctive	_____
imitating	_____	cling to	_____
splinter	_____	reflection	_____

EXERCISE 10

The first word in each group below is the keyword. All the words under each keyword (the related words) have similar meaning. Read each group and try to remember which words belong to each keyword.

25. **to care for**
    minister
    tend

26. **small piece**
    sliver
    scrap

27. **thought**
    meditation
    reflection

28. **to join**
    unite
    link

attend to	fragment	cogitation	merge
watch over	crumb	contemplation	couple
nurse	splinter	conception	fasten

29. to hold on to

adhere
grasp
stick
cling
clasp

30. automatic

involuntary
instinctive
reflex
spontaneous
intuitive

31. start

onset
genesis
inception
commencement
origin

32. tool

apparatus
gadget
device
utensil
appliance

33. to sleep

slumber
doze
hibernate
snooze
repose

34. food

comestibles
cuisine
edibles
nourishment
sustenance

35. to copy

emulate
mimic
ape
imitate
mime

36. together (with)

side by side
with
in conjunction
with
hand in hand
with
in combination
with
concomitant

EXERCISE 11

A. The 12 groups of related words are written below without keywords. Write the correct keyword over each keyword group.

B. Each group of related words has *one* word that does not belong in the group. Find that word, cross it out, and write it under the group to which it belongs.

KEYWORDS

automatic	**together (with)**	**start**	**to hold on to**
to care for	**thought**	**to copy**	**to join**
to sleep	**small piece**	**tool**	**food**

25. _____

minister
tend
emulate
watch over
nurse

_____

26. _____

commencement
scrap
fragment
crumb
splinter

_____

27. _____

meditation
reflection
cogitation
contemplation
edibles

_____

28. _____

unite
link
merge
slumber
fasten

_____

29. _____

adhere
attend to

30. _____

involuntary
instinctive

31. _____

onset
genesis

32. _____

apparatus
gadget

stick	reflex	inception	device
cling	concomitant	appliance	utensil
clasp	intuitive	origin	conception
_____	_____	_____	_____

33. _____ 34. _____ 35. _____ 36. _____

grasp	comestibles	couple	side by side
doze	cuisine	mimic	with
hibernate	sliver	ape	in conjunction
snooze	nourishment	imitate	with
repose	sustenance	mime	hand in hand
			with
			in combination
			with
			spontaneous

_____   _____   _____   _____

EXERCISE 12

Each sentence below contains one keyword, which is in heavy type.

A. Find the word below each sentence that is *not* a related word for the keyword. Circle that word. (The keyword numbers from Exercise 10 are in parentheses. These will help you if you need to look back.)

B. After completing instruction A, write each circled word under the keyword in the sentence to which it belongs.

1. The problem could not be solved without considerable **thought.**

    a. reflection   b. apparatus   c. contemplation   d. cogitation (27)

2. Primates learn by **copying** the actions of others.

    a. adhering   b. mimicking   c. imitating   d. aping (35)

3. Early man used rocks as a **tool** for killing animals.

    a. device   b. utensil   c. apparatus   d. genesis (32)

4. An increased heartbeat is an **automatic** reaction to fear.

    a. reflex   b. instinctive   c. in combination with
    d. spontaneous (30)

5. Anthropologists found **small pieces** of bone buried next the statue.

    a. scraps   b. slivers   c. meditations   d. splinters (26)

6. How to grow enough **food** to feed the world's population is a serious problem today.

    a. nourishment   b. comestibles   c. edibles   d. fragments (34)

7. After the explosion, doctors were brought in to **care for** the injured.

   a. attend to   b. link   c. tend to   d. nurse   (25)

8. Flies are able to walk on the ceiling because their feet have a substance that allows them to **hold on to** any surface.

   a. minister   b. grasp   c. cling to   d. stick to   (29)

9. Cats love to **sleep** in the warm sun.

   a. doze   b. slumber   c. link   d. repose   (33)

10. Tendons **join** muscles to bones.

    a. snooze   b. couple   c. fasten   d. unite   (28)

11. Better hunting techniques, **together with** agricultural developments, allowed humans to live in one place.

    a. in conjunction with   b. involuntary   c. hand in hand with
    d. side by side with   (36)

12. The **start** of more or less permanent settlements was probably in the Middle Stone Age.

    a. inception   b. origin   c. commencement   d. sustenance   (31)

EXERCISE 13

In each blank write the keyword that corresponds to the word in heavy type in the sentence. The number in parentheses can be used to check your answer.

1. The analysis of teeth and jaws is **crucial** to the understanding of how modern man evolved. _____ (19)

2. The **site** of the discovery of Neanderthal man was Gibraltar. _____ (14)

3. Radiocarbon dating has greatly **increased** our knowledge of the history of mankind. _____ (11)

4. The development of irrigation **promoted** agriculture in dry areas. _____ (5)

5. The computer is a **device** that is changing our society. _____ (32)

6. Fossilized **scraps** of food and bone allow anthropologists to reconstruct many aspects of early societies. _____ (26)

7. Modern medical advances have **extended** the average life expectancy by several years. _____ (3)

8. As the climate of the earth changed, the number of dinosaurs **dwindled.**
   _____ (15)

9. Careful observations and notes pay off **in the long run.**
   _____ (2)

10. When two cultures come into contact, they sometimes **merge.**
    _____ (28)

11. The evolutionary process **modifies** plants and animals in order to increase their chances for survival.   _____ (7)

12. The earliest **predecessor** of humans is the primate.
    _____ (16)

13. Human babies are born with the ability to **clasp** an object.
    _____ (29)

14. People who live in a new culture must adapt to a different **cuisine,** a sometimes very difficult process.   _____ (34)

15. Blinking one's eyes is an example of a **reflex** action.
    _____ (30)

16. Many **amateur** anthropologists made important discoveries.
    _____ (22)

17. Some animals **hibernate** during the winter months.
    _____ (33)

18. Charles Darwin published his book on the **origin** of the species in 1859.
    _____ (31)

19. The house was difficult to repair because its walls were not **plumb.**
    _____ (8)

20. The **manifestation** of a cultural phenomenon is usually a logical outgrowth of some physical aspect in the life-style of the people.
    _____ (17)

21. Every society tries to arrange for some kind of an **equitable** distribution of wealth among its people.   _____ (23)

22. The **migration** of nomadic peoples is influenced by food and water supplies as well as the weather.   _____ (18)

23. Although some people still consider Darwin's theory of evolution to be **controversial,** it is widely accepted in the scientific community.
    _____ (12)

24. How ancient man was able to **traverse** some of the great mountain ranges remains a mystery.   _____ (6)

25. The mother showed great patience in dealing with the **toddler.**
    _____ (21)

26. The **outcome** of the experiments by Gregor Mendel was a deeper understanding of heredity. _____ (20)

27. Comparative anatomy **incorporates** studies in physiology, serology, and genetics. _____ (24)

28. Scientists have wondered whether **contemplation** is possible without language. _____ (27)

29. The **volume** of the cranium (the bones that surround the brain) increased as modern man evolved. _____ (13)

30. For decades scientists **presumed** that the continents were always separated by bodies of water. _____ (10)

31. Children learn a lot by **mimicking** adults. _____ (35)

32. The physical characteristics of *Homo erectus* have been **thoroughly** examined. _____ (4)

33. One **potential** source of problems between nations is cultural misunderstanding. _____ (9)

34. Cultural anthropologists must understand theoretical aspects **in conjunction with** techniques of good fieldwork. _____ (36)

35. Many observations that were thought to be **frivolous** turned out to be very significant. _____ (1)

36. In most societies women **tend** to the children and the home while men obtain food. _____ (25)

EXERCISE 14

Solve the puzzle by writing the correct keyword for each of the words given below. The numbers in parentheses can be used to check your answers, but try to complete the puzzle without using them.

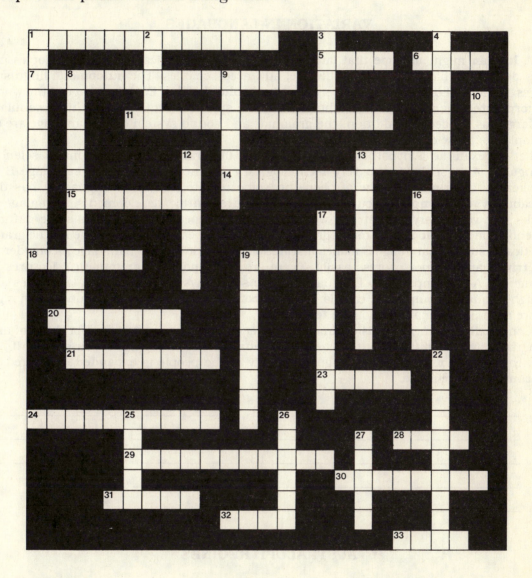

ACROSS

1. decrease (15)
5. gadget (32)
6. comestibles (34)
7. presuppose (10)
11. contestable (12)
13. lastly (2)
14. stick (29)
15. encourage (5)
18. upshot (20)
19. materialization (17)
20. entail (24)
21. draw out (3)

23. tot (21)
24. entirely (4)
28. fasten (28)
29. superficial (1)
30. side by side with (36)
31. whereabouts (14)
32. mass (13)
33. ape (35)

DOWN

1. enlarge (11)
2. repose (33)
3. inception (31)

4. likely (9)
8. apprentice (22)
9. cogitation (27)
10. vital (19)
12. nurse (25)
13. ancestor (16)
16. locomotion (18)
17. crumb (26)
19. intuitive (30)
22. upright (8)
25. corresponding (23)
26. vary (7)
27. span (6)

EXERCISE 15

Some of the words in the following reading passages are in heavy type. Read the passages and write the keywords for each in the blanks below.

VARIATION IN LANGUAGES

A **layman** might **assume** that languages of less technologically advanced peoples are less developed than languages of literate, advanced societies. The **outcome** of linguistic investigations shows that this observation is **absolutely** false. Each language of the world **incorporates** the amount of vocabulary that its speakers require, and this vocabulary **enlarges** as needed. In addition, the grammar and sound system of any language are as complex as those of any other language.

Let us examine a hypothetical situation that illustrates the conclusions of science. Language A is spoken by a very technologically advanced people, and Language B is spoken by a "primitive" tribe of people in some remote **location.** Language A has the vocabulary to **promote** discussions of advanced scientific developments. Language B lacks this vocabulary, but it has words to allow its speakers to discuss some natural phenomena of the **locale** in much greater detail than speakers of Language A. The grammatical system of Language B makes distinctions that speakers of Language A consider to be **trivial** and cannot express easily. There are **corresponding** grammatical features of Language A as compared to Language B. The sound systems of the two languages are roughly equal in complexity: each language **is comprised of** only 25–50 sounds, although more than 500 human sounds are **feasible.**

Complexity, then, is a misleading term when comparing languages. Speakers of any language are able to talk about all the phenomena that are **vital** within their society. If the environment is **modified,** the language facility of the people is **expanded** or **altered** to **encompass** the change.

1. _____   6. _____   11. _____   16. _____

2. _____   7. _____   12. _____   17. _____

3. _____   8. _____   13. _____   18. _____

4. _____   9. _____   14. _____

5. _____   10. _____   15. _____

AUSTRALOPITHECINES

In 1924, Professor Raymond Dart found the fossilized **fragments** of one of man's early **predecessors** in South Africa: *Australopithecus africanus,* or "southern ape of Africa." The skeleton was identified as that of a five- to seven-year-old **offspring,** and represented the earliest discovery of a bipedal (walking on two legs) animal.

When the skeleton was first discovered, it was **debatable** whether or not the animal was bipedal. Dart proved that the child walked in an **upright** position by examining the bones closely. The foramen magnum, the hole at the base of the skull through which the nerves of the spinal column pass, faced downward. This fact, **in combination with** the structure and number of its vertebrae, or backbones, indicated that **locomotion** was accomplished in a **perpendicular** position.

Since Dart's discovery, more than 100 other australopithecines have been recovered, allowing scientists to reconstruct the biped with great accuracy. The **capacity** of the cranium (the bone surrounding the brain) indicates that the **volume** of the brain was less than half that of modern man's. No **utensils** have been unearthed with australopithecine remains; however, it is **conceivable** that the earliest tools were made from bone rather than stone and were, therefore, not preserved.

The discovery of australopithecine hominids was **major** evidence in support of the theory that modern man is a **manifestation** of an evolutionary process from a primate **ancestor.** Anthropologists hope **ultimately** to discover fossils that will **link** modern man to his evolutionary **genesis.**

1. _____   6. _____   11. _____   16. _____
2. _____   7. _____   12. _____   17. _____
3. _____   8. _____   13. _____   18. _____
4. _____   9. _____   14. _____
5. _____   10. _____   15. _____

ADAPTING TO TREE LIFE

As forests spread over certain areas, it became advantageous for animals to be able to live safely in trees. As a result, new skills in **mobility** and obtaining **sustenance** became necessary.

The forelimbs of early primates **shrank** [past tense of **shrink**], and their hindlimbs **elongated,** allowing them to **grasp** branches firmly and to **traverse** great distances without touching land, where travel was more dangerous. Their fingers and toes **extended,** allowing them to **clasp** objects and bring them closer for examination. This ability to **cling** to objects played an important role in their future ability to **slumber** in the trees, to **tend to** their **infants,** and to make tools.

Good eyesight was also **crucial** in this new environment. So eyesight improved, and the eyes moved to the front of the head. This **shifting** of the eyes came **hand in hand with** a **decrease** in the size of the nose. The sense of smell, which was **vital** on the land, became not so important in the trees.

A **momentous** development in these animals was the tendency toward **cogitation,** directly related to the growth of the brain. Rather than being a **purely intuitive** process, animal behavior could now be significantly **transformed** by the very fact that some animals could now **emulate** the actions of their **peers.**

1. _____   7. _____   13. _____   19. _____
2. _____   8. _____   14. _____   20. _____
3. _____   9. _____   15. _____   21. _____
4. _____   10. _____   16. _____   22. _____
5. _____   11. _____   17. _____   23. _____
6. _____   12. _____   18. _____   24. _____

EXERCISE 16

Read the following articles. Do *not* use a dictionary. At least one related word from each of the keyword groups is in these articles. Try to remember the proper keywords as you read.

Prereading Introduction

Thousands of years ago, early man walked on all fours—that is, walked using both legs and arms. The development of the ability to walk on two legs, which is called bipedalism, made a very important contribution to the evolution of man as we know him today.

The following article examines the development of bipedalism. Since every change that a successful species undergoes produces some advantage(s), the article begins by giving theories about why bipedalism was successful—that is, what advantages man enjoyed as a result of becoming bipedal. Bipedalism obviously had a profound effect on the later development of culture. The article continues by examining how bipedalism influenced tool making and how tools made bipedalism useful. Also of cultural interest is how bipedalism influenced the role of males and females in the group. The third major area covered by the article involves physiological changes that affected the human body as a result of bipedalism, including such topics as development of the brain and changes in the process of carrying and giving birth to infants.

After reading the article, you should answer the following questions:

1. Discuss how each of the following may have contributed to the evolution of bipedalism:
   a. living in savannas (land covered by tall grass)
   b. food gathering
   c. tool making and using
2. Why would natural selection favor tool-making hominids?
3. Why is the human baby born with bones in its skull that are not completely formed?
4. How did bipedalism help create a division of labor by sex?

THE DEVELOPMENT OF BIPEDALISM*

Perhaps the most crucial change in early hominid[a] evolution was the development of bipedalism, or two-legged locomotion, combined with a fully upright posture.[b] In the opinion of many anthropologists, bipedalism was adaptive to life amid the tall grasses of the savanna.[c] True, an upright animal is more conspicuous, but stereoscopic or depth vision, originally an adaptation to tree life, combined with an erect posture, may have made it easier to spot ground predators[d] as well as potential prey.[e] It has been suggested that ancestral primates "were sometimes forced to move through the tall grass between forest areas and that, since this necessitated raising

---
*Carol R. Ember and Melvin Ember, *Anthropology.* © 1973, pp. 100–103. Reprinted by permission of Prentice-Hall, Inc., Englewood Cliffs, N.J.

their level of vision, bipedal abilities would have had selective advantages."[1] This theory does not adequately account for the development of bipedalism, however. Baboons and some other Old World monkeys live in savanna-type environments, yet although they can and do stand erect, they have not evolved fully bipedal *locomotion*.

Another theory explains bipedalism as an adaptation to new ways of food gathering consistent with terrestrial[f] life. The dwindling forests had reduced not only living sites, but food resources as well. In their new niche, those primates who became terrestrial gathered fruits and vegetables from the ground, and they probably needed to transfer food from one locale to another. Standing on two feet freed the hands for carrying and would have been adaptive.[g] Food carrying may also be related to the development of modified bipedalism in nonhuman primates.[h] Jane Goodall has seen chimpanzees "loading their arms with choice wild fruits, then walking erect for several yards to a spot of shade before sitting down to eat."[2] But still, food carrying is only a part-time activity and would not necessarily favor full-time bipedalism. Other factors, then, must have been involved in the evolution from a four-legged to a two-legged animal.

Sherwood Washburn has suggested that the use of tools furthered the evolution of bipedalism: carrying tools would have prevented the hands from being used for locomotion. With increased tool use, natural selection would have favored the use of the hindlegs alone for locomotion, leaving the hands free.[3]

Bipedalism and the Evolution of Culture

Although the circumstances that favored the development of bipedalism are still controversial, the immensity of its impact on human evolution, and on the emergence of culture in particular, is undisputed. Not only did bipedalism influence the development of tool making and the expansion of the brain, it had profound effects on human social behavior as well. For example, the time required to care for the human infant and the early definition of male and female roles can be traced, in part, to the influence of bipedalism.

Bipedalism, Tool Making, and the Expansion of the Brain

The origin of tool making is still not completely understood. Grasping hands and stereoscopic vision, characteristics of man's primate ancestors, preadapted terrestrial primates for the use of tools. The ability to grasp and to perceive objects in three dimensions facilitates the use and making of tools. But the fact that nonhuman primates also have these characteristics implies that they alone cannot account for the origin of human tool making. Clearly, some other factor or factors must have also been involved.

Traditionally the development of bipedalism in hominids was thought to be crucial for the origin of tool use and tool making, since bipedalism would have freed the hands for such activities. More recently, it has been thought that the sequence was reversed—that tool use and tool making came first—and their advantages were so profound that natural selection would have favored a more complete bipedalism in a tool-using and tool-making terrestrial primate. That is, in the absence of large body size and large canines,[i] a terrestrial primate living in a grassland environment full of predators would have been at a great disadvantage if he did not use tools at least to protect himself. Thus, those terrestrial primates that were more efficient tool users, perhaps because they were more completely bipedal, would have been able to survive in the grassland environment. It may be, however, that both of these theories are correct: bipedalism interacted with tool use and tool making, each one favoring an increase in the other. The benefits derived from efficient tool use would favor a more complete bipedalism, which in turn would free the hands even further for tool use and tool making.

[1]Kenneth Oakley, "On Man's Use of Fire, with Comments on Tool-Making and Hunting," in S. L. Washburn, ed., *Social Life of Early Man* (Chicago: Aldine, 1964), p. 186.
[2]Jane van Lawick-Goodall, "My Life among Wild Chimpanzees," *National Geographic* (August 1963), pp. 274–308.
[3]Sherwood Washburn, "Tools and Human Behavior," *Scientific American*, Vol. 203 (September 1960), p. 69.

Not only did tool making increase in sophistication[j] from *Australopithecus* to *Homo erectus*, but the volume of the brain also expanded, probably in conjunction with the selective forces that adapted the hominids to open-country life. The australopithecine cranial[k] capacity ranged from about 450 to 580 cc. The next known hominid, *Homo habilis*, had a capacity of about 600 cc. *Homo erectus*'s cranial capacity ranged from 775 to 1,300 cc. However, it should be noted that the australopithecine cranial capacity was already relatively large, considering that most of the australopithecines probably only weigh 50–100 pounds. (*Homo erectus* was about the size of modern man.) Since at least some of the australopithecines were tool makers, the emergence of tool making may have favored the expansion of the brain. Given that tool making was crucial to the survival of our ancestors in the grassland environment, natural selection may have favored not only increasing bipedalism, but also increasing motor and conceptual[l] skills, perhaps made possible by an enlarged brain. The increasing brain size may in turn have favored the evolution of more sophisticated tool making.

Other Consequences of Bipedalism and Tool Making

Not only can tool making, the enlargement of the brain, and perhaps language be linked in some way to the development of bipedalism, but several other human characteristics may be related to bipedalism as well. A prolonged period of infant dependency, division of labor between men and women, and food sharing may be traceable, in part, to two-legged walking.

The human pelvis[m] is primarily adapted for upright, two-legged walking and running. As natural selection favored increasing brain size, it also favored the widening of the female pelvis to allow larger-brained babies to be born. But there was probably a limit to how far the pelvis could widen and still be adapted to bipedalism. Something had to give, and that something was the degree of physical development of the human infant at birth: the human infant is born with cranial bones so plastic that they can overlap. (The bones at the top of the head do not even close until considerably after birth.) By being born before the cranial bones have hardened, the human infant with an enlarged brain could still pass through the mother's pelvis. But unable to cling like a monkey or an ape to its mother while nursing,[n] the utterly dependent newborn must be carried in her free hands.

Another effect of bipedalism, perhaps a consequence of lessened maturity at birth, was the prolongation of infant and child dependency that is so distinctively human. As compared with other animals, we not only spend the longest proportion of our life span, but also the longest absolute period of time, in a dependent state. This prolongation of dependency may have also been favored by the increasing complexity of human life, which required more time spent in social learning. Thus, prolonged infant dependency has been of great significance in human cultural evolution.

The development of hunting and division of labor by sex were other changes, related to bipedalism, that probably occurred by the time of *Homo erectus*, some 500,000 years ago. Tools made possible the development of hunting by man—for man is not naturally equipped for the killing and butchering of other animals. He did not have large canines, claws,[o] or great size. There are definite signs of hunting found with *Homo erectus*, and australopithecines probably hunted too. The development of hunting, combined with the prolongation of infant and child dependency, may have fostered the development of a division of labor by sex, with the men doing the hunting, and women doing the child tending and other work closer to home. If women have to carry babies and young children, they cannot easily chase animals that may run for some distance. Since the men would have been freer to do so, they probably became the hunters early in human evolution. While the men were away hunting, the women may have gathered wild plants and hunted some wild animals within a radius that could be traversed while carrying young children. This division of labor by sex may have given rise to another distinctively human characteristic: the sharing of food.

What is the evidence that the physical and cultural changes we have been discussing occurred during the evolution of the hominids? Fossil fragments from the late Pliocene and early Pleistocene indicate that new creatures, upright-walking primates since named the australopithecines, had emerged in the shrinking African forests to roam on the plains-like savannas, then forming over much of the earth's surface. Fossil fragments dating from later in the Pleistocene indicate the appearance of the first man—*Homo erectus.*

Notes

*a*hominid: an early ancestor of modern man.
*b*posture: the way a person holds his or her body when walking or sitting.
*c*savanna: flat, grass-covered land in tropical regions.
*d*predators: animals that live by killing and eating others.
*e*prey: an animal that is hunted as a source of food.
*f*terrestrial: on the ground (as opposed to in the trees).
*g*adaptive: useful in helping an animal to live in its environment.

*h*primates: a category of animals that includes monkeys, apes, and humans.
*i*canines: sharply pointed front teeth.
*j*increase in sophistication: become more complex, less simple.
*k*cranial: of or related to the bones of the head.
*l*motor and conceptual: physical and mental.
*m*pelvis: that part of one's bones which supports the backbone and to which the legs are attached.
*n*nursing: drinking milk from the mother.
*o*claws: an animal's long, sharp fingernails and toenails.

Prereading Introduction

"Culture" is a word that is often used when discussing some advanced art form. However, from an anthropological point of view, culture has a much broader meaning.

The next article first explains what is meant in anthropology by the term "culture." It then continues with the definition by contrasting learned behavior and innate behavior—that is, behavior that an animal knows from birth. Several examples are given for each type of behavior in the animal world.

After reading this article, you should answer the following questions:

1. When an anthropologist uses the term "culture," what does he or she mean?
2. Using food as an example, show how this aspect of human life is both cultural and noncultural.
3. Why is hibernation not considered to be a cultural trait?
4. The authors use an example of monkeys in Japan and sweet potatoes to illustrate a cultural acquisition. Explain that example.
5. What aspect of life separates monkeys, apes, and humans from other animals?

TOWARDS A DEFINITION OF CULTURE*

In everyday usage the word "culture" refers to a desirable quality that we can acquire by attending a sufficient number of plays and dance concerts and trudging through several miles of art galleries. The anthropologist, however, has a different definition. In the following extract, Ralph Linton makes clear how the layman's defi-

*Carol R. Ember and Melvin Ember, *Anthropology,* © 1973, pp. 21–22. Reprinted by permission of Prentice-Hall, Inc., Englewood Cliffs, N.J.

nition of "culture" differs from that of the anthropologist.

> It [culture] refers to the total way of life of any society, not simply to those parts of this way which the society regards as higher or more desirable. Thus culture, when applied to our own way of life, has nothing to do with playing the piano or reading Browning. For the social scientist such activities are simply elements within the totality of our culture. This totality also includes such mundane[a] activities as washing dishes or driving an automobile, and for the purposes of cultural studies these stand quite on a par with "the finer things of life." It follows that for the social scientist there are no uncultured societies or even individuals. Every society has a culture, no matter how simple this culture may be, and every human being is cultured, in the sense of participating in some culture or other.[1]

Culture, then, refers to innumerable aspects of life; it encompasses the behavior, beliefs, and attitudes, as well as the products of human activity, that are characteristic of a particular society or population. The Shinto and Buddhist religions and a strong sense of respect for the elderly are as much a part of Japanese culture as chopsticks and Kabuki theater. Each of us is born in a complex culture which will strongly influence how we will live and behave for the remainder of our lives.

Culture Is Learned

Culture is learned behavior; it does not rely on biological transmission or genetic inheritance.[b] It is necessary to make this point in order to differentiate the cultural behaviors of man and the other primates from behavior which is almost purely instinctual in origin.

All human beings are born with instinctual behaviors and drives which, although they are not considered parts of culture, do influence culture. For example, the need for nourishment is a basic need that is not cultural. But *how* that need is satisfied—what and how we eat—is part of our culture. Thus, all people eat, but different cultures approach this basic activity in vastly different ways. In the time of Rich-

ard the Lion-Hearted (1157–1199), for example, eating utensils did not grace[c] the English table. When people gathered together at mealtime, food was simply placed in large bowls in the center of the table, and everyone took what he wanted, eating with his fingers. As time went on, Englishmen began to eat with wooden or metal utensils. We eat because we must; but the use of eating utensils is a learned habit and thus part of our culture.

Instinctive behaviors, on the other hand, are not learned. A bear would hibernate in winter even if it were isolated from others of its species and could not imitate (that is, learn) the behavior of its forebears. An inherited pattern of behavior would make it physiologically necessary for it to do so. Because hibernation is not learned behavior, it cannot be considered a cultural trait held in common by a community of bears. Similarly, the sociable ants, for all their organized behavior, cannot be said to share a culture. They divide their labor, construct their nests, and form their raiding columns[d] all without having been taught to do so and without imitating the behavior of other ants.

Monkeys, however, learn a great deal from their parents and peers. For example, in 1953, a group of scientists at the Japan Monkey Center were able to observe how a particular behavioral innovation[e] spread from monkey to monkey, eventually becoming a part of the group's culture, independent of genetic factors. The scientists left some sweet potatoes out on the beach, near the place where a group of Japanese monkeys lived. Attracted by the food, a young female began to wash the sand off the potatoes by plunging them into a nearby brook.[f] Previously the monkeys had rubbed their food clean, but this washing behavior spread throughout the group and eventually replaced their former habit. After a number of years, 80 to 90 percent of the monkeys were washing their sweet potatoes. This learned habit had become a part of the monkeys' culture.[2]

Experimenters have shown that apes

---

[1]Ralph Linton, *The Cultural Background of Personality* (New York: Appleton-Century Crofts, 1945), p. 30.

[2]Jun'ichiro Itani, "The Society of Japanese Monkeys," *Japan Quarterly,* Vol. 8 (1961), pp. 421–430.

and monkeys learn a wide variety of behaviors—some as basic as those involved in maternal[g] care, and some as frivolous as the taste for candy. In fact, monkeys have relatively long childhoods as compared with other animals, and they must learn much before they can function as adults. Learning accounts for a relatively higher proportion of their behavior than is the case with many other animals. Man has the longest childhood of any animal. He is unique in the number and complexity of the learned behavior patterns that he transmits to his young. And he has a unique way of transmitting his culture: through language.

Notes

[a]mundane: ordinary, worldly, common.
[b]genetic inheritance: biological qualities a child receives from its parents.
[c]did not grace: were not present on.

[d]raiding columns: lines of ants that go in search of food.
[e]innovation: new idea.
[f]brook: small river.
[g]maternal: motherly.

Exercise 17

The following exercises show how different word forms are derived in English. Try to remember the endings and what parts of speech they indicate.

A. Words that end in -ly are usually adverbs:

> **Examples:** frivolous → frivolously
> vertical → vertically

Put the letter of the correct keyword in the blank after each derived word. Some keywords are used more than one time:

a. basic   b. complicated   c. unending   d. exact   e. unclear
   f. numberless

1. vague → vaguely _____

2. precise → precisely _____

3. I heard the sound of the distant voices **indistinctly.** _____

4. The people of that area are known for their **intricately** made gold jewelry. _____

5. Studying the history of early man is made **infinitely** more difficult by the absence of a written language. _____

6. I will be **eternally** grateful to you if you will help me with this task. _____

7. Man is not **inherently** good or evil. _____

B. Words that end in *-able* (or *-ible*) are usually adjectives formed from verbs. This ending means that one is able to perform the action of the verb on the noun.

> **Example:** The cloth is **stretchable**.
> **Meaning:** One is able to lengthen the cloth (by pulling it).
> **Example:** The river was high but **fordable**.
> **Meaning:** One was able to cross the river.

a. hold back   b. fight   c. use   d. arrange   e. name   f. stop

1. combat → combatable ____

2. identify → identifiable ____

3. The sad truth was that the accident was **preventable.** ____

4. Lists that are **categorizable** are easier to remember than those that are not. ____

5. Because the man had no special skill, he was not **employable.** ____

6. Fear is a feeling that can build up until it is no longer **restrainable.** ____

7. The writings of that author are **classifiable** into three main periods. ____

C. Words ending in *-(i)al* or *-(u)al* are sometimes adjectives formed from nouns and sometimes nouns formed from verbs.

> **Examples:**   to traverse → traversal (noun)
> fragment → fragmental (adjective)

a. good   b. say no to   c. people   d. environment   e. respect
f. world

1. deference → deferential ____

2. globe → global ____

3. The main **residential** area of the city was in the northern part. ____

4. The **refusal** of the government to cooperate eventually led to war. ____

5. The sun and clean air in Arizona are **beneficial** to patients with breathing difficulties. ____

6. The president's **denial** of the request to allocate more money for education caused a lot of people to be unhappy. ____

7. If you are unable to understand a word while reading, you should look for **contextual** clues to help you before turning to a dictionary. ____

8. The police called for the immediate **dispersal** of the crowd of people. ____

D. Words ending in *-er* or *-or* are often nouns formed from verbs. This ending means the person or thing that performs the action of the verb.

> **Example:** The zipper is the most widely used **fastener** today.
> **Meaning:** The zipper is the most widely used thing that fastens.

Example: The **imitator** looked like the president.
Meaning: The person who imitated the president looked like him or her.

a. hold back   b. unending   c. stop   d. name   e. use   f. arrange

1. inhibit → inhibitor ____

2. sort → sorter ____

3. The ropes put along the side of the road served as a temporary **restrainer,** keeping the people away from the race. ____

4. The government is the leading **employer** of students who graduate with degrees in certain areas. ____

5. Oral tradition is the **perpetuator** of many superstitutions. ____

6. A stop sign is the **designator** of the end of a major section of the test. ____

In summary:

1. Words that end in *-ly* are usually _____.

2. Words that end in *-(i/u)al* are either _____ or _____. Context will show you which is which.

3. Words that end in *-er* or *-or* are often _____ formed from _____ . What does this ending mean? _____
_____

4. Words that end in *-able* (or *-ible*) are usually _____ formed from verbs. What does this ending mean? _____

5 Biology

EXERCISE 1

In the following paragraph some of the words are in heavy type. Find the keyword from the list below that is closest in meaning to each of these words, and write the keyword in the proper blank underneath the paragraph. Check your answers by looking at Exercise 2.

KEYWORDS

to find	**neighboring**	**part**	**to excite**
no matter	**exactness**	**likeness**	**see-through**
following	**strength**	**similar**	**going back**

Mosquitoes are tiny insects with **diaphanous** wings that are found in almost every part of the world. The only **ingredients** necessary for their survival are water and blood. Water is necessary for reproduction. Mosquitoes must live in areas **adjoining** calm water in which they can lay their eggs. Blood is necessary for food. Mosquitoes are able to **determine** the location of a source of warm blood with amazing **exactitude** because they are **aroused** by the heat of a warm-blooded animal. Since the contrast between air temperature and body temperature is greater at night, they seek food after the sun sets and **retreat** to the cover of long grass or leaves by day. When they draw blood from their prey, they inject a chemical **akin** to that used by doctors to stop the blood from clotting (drying up). This chemical makes their bites itch with a **vehemence** that is surprising: how can such small things create such large swellings that itch for the **ensuing** several days! The female is the troublemaker. Male mosquitoes, though exact **facsimiles** of the female to the human eye, differ from her in two important ways: they do not bite, and they make a buzzing sound as they fly. So, **regardless of** the disturbing sound they make, they are harmless.

diaphanous	_____	ingredients	_____
adjoining	_____	determine	_____
exactitude	_____	aroused	_____
retreat	_____	akin	_____
vehemence	_____	ensuing	_____
facsimiles	_____	regardless of	_____

EXERCISE 2

The first word in each group below is the keyword. All the words under each keyword (the related words) have similar meaning. Read each group and try to remember which words belong to each keyword.

1. **see-through**
   limpid
   translucent
   sheer
   diaphanous
   transparent

2. **part**
   element
   constituent
   facet
   aspect
   ingredient

3. **following**
   later
   ensuing
   next
   subsequent
   succeeding

4. **similar**
   akin
   comparable
   kindred
   analogous
   like

5. **going back**
   retreat
   withdrawal
   regression
   backsliding
   reversal

6. **likeness**
   representation
   image
   model
   reproduction
   facsimile

7. **to find**
   locate
   ascertain
   determine
   pinpoint
   unearth

8. **to excite**
   stimulate
   inspire
   arouse
   inflame
   titillate

9. **neighboring**
   adjoining
   bordering
   proximate
   contiguous
   adjacent

10. **strength**
    stamina
    forcefulness
    intensity
    vigor
    vehemence

11. **exactness**
    accuracy
    acuity
    precision
    sureness
    exactitude

12. **no matter**
    regardless of
    in spite of
    notwithstanding
    despite
    leaving aside

EXERCISE 3

A. The 12 groups of related words are written below without keywords. Write the correct keyword over each keyword group.

B. Each group of related words has *one* word that does not belong in the group. Find that word, cross it out, and write it under the group to which it belongs.

KEYWORDS

to find	neighboring	part	to excite
no matter	exactness	likeness	see-through
following	strength	similar	going back

1. _____
   diaphanous
   limpid

2. _____
   facet
   ingredient

3. _____
   subsequent
   sheer

4. _____
   succeeding
   akin

translucent	facsimile	next	like
proximate	aspect	later	kindred
transparent	element	ensuing	comparable
_____	_____	_____	_____

5. _____ 6. _____ 7. _____ 8. _____

regression	image	arouse	titillate
withdrawal	acuity	unearth	inflame
retreat	representation	locate	determine
reversal	reproduction	ascertain	inspire
constituent	model	pinpoint	stimulate
_____	_____	_____	_____

9. _____ 10. _____ 11. _____ 12. _____

contiguous	vehemence	stamina	despite
adjacent	intensity	accuracy	analogous
notwithstanding	forcefulness	precision	regardless of
bordering	vigor	sureness	leaving aside
adjoining	backsliding	exactitude	in spite of
_____	_____	_____	_____

EXERCISE 4

Each sentence below contains one keyword, which is in heavy type.

A. Find the word below each sentence that is *not* a related word for the keyword. Circle that word. (The keyword numbers from Exercise 2 are in parentheses. These will help you if you need to look back.)

B. After completing instruction A, write each circled word under the keyword in the sentence to which it belongs.

1. The insect has wings that are **see-through.**

    a. transparent   b. diaphanous   c. sheer   d. akin   (1)

2. The heart must pump blood with sufficient **strength** to allow it to reach all parts of the body.

    a. vigor   b. facet   c. forcefulness   d. vehemence   (10)

3. The smell of blood **excites** many animals.

    a. arouses   b. inflames   c. ascertains   d. titillates   (8)

4. Birds from **neighboring** territories are quickly chased away.

    a. regardless of   b. adjacent   c. proximate   d. bordering   (9)

5. Mendel's work with peas allowed him to **find** the fundamental law of genetics.

   a. determine   b. stimulate   c. pinpoint   d. unearth (7)

6. Robert Hooke drew the first **likeness** of a cell some 300 years ago.

   a. representation   b. image   c. regression   d. facsimile (6)

7. The development of the microscope allowed Hooke to work with an **exactness** that was not possible before.

   a. precision   b. intensity   c. sureness   d. exactitude (11)

8. Fingernails on humans are **similar to** scales on fish.

   a. comparable to   b. analogous to   c. regardless of   d. like (4)

9. In evolutionary terms there is no **going back;** everything must contribute to progress.

   a. backsliding   b. reversal   c. retreat   d. adjoining (5)

10. One very important **part** of many animals' defense is camouflage.

    a. model   b. aspect   c. element   d. constituent (2)

11. Physical characteristics of both parents combine to determine the physical appearance of **following** generations.

    a. subsequent   b. succeeding   c. later   d. translucent (3)

12. **No matter** the environment, insects are able to adapt.

    a. Ensuing   b. Despite   c. In spite of   d. Notwithstanding (12)

EXERCISE 5

In the following paragraph one word in each sentence is in heavy type. Find the keyword from the list below that is closest in meaning to each of these words, and write it in the proper blank underneath the paragraph. Check your answers by looking at Exercise 6.

KEYWORDS

very good	**slope**	**simple**	**to join together**
to give off	**receiver**	**to confuse**	**to spread out**
to equalize	**type**	**to notice**	**continuation**

The mosquito population of the world continues to follow an upward **slant.** Because they have a **superb** system for adapting, they have **disseminated** to almost every corner of the globe. Mosquitoes carry diseases which they sometimes pass on to the **recipients** of their bites through the chemicals they **secrete** during the process of obtaining blood. For this reason, as well as for others, people from all over the world have **blended** their efforts to kill off these little pests, but with little success. A **coarse** method such as spraying a poisonous gas into the air only works for a few days. Putting poison on the water is only temporarily successful—the mosquitoes simply develop a new **breed** that is not affected by the poison. Scientists have also tried releasing females that cannot lay eggs. The male mosquitoes cannot **detect** whether the females are sterile, so they mate with them with no results. However, egg-laying (fertile) females soon **offset** the small number of sterile ones because of the number of offspring they are able to produce. Spraying chemicals designed to **disorient** the mosquitoes so that males and females cannot find each other has also been unsuccessful. No matter what approach the scientists use, the mosquitoes always find some way to insure their **perpetuation.**

slant	_____	superb	_____
disseminated	_____	recipients	_____
secrete	_____	blended	_____
coarse	_____	breed	_____
detect	_____	offset	_____
disorient	_____	perpetuation	_____

EXERCISE 6

The first word in each group below is the keyword. All of the words under each keyword (the related words) have similar meaning. Read each group and try to remember which related words go with each keyword.

13. **simple**
coarse
crude
elementary
unrefined
primitive

14. **to equalize**
compensate
offset
counterbalance
counteract
make up for

15. **to join together**
coalesce
blend
fuse
mingle
amalgamate

16. **type**
breed
caste
category
denomination
species

17. **to confuse**
mix up
disorient
mislead
befuddle
fluster

18. **receiver**
heir
recipient
beneficiary
inheritor
consignee

19. **continuation**
survival
perpetuation
prolonging
endurance
continuity

20. **to give off**
discharge
emit
radiate
secrete
exude

21. **very good**
superb
sensational

22. **to notice**
perceive
sense

23. **slope**
pitch
gradient

24. **to spread out**
suffuse
disseminate

spectacular	detect	slant	scatter
marvelous	spot	grade	proliferate
magnificent	discern	ramp	diffuse

EXERCISE 7

A. The 12 groups of related words are written below without keywords. Write the correct keyword over each keyword group.

B. Each group of related words has *one* word that does not belong in the group. Find that word, cross it out, and write it under the group to which it belongs.

KEYWORDS

very good	slope	simple	to join together
to give off	receiver	to confuse	to spread out
to equalize	type	to notice	continuation

13. _____ 14. _____ 15. _____ 16. _____

crude	offset	mingle	breed
unrefined	compensate	fuse	gradient
primitive	fluster	coalesce	denomination
coarse	counteract	suffuse	species
magnificent	make up for	blend	category

_____ _____ _____ _____

17. _____ 18. _____ 19. _____ 20. _____

disorient	recipient	perpetuation	exude
mislead	inheritor	survival	discharge
counterbalance	heir	beneficiary	emit
befuddle	consignee	continuity	sense
mix up	caste	endurance	radiate

_____ _____ _____ _____

21. _____ 22. _____ 23. _____ 24. _____

marvelous	spot	slant	disseminate
sensational	perceive	prolonging	proliferate
superb	discern	grade	amalgamate
elementary	detect	pitch	diffuse
spectacular	secrete	ramp	scatter

_____ _____ _____ _____

EXERCISE 8

Each sentence below contains one keyword, which is in heavy type.

A. Find the word below each sentence that is *not* a related word for the keyword. Circle that word. (The keyword numbers from Exercise 6 are in parentheses. These will help you if you need to look back.)

B. After completing instruction A, write each circled word under the keyword in the sentence to which it belongs.

1. All living things change in order to insure their **continuation.**

    a. survival   b. category   c. continuity   d. endurance   (19)

2. The thyroid gland **gives off** chemicals that influence growth.

    a. exudes   b. secretes   c. mixes up   d. discharges   (20)

3. The lower the order of animal, the more **simple** is its brain.

    a. primitive   b. elementary   c. coarse   d. superb   (13)

4. Every **type** of animal has evolved special defensive abilities.

    a. pitch   b. species   c. breed   d. caste   (16)

5. One of the functions of the brain in all vertebrates (animals with backbones) is to **join together** all of the information from the sensory organs.

    a. blend   b. fuse   c. amalgamate   d. disseminate   (15)

6. An animal with poor sight usually **equalizes** this deficiency by a well-developed sense of smell.

    a. offsets   b. compensates for   c. detects   d. counterbalances   (14)

7. The **slope** of the mountain was so steep that the scientists were unable to drive to the top.

    a. slant   b. heir   c. gradient   d. grade   (23)

8. The keen ability of the deer to smell allows them to **notice** an enemy before it is visible.

    a. sense   b. perceive   c. discern   d. emit   (22)

9. The coloration of some insects is designed to **confuse** enemies.

    a. mislead   b. befuddle   c. make up for   d. fluster   (17)

10. The results of the experiment to control polio were **very good.**

    a. magnificent   b. crude   c. spectacular   d. sensational   (21)

11. Some plants have seeds that are very light so that the wind can **spread** them **out.**

    a. scatter   b. coalesce   c. diffuse   (24)

12. Genes transmit characteristics from the parents to the **receiver.**

    a. perpetuation   b. recipient   c. heir   d. beneficiary   (18)

EXERCISE 9

In the following paragraph some of the words are in heavy type. Find the keyword from the list below that is closest in meaning to each of these words, and write the keyword in the proper blank underneath the paragraph. Check your answers by looking at Exercise 10.

KEYWORDS

post	**irregular**	**to bother**	**signal of danger**
to eat	**rightly**	**gaslike**	**marriage (adjective)**
false	**to cover**	**different**	**to begin**

Animals have many **dissimilar** ways to defend themselves. If, for example, something **annoys** a skunk (a furry black and white animal), it gives off a **gaseous** liquid that soon **blankets** the area with a very bad smell. Many animals are colored in an **unsystematic** way so that they are difficult to see in their environment. Many birds have specific sounds that they use as a **warning** to others. The mockingbird has an additional method of defense. If a cat, for example, comes too close to its nest, the mockingbird **initiates** a set of actions to protect its **marital** partner and their offspring. It will dive down at the cat in a series of **pseudo-** attacks, flying from one **support** to another. The cat becomes confused and decides to look elsewhere for something to **feed on.** The mockingbird then returns to its nest, **appropriately** proud of itself and ready to attack again if necessary.

dissimilar	_____	annoys	_____
gaseous	_____	blankets	_____
unsystematic	_____	warning	_____
initiates	_____	marital	_____
pseudo-	_____	support	_____
feed on	_____	appropriately	_____

EXERCISE 10

The first word in each group below is the keyword. All the words under each keyword (the related words) have similar meaning. Read each group and try to remember which words belong to each keyword.

25. **rightly**	26. **post**	27. **to cover**	28. **gaslike**
fittingly	column	blanket	vaporous
aptly	stake	carpet	gasiform

legitimately	pole	envelop	volatile
appropriately	support	wrap	vaporized
suitably	prop	coat	gaseous

29. **signal of danger**

warning
alarm
siren
caution
alert

30. **to bother**

upset
vex
annoy
irritate
disturb

31. **to eat**

ingest
feed on
devour
dine (on)
swallow

32. **marriage (adjective)**

matrimonial
conjugal
marital
nuptial
connubial

33. **different**

distinct
discrete
dissimilar
divergent
incongruous

34. **false**

counterfeit
pseudo-
synthetic
bogus
fake

35. **irregular**

inconsistent
unsystematic
intermittent
erratic
abnormal

36. **to begin**

initiate
launch
found
trigger
set in motion

EXERCISE 11

A. The 12 groups of related words are written below without keywords. Write the correct keyword over each keyword group.

B. Each group of related words has *one* word that does not belong in the group. Find that word, cross it out, and write it under the group to which it belongs.

KEYWORDS

post	irregular	to bother	signal of
to eat	rightly	gaslike	danger
false	to cover	different	marriage (adjective)
			to begin

25. _____

aptly
divergent
suitably
fittingly
appropriately

_____

26. _____

siren
stake
support
column
pole

_____

27. _____

carpet
wrap
dine
blanket
coat

_____

28. _____

gaseous
volatile
gasiform
connubial
vaporous

_____

29. _____

caution
warning

30. _____

irritate
annoy

31. _____

devour
ingest

32. _____

conjugal
marital

alert	found	feed on	nuptial
alarm	disturb	swallow	matrimonial
prop	upset	vex	vaporized
_____	_____	_____	_____

33. _____   34. _____   35. _____   36. _____

incongruous	counterfeit	abnormal	launch
distinct	synthetic	bogus	trigger
discrete	intermittent	erratic	set in motion
legitimately	pseudo-	inconsistent	initiate
dissimilar	fake	unsystematic	envelop
_____	_____	_____	_____

EXERCISE 12

Each sentence below contains one keyword, which is in heavy type.

A. Find the word below each sentence that is *not* a related word for the keyword. Circle that word. (The keyword numbers from Exercise 10 are in parentheses. These will help you if you need to look back.)

B. After completing instruction A, write each circled word under the keyword in the sentence to which it belongs.

1. In the insect world, sometimes the offspring **eat** the mother.

    a. devour   b. feed on   c. carpet   d. dine on   (31)

2. The walking stick (an insect) is **rightly** named because it so closely resembles a stick with legs.

    a. matrimonial   b. appropriately   c. fittingly   d. suitably   (25)

3. Scientists put sweet liquid on **posts** to attract bees.

    a. stakes   b. warnings   c. columns   d. props   (26)

4. The arrival of warm weather **begins** a whole series of transformations in the animal and plant world.

    a. initiates   b. sets in motion   c. launches   d. ingests   (36)

5. Some insects spray a **gaslike** substance to protect themselves.

    a. gaseous   b. vaporized   c. aptly   d. volatile   (28)

6. The presence of lions in the area does not always **bother** other animals.

    a. upset   b. annoy   c. trigger   d. vex   (30)

7. The pollution from the factory **covered** the water.

    a. disturbed   b. coated   c. blanketed   d. enveloped   (27)

8. The **marriage** ceremony varies from culture to culture.

   a. nuptial   b. connubial   c. marital   d. discrete   (32)

9. After receiving the hormones, the animal's behavior was **irregular.**

   a. erratic   b. abnormal   c. unsystematic   d. fake   (35)

10. The cry of certain birds serves as a **signal of danger** to other birds and animals in the area.

    a. (an) alarm   b. (an) alert   c. pole   d. caution   (29)

11. The amphibians branched out into **different** families.

    a. vaporous   b. discrete   c. divergent   d. dissimilar   (33)

12. The coat was very expensive although it was made of **false** fur.

    a. synthetic   b. bogus   c. inconsistent   d. counterfeit   (34)

EXERCISE 13

In each blank write the keyword that corresponds to the word in heavy type in the sentence. The number in parentheses can be used to check your answer.

1. The eyesight of birds must be very sharp in order to allow them to move with the **precision** necessary for flight. _____ (11)

2. Snakes are able to **swallow** animals that are several times their diameter. _____ (31)

3. In insects, blood usually flows from the back of the heart to the front, although **reversal** of flow does occur in some types. _____ (5)

4. The body of an arthropod is **wrapped** in a hard external skeleton. _____ (27)

5. **In spite of** the characteristics of an environment, insects are able to adapt successfully. _____ (12)

6. This fact has allowed insects to **proliferate.** _____ (24)

7. In Africa, some termites build nests that look like huge **columns.** _____ (26)

8. The migration habits of some fish make it very difficult for scientists to **pinpoint** where they lay their eggs. _____ (7)

9. Some insects **discharge** a bitter-tasting chemical when attacked. _____ (20)

10. An insect may lay thousands of eggs in order to insure its **survival.**
    _____ (19)

11. Many birds have coloration that allows them to **blend** in with their
    environment. _____ (15)

12. Some fish have developed **primitive** lungs to allow them to live on land for a
    short period of time. _____ (13)

13. Male bees live just for a few days, functioning only during the **conjugal**
    flight with a queen bee. _____ (32)

14. When a bee's hive (nest) becomes too crowded, the queen moves to an
    adjacent area. _____ (9)

15. Here the queen **founds** a new hive. _____ (36)

16. The worker bees have **distinct** jobs within the hive.
    _____ (33)

17. One of the tasks of a worker bee is to give an **alarm** in case of attack.
    _____ (29)

18. This signal **inflames** the other workers, who then go out to look for the
    source of danger. _____ (8)

19. Ants, termites, and wasps have **comparable** systems of social behavior.
    _____ (4)

20. The **inheritor** of a certain characteristic may be able to survive more
    successfully than its peers. _____ (18)

21. This characteristic will be passed on to **subsequent** generations.
    _____ (3)

22. In this manner, all **species** of living things improve their ability to live in
    their environment. _____ (16)

23. Some insects communicate by **volatile** chemicals. _____ (28)

24. Certain **aspects** of a frog's body allow it to live successfully in a variety of
    environments. _____ (2)

25. A baby frog (tadpole) has a tail that is **suitably** formed for swimming.
    _____ (25)

26. The adult frog has **marvelous** eyesight. _____ (21)

27. Good vision allows the frog to **discern** the slightest movement of an insect.
    _____ (22)

28. **Erratic** behavior in most living things is usually caused by some sort of
    chemical imbalance. _____ (35)

29. Research that is not done very carefully is sometimes called **pseudo**-scientific. _____ (34)

30. The backwards **slant** of the wings of birds allows air to travel more quickly across the bottom of the wing than across the top. _____ (23)

31. The shape of the wing, combined with the **forcefulness** of its movement, explains how birds can fly. _____ (10)

32. Some fish are almost **transparent,** which makes them difficult to see in shallow water. _____ (1)

33. The coloration of some butterflies is designed not to camouflage the insect, but rather to **mislead** their enemies. _____ (17)

34. This coloration **compensates** for the fact that these types of butterflies have no other defensive capabilities. _____ (14)

35. Some fish have chemicals that **irritate** the skin of its enemies. _____ (30)

36. Some insects do not have well-developed eyesight, so they see only poor **images** of things in their environment. _____ (6)

EXERCISE 14

Solve the puzzle by writing the correct keyword for each of the words given below. The numbers in parentheses can be used to check your answers, but try to complete the puzzle without using them.

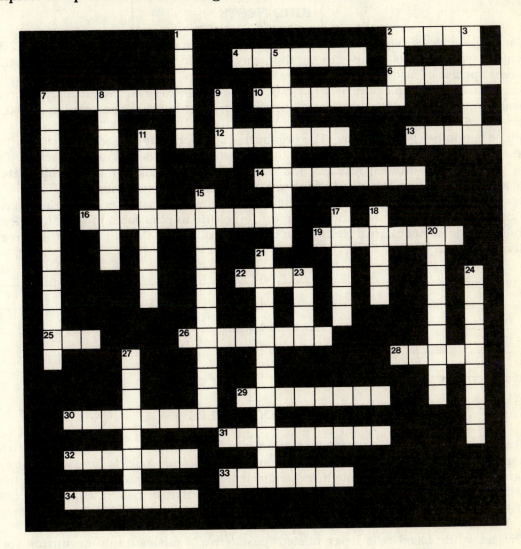

ACROSS

2. counterfeit (34)
4. volatile (28)
6. spot (22)
7. vehemence (10)
10. marvelous (21)
12. fittingly (25)
13. envelop (27)
14. later (3)
16. contiguous (9)
19. representation (6)
22. prop (26)
25. devour (31)
26. consignee (18)
28. ramp (23)
29. conjugal (32)
30. notwithstanding (12)
31. reversal (5)
32. like (4)
33. mix up (17)
34. discharge (20)

DOWN

1. annoy (30)
2. unearth (7)
3. titillate (8)
5. sheer (1)
7. caution (29)
8. precision (11)
9. constituent (2)
11. unsystematic (35)
15. blend (15)
17. primitive (13)
18. launch (36)
20. disseminate (24)
21. endurance (19)
23. denomination (16)
24. incongruous (33)
27. counteract (14)

EXERCISE 15

Some of the words in the following reading passages are in heavy type. Read the passages and write the keywords for each in the blanks below.

BIRD NESTS

There is a wide variety of bird nests in the world. One **aspect** that contributes to the **divergent** types of nests is the material that is available in an area. Another **factor** is that different **species** of birds lay eggs that are **dissimilar.**

Size is a good example of variety in nests. A hummingbird's nest weighs only a couple of grams and is difficult to **locate;** in contrast, an eagle builds a **spectacular** nest that may weigh 850 kilograms.

Shape is another good example. The ovenbird is **appropriately** named because it builds a nest on the ground that is **analogous** to an oven in shape as well as in function. Old world weavers of southwest Africa combine their efforts to build a roof that **blankets** a large area of a tree. Penguins in Antarctica build **crude** nests out of stones.

Despite the **inconsistent** size and shape of bird nests, they all serve the same basic purpose: to protect the birds and the product(s) of the **nuptial facet** of their lives from enemies in the **adjacent** area. Nests allow birds to **proliferate,** thus insuring the **perpetuation** of the species.

1. _____   6. _____   11. _____   16. _____
2. _____   7. _____   12. _____   17. _____
3. _____   8. _____   13. _____   18. _____
4. _____   9. _____   14. _____
5. _____   10. _____   15. _____

WHITE BLOOD CELLS

When you cut yourself, you **set in motion** a process within your body to repair the damage. White blood cells in your bloodstream are constantly looking for areas that are **irritated.** When they **discern** rough tissue or **elements** that are positively charged, they are **stimulated** into action. They **emit** a chemical **alert** that brings in white blood cells from **adjoining** areas, and they all begin to **feed on** bacteria, dirt, and dead or injured cells that lack the **stamina** to continue to fight.

Why are white blood cells never **misled** [past tense of **mislead**] into **devouring** your body's own healthy cells? Every cell that your body produces is the **recipient** of a complex chemical code that allows white blood cells to recognize it with great **accuracy,** thus leaving it alone. If bacteria could develop a **facsimile** of this code, these **counterfeit** cells could **befuddle** your body's defenses and **launch** a successful attack.

1. _____   6. _____   11. _____   16. _____
2. _____   7. _____   12. _____   17. _____
3. _____   8. _____   13. _____   18. _____
4. _____   9. _____   14. _____
5. _____   10. _____   15. _____

COMMUNICATION BETWEEN BEES

Scientists have discovered how a bee communicates the location of food to other members of the hive. They placed a sweet substance on **stakes** at different locations around a hive and studied the dance the bee performs after it **ascertains** the source of food. This is what they found:

When it returns to the hive, the bee dances on a vertical surface in one of two **distinct** patterns. If the source is near the hive, the bee does a circle dance, making a circle first in one direction and then in the other. This **reversal** of circles **stimulates** other bees to **scatter** in all directions near the hive to **determine** where the food is.

If the source of food is farther away from the hive, the returning bee completes only half of the circle. It then moves in a straight line across the circle. The **slant** of this line is equal to the angle of flight from the sun to the source. The bee then completes the circle in the opposite direction. In each **succeeding** circle it repeats the line across the middle on the same **gradient.** Distance from the hive is communicated by the number of moves and the amount of sound the bee makes while dancing.

Thus worker bees are able to **blend** their efforts, **pinpointing** sources of food for other workers with amazing **exactitude.** The result is increased efficiency in producing that **translucent** liquid that is so necessary for the **survival** of the hive.

1. _____ 5. _____ 9. _____ 13. _____

2. _____ 6. _____ 10. _____ 14. _____

3. _____ 7. _____ 11. _____ 15. _____

4. _____ 8. _____ 12. _____

EXERCISE 16

Read the following articles. Do *not* use a dictionary. At least one related word from each of the keyword groups is in these articles. Try to remember the proper keywords as you read.

Prereading Introduction

All living things use chemicals, both internally and externally, in a wide variety of ways. One of the more recent discoveries in the area of chemicals and their effects on animal behavior is the existence of pheromones. These are chemicals that are secreted into the external environment of the animal in order to communicate between members of the same species.

The following article examines the phenomenon of pheromones. After giving a brief definition and introduction to the concept, the author gives several examples of how pheromones are used in the animal world by such diverse animals as moths, bees, ants, and mice.

After reading the article, you should answer the following questions:

1. What are pheromones?
2. What is the possible significance of pheromones?
3. Give an example of the effect of a primer pheromone.
4. How does the male silk moth use pheromones to find a female silk moth?
5. How are pheromones being used as insecticides?
6. What is the purpose of a trail pheromone? An alarm pheromone?
7. Why are new queen bees, ants, or termites unable to develop after a queen begins laying eggs?
8. What happens to female mice when they are crowded into a cage with no males?

PHEROMONES*

In recent years it has been appreciated that the behavior of animals may be influenced not only by hormones (chemicals released into the internal environment by endocrine glands that regulate and coordinate the activities of other tissues) but also by **pheromones**—substances released into the *external* environment by *exocrine* glands that influence the behavior of other members of the same species. We are accustomed to thinking that information can be transferred from one animal to another by sight or sound; pheromones represent a means of communication, a means of transferring information, by smell or taste. Pheromones evoke[a] specific behavioral, developmental or reproductive responses in the recipient; these responses may be of great significance for the survival of the species.

Some pheromones act on the recipient's central nervous system and produce an immediate effect on its behavior. Among these **releaser** pheromones are the **sex attractants** of moths and the **trail pheromones** and **alarm substances** secreted by ants. Other **primer** pheromones trigger a chain of physiological events in the recipient that affect its growth and differentiation. The regulation of the growth of locusts[b] and the control of the number of reproductives and soldiers in termite[c] colonies are controlled by primer hormones.

The sex attractants of moths[d] provide some of the more spectacular examples of pheromones. . . . The male silk moth has an extremely sensitive receptor in his antennae[e] for sensing the attractant. When an investigator records the nerve impulses coming from the antennae, he finds that these electroantennagrams show specific responses to bombykol and not to other substances. The male silk moth cannot determine the direction of the source by flying up a concentration gradient[f] because the molecules[g] are nearly uniformly dispersed except within a few meters of the source. Instead, he responds to the stimulus by flying *upwind* to the source. With a gentle wind, the bombykol given off by a single female moth covers an area several thousand meters long and as much as 200 meters wide. An average silkworm contains some 0.01 mg. of bombykol. It can be shown experimentally that a male responds appropriately when as little as 10,000 molecules of attractant are allowed to diffuse from a source 1 cm. away from him. He can have received only a few hundred of these molecules, perhaps less. Thus, the amount of attractant in one female moth could stimulate more than one billion males!

. . . Sex attractants have been tested as possible specific insecticides.[h] By putting sex attractant on stakes placed every 10 meters in a large field, investigators could blanket the air with sex attractant, thus confusing the males and greatly decreasing the probability of their finding females and mating with them.

The fire ants, when returning to the nest after finding food, secrete a trail pheromone that marks the trail so that other ants can find their way to the food. The trail pheromone is volatile and evaporates within two minutes, so that there is little danger of ants being misled by old trails. Ants also release alarm substances when disturbed, and this (rather like ringing the bell in a firehouse) in turn transmits the alarm to ants in the vicinity. These alarm substances have a lower molecular weight than the sex attractants and are less specific, so that members of several different species respond to the same alarm substance.

Worker bees, on finding food, secrete **geraniol,** a 10-carbon, branched chain alcohol, in order to attract other worker bees to the food. This supplements the information conveyed by their wagging dance. Queen bees secrete 9-ketodecanoic acid, which, when ingested by worker· bees, inhibits the development of their ovaries[i] and their ability to make royal cells in which new queens might be reared. This substance also serves as a sex attrac-

tant to male bees during the queen's nuptial flight.

In colonial insects, such as ants, bees and termites, pheromones play an important role in regulating and coordinating the composition and activities of the population. A termite colony includes morphologically[j] distinct queen, king, soldiers and nymphs or workers. All develop from fertilized eggs; however, queens, kings and soldiers each secrete inhibitory pheromones that act on the corpus allatum of the nymphs and prevent their developing into the more specialized types. If the queen dies, there is no longer any "antiqueen" pheromone released and one or more of the nymphs develop into queens. The members of each colony will permit only one queen to survive, devouring any excess ones. Similarly, the loss of the king termite or a reduction in the number of soldiers permits other nymphs to develop into the specialized castes to replace them.

Primer pheromones occur in mammals as well as in insects. When four or more female mice are placed in a cage, there is a greatly increased frequency of pseudopregnancy. If their olfactory bulbs[k] are removed, this effect disappears. When more females are placed together in a cage, their estrous cycles[l] become very erratic. However, if one male mouse is placed in the cage, his odor can initiate and synchronize[m] the estrous cycles of all the females (the "Whitten effect") and reduce the frequency of reproductive abnormalities. Even more curious is the finding (the "Bruce effect") that the odor of a strange male will block pregnancy in a newly impregnated female mouse.

Notes

[a]evoke: cause to happen.
[b]locusts: a type of insect known for flying together in huge numbers, eating everything that is green.
[c]termite: an insect that eats wood.
[d]moth: an insect that looks like a butterfly. It can usually be seen at night flying around any source of light.
[e]antennae: two rather long growths from the

head of insects. They are used to smell or feel objects.
[f]flying up a concentration gradient: flying in the direction in which the smell is strongest.
[g]molecules: the simplest unit of something that keeps its physical and chemical properties.
[h]insecticides: chemicals used to control the population of insects.

[i]ovaries: the egg-producing part of the female body.

[j]morphologically: structurally; in shape or form.

[k]olfactory bulbs: that portion of the body that receives smells.

[l]estrous cycle: a regularly recurring period in nonhuman mammals when pregnancy is possible.

[m]synchronize: to cause to occur at the same time.

Prereading Introduction

The next article deals with the structure and functioning of the eye of arthropods, any of a number of species of animals that have no backbone and are covered by layers of some type of hard material.

The first paragraph discusses the structure of the compound eye and shows how each part works to produce sight. The rest of the article discusses how a compound eye functions in different types of light and explains what type of image the arthropod receives. Whether or not an arthropod sees distinct images or merely shapes and motion is also covered. The final paragraph compares how well arthropods can detect flicker, or blinking pulses of light.

After reading this article, you should answer the following questions:

1. What is a compound eye? How does it differ from the human eye?
2. Do arthropods see several images of the same object?
3. Arthropod eyes cannot adjust to varying intensities of light. How do they compensate for this inability?
4. What determines whether a spider or an insect can perceive objects?
5. Can any insect discriminate color?
6. How do flies, for example, perceive a motion picture or the light from a light bulb? Why?
7. What is the main advantage of an insect's "high critical flicker fusion rate"?

THE COMPOUND EYE OF ARTHROPODS*

Most arthropods have eyes. Some are simple, having only a few photoreceptors,[a] others are large, with thousands of retinal cells. A transparent lens-cornea is the usual skeletal contribution to the eye,[b] and the focus is usually fixed since the immovable lens is continuous with the surrounding exoskeleton.[c] Insects and many crustaceans, such as crabs and shrimp, have a **compound eye,** so called because it is composed of many long cylindrical[d] units, each of which possesses all of the elements for light reception. Each unit, called an **ommatidium,** contains an outer cornea, a middle crystalline cone and an inner **retinula.** On the external surface, the cornea of each ommatidium is distinct and forms one facet of the compound eye. The cornea functions as the lens and the crystalline cone funnels light down to the retinula, which is equivalent to the retina and is composed of a rosette of seven monopolar neurons. Their inner photosensistive surfaces (rhabdomeres) together form a central **rhabdome.** Movable screening pigment[e] is commonly present between adjacent ommatidia.

The term "compound eye" implies that each ommatidium forms a separate image, but this is untrue and misleading. The seven retinula cells function as a single photoreceptor unit and together transmit a single signal. The image formed by the entire eye, although sometimes called

*From *Introduction to Animal Biology* by Claude A. Villee, Warren F. Walker, and Robert D. Barnes, pp. 176–78. Copyright © 1979 by W. B. Saunders Co. Reprinted by permission of W. B. Saunders, CBS College Publishing.

mosaic,[f] depends upon all of the signals transmitted by the ommatidia and thus is really no different from that of other types of eyes. Compound eyes may function differently in bright light than they do in weak light. In bright light the screening pigment is extended between the ommatidium and each retinula responds only to the light received by its facet and crystalline cone. This type of image, called an **apposition**[g] **image,** is believed to be especially effective in detecting movement, for slight changes in the position of the moving object will stimulate different ommatidia.

In weak light the screening pigment is contracted, and the light received by an ommatidium can cross over to adjacent units; thus, a retinula may be fired by the light received through several ommatidia. Under these conditions the eye is said to form a **superposition image,** but it is unlikely that there is any object discrimination at all. Rather, the eye is detecting changes in general light intensity or the position of a bright light source or shadow. Although the eyes of some arthropods can adapt to bright or dim light, the compound eyes of most species are usually adapted for functioning in either bright or weak light, but not in both. They are either diurnal or nocturnal[h] or live in habitats in which there is reduced light; hence, the eyes usually function under only limited light conditions.

Visual acuity varies greatly and depends upon the number of photoreceptors present, regardless of the type of eye. The eyes of some hunting spiders and the compound eyes of many insects and some crabs appear to be capable of detecting objects. In all of these species the number of photoreceptors is very great. The eye of the dragon fly, for example, has 10,000 ommatidia, and the eye of a wolf spider has 4500 photoreceptors. However, when one compares these numbers with the 130 million photoreceptors in the human eye, it is evident that the images formed in even the most highly developed arthropod eye must be very crude. Color discrimination has been demonstrated in several arthropods and is an important adaptation of bees and other insects that depend on flowers as a food source.

Although the compound eye of the arthropod forms only coarse images, it compensates for this by being able to follow flicker to high frequencies. Flies are able to detect flickers of up to approximately 265 per second, whereas the human eye can detect flickers of only 45 to 53 per second. Because flickering lights fuse above these values, we see motion pictures as smooth movement and the ordinary 60 cycle light in a room as a steady light. To an insect, both motion pictures and light must flicker horribly. Because the insect has such a high critical flicker fusion rate, any movement of prey or enemy is immediately detected by one of the eye units. Hence, the compound eye is peculiarly well suited to the arthropod's way of life.

Notes

[a]photoreceptors: cells especially designed to be sensitive to light.
[b]the usual skeletal contribution to the eye: normally part of the overall external hard covering of the arthropod's body.
[c]exoskeleton: hard outer covering.
[d]cylindrical: shaped like a cylinder.

[e]screening pigment: coloring used to protect the eye.
[f]mosaic: composed of several small parts.
[g]apposition: placing side by side.
[h]diurnal or nocturnal: active during the day or active during the night.

EXERCISE 17

The following exercises show how different word forms are derived in English. Try to remember the endings and what parts of speech they indicate.

A. Words that end in *-ize* are usually verbs.

> **Examples:** category → categorize (to put into categories)
> equal → equalize (to make equal)

Put the letter of the correct keyword in the blank after each derived word. Some keywords are used more than one time:

a. cruelty   b. reason   c. unending   d. appearance   e. fright
f. thought   g. place   h. unreality   i. angry

1. terror → terrorize _____

2. antagonistic → antagonize _____

3. The man tried to **rationalize** his actions by telling himself that he had no other choice. _____

4. The storm that the weatherman predicted never **materialized.** _____

5. The treatment that the child received at home **brutalized** him. _____

6. The medicine that the doctor gave me **localized** the pain to my right shoulder. _____

7. The student **fantasized** about becoming a famous sports star. _____

8. One of the problems involved with learning to program a computer is the difficulty of **conceptualizing** some of the commands. _____

9. Although the singer died at an early age, she was **eternalized** by her music. _____

B. Words that end in *-ify* are usually verbs.

> **Example:**   intensity → intensify (to make more intense)

a. fright   b. size   c. exact   d. characteristic

1. horror → horrify _____

2. The insurance company returned my application because I failed to **specify** what kind of automobile I had. _____

3. The hot weather only served to **magnify** the anger and frustration of the people working on the project. _____

4. For some reason, the dog was **terrified** of thunderstorms. _____

5. Basically I agree with your conclusion, but I want the opportunity to **qualify** my response. _____

C. Words that end in *-ant* or *-ent* are often nouns formed from verbs. The ending is very similar to *-er/-or:* it shows the thing or person that performs the action of the verb.

> **Examples:** stimulate → stimulant (that thing that stimulates)
> counteract → counteractant (that thing that counteracts)

a. change   b. hold back   c. hold on to   d. fight   e. care for
f. help

1. assist → assistant _____

2. The weather was a **variant** that the racing team hadn't considered. _____

3. The actor took appetite **suppressants** in an effort to lose weight. _____

4. All of the **attendants** at the wedding were relatives of the bride. _____

5. The audience began to cheer as the **combatants** came out for another round of boxing. _____

6. **Adherents** of both political parties attended the meeting. _____

In summary:

1. One ending changes a verb into a noun much as *-er/-or* does. What is that ending? _____

2. Two different endings are used to make verbs. The meaning of these verbs is always closely related to the words from which they are derived. What are the endings? _____ and _____.

6 U.S. Government

EXERCISE 1

In the following paragraph one word in each sentence is in heavy type. Find the keyword from the list below that is closest in meaning to each of these words, and write the keyword in the proper blank underneath the paragraph. Check your answers by looking at Exercise 2.

KEYWORDS

unfair	hand out	revolution	make peace
public	evil	depend on	earlier example
death	goodness	cancel	spread through

People **rely on** the government to make the right decisions. So, if the leader of a government is **corrupt,** problems can develop quickly. The leader's attitude **permeates** every aspect of the government. The decisions that his government makes are often **unjust.** If the people become too dissatisfied with the government, they may begin a **rebellion.** Their efforts may result in the **demise** of the old government. The **integrity** of the new leader can change everything. These changes can allow the government to **reconcile** the differences between the opposing sides, but the cost, in terms of human lives and suffering, is sometimes high. English law, which was the **antecedent** for American law, provides ways to change the government and the laws it makes without bloodshed. Because the leaders of a government are elected, they must be sensitive to **community** pressures. If, for example, a law proves to be very unpopular, they must take steps either to have it **rescinded** or to have it changed. The government must also try to be fair and honest about the manner in which it **allocates** money.

rely on	_____	corrupt	_____
permeates	_____	unjust	_____
rebellion	_____	demise	_____
integrity	_____	reconcile	_____
antecedent	_____	community	_____
rescinded	_____	allocates	_____

EXERCISE 2

The first word in each group below is the keyword. All the words under each keyword (the related words) have similar meaning. Read each group and try to remember which related words go with each keyword.

1. **earlier example**
   precedent
   antecedent
   prototype
   exemplar
   archetype

2. **death**
   fatality
   demise
   expiration
   decease
   extinction

3. **to make peace**
   reconcile
   conciliate
   pacify
   appease
   bring to terms

4. **evil**
   immoral
   wicked
   sinful
   corrupt
   vile

5. **to cancel**
   repeal
   annul
   abrogate
   nullify
   rescind

6. **goodness**
   morality
   righteousness
   ethic
   virtue
   integrity

7. **to hand out**
   dispense
   allocate
   grant
   dole out
   bestow

8. **unfair**
   unjust
   inequitable
   injurious
   undue
   unrighteous

9. **to depend on**
   rely on
   lean on
   count on
   bank on
   put faith in

10. **revolution**
    revolt
    uprising
    insurrection
    mutiny
    rebellion

11. **to spread through**
    pervade
    permeate
    saturate
    infiltrate
    seep

12. **public**
    civil
    civic
    communal
    societal
    community

EXERCISE 3

A. The 12 groups of related words are written below without keywords. Write the correct keyword over each keyword group.

B. Each group of related words has *one* word that does not belong in the group. Find that word, cross it out, and write it under the group to which it belongs.

KEYWORDS

unfair	hand out	revolution	make peace
public	evil	depend on	earlier example
death	goodness	cancel	spread through

1. _____   2. _____   3. _____   4. _____
   exemplar   demise   conciliate   undue
   precedent   fatality   reconcile   sinful

prototype	extinction	bestow	immoral
archetype	ethic	bring to terms	corrupt
mutiny	expiration	pacify	wicked
_____	_____	_____	_____

5. _____   6. _____   7. _____   8. _____

repeal	integrity	dole out	communal
nullify	morality	dispense	inequitable
rescind	decease	lean on	injurious
annul	virtue	allocate	unjust
seep	righteousness	grant	unrighteous
_____	_____	_____	_____

9. _____   10. _____   11. _____   12. _____

bank on	uprising	pervade	civic
appease	insurrection	permeate	societal
put faith in	revolt	infiltrate	vile
count on	rebellion	saturate	civil
rely on	antecedent	abrogate	community
_____	_____	_____	_____

EXERCISE 4

Each sentence below contains one keyword, which is in heavy type.

A. Find the word below each sentence that is *not* a related word for the keyword. Circle that word. (The keyword numbers from Exercise 2 are in parentheses. These will help you if you need to look back.)

B. After completing instruction A, write each circled word under the keyword in the sentence to which it belongs.

1. Pollution has caused the **death** of millions of birds.

   a. demise   b. fatality   c. archetype   d. extinction   (2)

2. Sometimes a third party can help **make peace between** two warring factions.

   a. pacify   b. conciliate   c. reconcile   d. infiltrate   (3)

3. Henry VIII wanted the church to **cancel** his marriage to Catherine of Aragon.

   a. rescind   b. repeal   c. nullify   d. bank on   (5)

4. The people soon learned that they could **depend on** the new president in time of trouble.

   a. put faith in   b. rely on   c. dole out   d. count on   (9)

5. The law was changed because of **public** pressure.

   a. injurious   b. community   c. civic   d. societal (12)

6. Almost every system of government has its **goodness.**

   a. integrity   b. ethics   c. revolts   d. morality (6)

7. Every year the government **hands out** billions of dollars for defense.

   a. dispenses   b. brings to terms   c. allocates (7)

8. Dishonesty became more and more common until it had **spread through** every department of the new government.

   a. permeated   b. pervaded   c. annulled (11)

9. The lawyer tried to prove that the magazine article contained statements that were **unfair.**

   a. undue   b. inequitable   c. unjust   d. wicked (8)

10. The history of almost every country is marked by **revolutions** of the people against the government.

   a. insurrections   b. expirations   c. rebellions   d. uprisings (10)

11. History books described the king as dishonest, **evil,** and cruel.

   a. civil   b. immoral   c. vile   d. corrupt (4)

12. The British House of Commons has been called the **earlier example of** all the representative assemblies.

   a. prototype of   b. virtue for   c. archetype of   d. precedent for (1)

EXERCISE 5

In the following paragraph one word in each sentence is in heavy type. Find the keyword from the list below that is closest in meaning to each of these words, and write it in the proper blank underneath the paragraph. Check your answers by looking at Exercise 6.

KEYWORDS

cure	**very old**	**desire**	**intelligence**
total	**be about**	**money**	**make into law**
almost	**economic**	**question**	**physical harm**

Politicians are always **querying** laws. Let's imagine that there is an **antiquated** law on the books. This law does not involve **injuries** to an individual. Instead, it **pertains to** what happens with our taxes. The government wastes its **assets** because of this law. The **yearning** to change this law is very strong. **Approximately** two-thirds of the politicians agree that the law must be changed. After much discussion, the politicians **legislate** a new system to control how money is spent. The **overall** effect of the new law is positive. The **monetary** policies produce benefits that are felt all over the country. While the new law is not a **remedy** for all of the problems that the government faces, it does provide assistance. The **sagacity** of the politicians thus serves the people in a very real way.

querying	_____	antiquated	_____
injuries	_____	pertains to	_____
assets	_____	yearning	_____
Approximately	_____	legislate	_____
overall	_____	monetary	_____
remedy	_____	sagacity	_____

EXERCISE 6

The first word in each group below is the keyword. All of the words under each keyword (the related words) have similar meaning. Read each group and try to remember which related words go with each keyword.

13. physical harm
injury
lesion
wound
abrasion
laceration

14. money
funds
capital
assets
revenue
wherewithal

15. total
cumulative
inclusive
entire
aggregate
overall

16. to question
challenge
dispute
query
suspect
distrust

17. intelligence
wisdom
sagacity
prudence
astuteness
shrewdness

18. to be about
concern
deal with
pertain to
have to do with
refer to

19. desire
will
yearning
craving
yen
longing

20. very old
ancient
antiquated
antique
primeval
archaic

21. economic
fiscal
financial
monetary
pecuniary
budgetary

22. cure
remedy
panacea
antidote
counteractant
curative

23. to make into law
enact
proclaim
decree
legislate
ordain

24. almost
quasi-
virtually
roughly
approximately
more or less

EXERCISE 7

A. The 12 groups of related words are written below without keywords. Write the correct keyword over each keyword group.

B. Each group of related words has *one* word that does not belong in the group. Find that word, cross it out, and write it under the group to which it belongs.

KEYWORDS

cure	**very old**	**desire**	**intelligence**
total	**be about**	**money**	**make into law**
almost	**economic**	**question**	**physical harm**

13. _____	14. _____	15. _____	16. _____
wound	assets	aggregate	query
lesion	funds	cumulative	ordain
abrasion	prudence	primeval	challenge
yen	wherewithal	entire	distrust
injury	capital	overall	suspect
_____	_____	_____	_____

17. _____	18. _____	19. _____	20. _____
sagacity	deal with	yearning	inclusive
astuteness	dispute	craving	archaic
shrewdness	refer to	laceration	ancient
wisdom	concern	will	antiquated
revenue	have to do with	longing	antique
_____	_____	_____	_____

21. _____	22. _____	23. _____	24. _____
fiscal	curative	legislate	virtually
counteractant	panacea	enact	more or less
monetary	remedy	pertain to	roughly
budgetary	antidote	decree	approximately
financial	quasi-	proclaim	pecuniary
_____	_____	_____	_____

EXERCISE 8

Each sentence below contains one keyword, which is in heavy type.

A. Find the word below each sentence that is *not* a related word for the keyword. Circle that word. (The keyword numbers from Exercise 6 are in parentheses. These will help you if you need to look back.)

B. After completing instruction A, write each circled word under the keyword in the sentence to which it belongs.

1. Abraham Lincoln is often given credit for **making into law** freedom for the slaves.

   a. decreeing   b. challenging   c. legislating   (23)

2. There are **almost** 250 million people living in the United States.

   a. approximately   b. more or less   c. aggregate   (24)

3. Some people believe that the federal government has the **money** to solve every economic problem.

   a. antidote   b. capital   c. assets   d. funds   (14)

4. The plan was never completed for **economic** reasons.

   a. monetary   b. fiscal   c. financial   d. archaic   (21)

5. The politician handled problems with an **intelligence** that he had developed during years of experience.

   a. (a) wisdom   b. astuteness   c. (a) sagacity   d. (a) longing   (17)

6. The driver of the automobile received only minor **physical harm** because he was wearing a seat belt when the accident occurred.

   a. injuries   b. wherewithal   c. wounds   d. lacerations   (13)

7. During the press conference, the reporters **questioned** some of the president's earlier statements.

   a. queried   b. disputed   c. referred to   (16)

8. The vice-president's comments **were about** the recent developments in the Far East.

   a. pertained to   b. concerned   c. dealt with   d. proclaimed   (18)

9. After serving for six years overseas, the ambassador had an intense **desire** to return to his native country.

   a. yearning   b. shrewdness   c. yen   (19)

10. The **very old** law was no longer useful or effective.

    a. budgetary   b. antiquated   c. ancient   (20)

11. The **total** opinion of the lawmakers favored a decrease in defense spending and an increase in social programs.

    a. overall   b. roughly   c. cumulative   (15)

12. It was believed that increased federal spending would serve as a **cure** for inflation.

    a. an abrasion   b. counteractant   c. remedy   d. panacea   (22)

EXERCISE 9

In the following paragraph one word in each sentence is in heavy type. Find the keyword from the list below that is closest in meaning to each of these words, and write the keyword in the proper blank underneath the paragraph. Check your answers by looking at Exercise 10.

KEYWORDS

order	**clean**	**examine**	**more than half**
slow	**obey**	**very small**	**make clear**
idea	**law**	**support**	**legal paper**

The government moves at a **deliberate** speed because of the importance of its actions. Each decision involves many **minute** details. Each of these details must be **scrutinized** very closely. If lawmakers decide to pass a new **ordinance,** several things must be considered. All decisions should help **the preponderance** of the people. This **concept** is basic in a democratic society. The details of the new ruling must be **spelled out.** The ruling must be **endorsed** by the people who vote for the lawmakers. Let's imagine that the lawmakers create rules requiring restaurants to be more **hygienic.** The politicians must then decide what types of **permits** are necessary. If a restaurant fails to **abide by** the rules, the lawmakers must decide what type of legal action must be taken. If all of these decisions are not made carefully, a judge can issue an **injunction** that will prevent the police from enforcing this new law.

deliberate	_____	minute	_____
scrutinized	_____	ordinance	_____
the preponderance	_____	concept	_____
spelled out	_____	endorsed	_____
hygienic	_____	permits	_____
abide by	_____	injunction	_____

EXERCISE 10

The first word in each group below is the keyword. All the words under each keyword (the related words) have similar meaning. Read each group and try to remember which related words go with each keyword.

25. **to obey**	26. **slow**	27. **order**	28. **to make clear**
comply with	gradual	injunction	interpret
follow	creeping	writ	explicate

conform to	leisurely	mandate	spell out
abide by	deliberate	directive	illuminate
adhere to	unhurried	summons	delineate

29. very small

minute
miniature
tiny
minuscule
infinitesimal

30. law

regulation
canon
edict
ordinance
statute

31. to support

back
be for
advocate
champion
endorse

32. clean

sanitary
hygienic
unpolluted
immaculate
spotless

33. idea

principle
concept
notion
hypothesis
premise

34. to examine

inspect
investigate
scrutinize
probe
delve into

35. legal paper

certificate
document
license
warrant
permit

36. more than half

majority
preponderance
bulk
plurality
lion's share

EXERCISE 11

A. The 12 groups of related words are written below without keywords. Write the correct keyword over each keyword group.

B. Each group of related words has *one* word that does not belong in the group. Find that word, cross it out, and write it under the group to which it belongs.

KEYWORDS

order	clean	examine	more than half
slow	obey	very small	make clear
idea	law	support	legal paper

25. _____

follow
conform to
abide by
probe
comply with

_____

26. _____

infinitesimal
leisurely
deliberate
gradual
unhurried

_____

27. _____

writ
directive
injunction
mandate
notion

_____

28. _____

explicate
advocate
illuminate
spell out
interpret

_____

29. _____

miniature
minute
unpolluted

30. _____

canon
ordinance
regulation

31. _____

be for
delineate
back

32. _____

hygienic
sanitary
spotless

tiny	statute	endorse	immaculate
minuscule	summons	champion	creeping
_____	_____	_____	_____

33. _____ 34. _____ 35. _____ 36. _____

edict	delve into	permit	preponderance
premise	inspect	certificate	lion's share
principle	adhere to	license	majority
hypothesis	scrutinize	document	bulk
concept	investigate	plurality	warrant
_____	_____	_____	_____

EXERCISE 12

Each sentence below contains one keyword, which is in heavy type.

A. Find the word below each sentence that is *not* a related word for the keyword. Circle that word. (The keyword numbers from Exercise 10 are in parentheses. These will help you if you need to look back.)

B. After completing instruction A, write each circled word under the keyword in the sentence to which it belongs.

1. People who do not **obey** the laws of the land end up in prison.

   a. abide by   b. comply with   c. adhere to   d. explicate (25)

2. The problems that the world faced a few centuries ago seem **very small** compared to the complexities of life today.

   a. tiny   b. gradual   c. minute   d. infinitesimal (29)

3. The spy **examined** the area very carefully.

   a. scrutinized   b. investigated   c. was for (34)

4. Many Americans do not like to reveal the person they **support** in an election.

   a. endorse   b. back   c. advocate   d. inspect (31)

5. Major change in government should be a **slow** process.

   a. spotless   b. deliberate   c. unhurried (26)

6. The grocery store was old and small, but it was **clean.**

   a. immaculate   b. hygienic   c. minuscule   d. sanitary (32)

7. The government is based on the **idea** that all men are created equal.

   a. notion   b. principle   c. hypothesis   d. regulation (33)

8. The new **law** was designed to protect property owners in the city.

   a. ordinance   b. edict   c. statute   d. license (30)

9. When the policeman came to the door, he was holding an **order** from a judge.

    a. (a) summons   b. injunction   c. (a) premise   d. (a) directive (27)

10. The Supreme Court writes opinions to **make clear** laws passed by the Congress.

    a. follow   b. interpret   c. spell out   d. delineate (28)

11. Every person who wants to do electrical work must first get a **legal paper.**

    a. permit   b. majority   c. certificate   d. document (35)

12. **More than half** of the people voted for a new subway system in the city.

    a. The bulk   b. The lion's share   c. A writ
    d. The preponderance (36)

EXERCISE 13

In each blank write the keyword that corresponds to the word(s) in heavy type in the sentence. The number in parentheses can be used to check your answer.

1. In the 1700s, the people living in America (colonists) began to **dispute** the right of the king of England to rule their country. _____ (16)

2. The colonists felt that paying taxes to England was **inequitable.**
_____ (8)

3. England could not find a way to **pacify** these people.
_____ (3)

4. Several **uprisings** occurred before war was declared in 1775.
_____ (10)

5. As in any war, the price was very high: there were many **injuries** and **fatalities** on both sides. _____ (13) _____ (2)

6. After this war, a **document** was approved that still guides the American governing process today: the U.S. Constitution. _____ (35)

7. It is the basic safeguard of **civic** liberty. _____ (12)

8. Because of the **will** of the people to be free from the rule of a king, three branches of government were established. _____ (19)

9. The power to **legislate** was given to the Congress. _____ (23)

10. Executive power was **granted** to the president. _____ (7)

11. The power to **interpret** the law was given to a supreme court.
_____ (28)

12. The legislative branch creates all of the federal **statutes.**

    _____ (30)

13. Its procedures must be careful and **deliberate.** _____ (26)

14. These laws **deal with** citizenship, the military, the mail, interstate

    commerce, and so on. _____ (18)

15. They also control the usage of federal **funds** that are generated by taxation.

    _____ (14)

16. Thus all of the **fiscal** policies must be approved by Congress.

    _____ (21)

17. The **cumulative** effect of all of these laws is to create a very complicated

    system of government. _____ (15)

18. The **tiny** details that these laws contain require years of study to

    comprehend. _____ (29)

19. The executive branch is headed by the president, who must be **backed** by

    the voters. _____ (31)

20. His personal and political **integrity** is carefully watched by the people.

    _____ (6)

21. An **immaculate** public image, however, is not enough.

    _____ (32)

22. If the **bulk** of the population is dissatisfied with the way things are going,

    the president will not be reelected. _____ (36)

23. The main responsibility of the executive branch is to see that all citizens

    comply with the law. _____ (25)

24. This branch of government **delves into** any violation of federal law.

    _____ (34)

25. The government **counts on** the judicial branch to decide whether laws agree

    with the Constitution. _____ (9)

26. This branch has the power to **nullify** laws passed by Congress.

    _____ (5)

27. Its power **pervades virtually** every aspect of society.

    _____ (11) _____ (24)

28. Everyone, including the president, must follow its **directives.**

    _____ (27)

29. Thus the basic **principle** underlying this system of government is

    separation of powers. _____ (33)

30. The people who wrote the Constitution had the **wisdom** to study historical law. _____ (17)

31. French and English law, based on **ancient** codes of social behavior, served as **precedents** for the Constitution. _____ (20)
   _____ (1)

32. Though the Constitution is not a **panacea,** it has proven to be effective.
   _____ (22)

33. It protects society against **immoral** actions in government.
   _____ (4)

EXERCISE 14

Below each puzzle is a list of related words. Write the keyword for each related word in the appropriate squares. After you have written in all of the keywords for one puzzle, read the word in the circles going down. This will be a related word for the first keyword in the *next* puzzle. The numbers in parentheses can be used to check your answers, but try to complete the puzzles without using them.

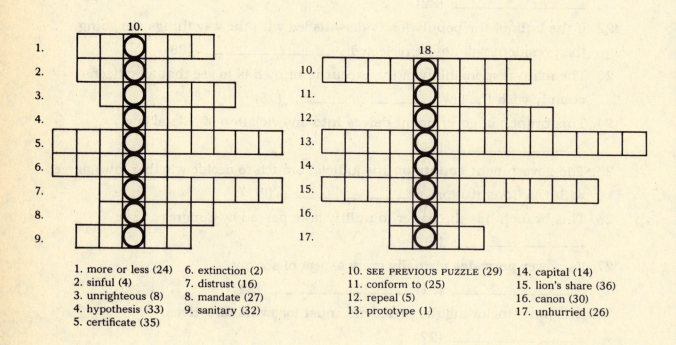

1. more or less (24)	6. extinction (2)
2. sinful (4)	7. distrust (16)
3. unrighteous (8)	8. mandate (27)
4. hypothesis (33)	9. sanitary (32)
5. certificate (35)	

10. SEE PREVIOUS PUZZLE (29)	14. capital (14)
11. conform to (25)	15. lion's share (36)
12. repeal (5)	16. canon (30)
13. prototype (1)	17. unhurried (26)

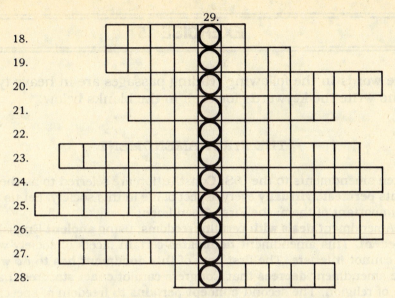

18.
19.
20.
21.
22.
23.
24.
25.
26.
27.
28.

29.

18. SEE PREVIOUS PUZZLE (12)
19. morality (6)
20. insurrection (10)
21. conciliate (3)
22. craving (19)
23. saturate (11)

24. wound (13)
25. astuteness (17)
26. illuminate (28)
27. champion (16)
28. concern (18)

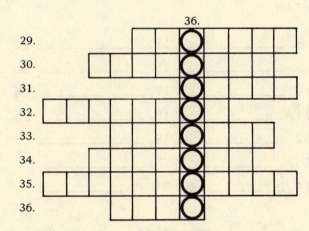

29.
30.
31.
32.
33.
34.
35.
36.

36.

29. SEE PREVIOUS PUZZLE (34)
30. put faith in (9)
31. entire (15)
32. financial (21)

33. dispense (7)
34. antique (20)
35. enact (23)
36. SEE THIS PUZZLE (22)

EXERCISE 15

Some of the words in the following reading passages are in heavy type. Read the passages and write the keywords for each in the blanks below.

THE FIRST AMENDMENT

The first ten amendments to the U.S. Constitution are referred to as the Bill of Rights. Their contents **permeate virtually** every aspect of life in this society. Let us **delve into** one of the most important of them: the First Amendment.

The First Amendment **deals with** certain freedoms, using **ancient** English common law as its **antecedent.** This amendment **delineates** certain facets of society with which the government cannot interfere. The first part of this **document has to do with** freedom of religion. The amendment **decrees** that Congress cannot **enact statutes** that prohibit the free exercise of religion. The second **concept pertains to** freedom of speech and freedom of the press. The third **principle** forbids Congress from **challenging** the right of people to meet peacefully, and the final area establishes the **premise** that the people have the right to ask the government for help if they are treated in an **unjust** manner.

Over the years since it was written, the government has **relied on** the **sagacity** of the Supreme Court to **interpret** the freedoms outlined in the First Amendment. The **cumulative** effect of its decisions has been a **gradual** evolution of a body of laws designed to protect the **virtues** of the First Amendment while safeguarding the **civil** rights of individuals.

1. _____	8. _____	15. _____	22. _____
2. _____	9. _____	16. _____	23. _____
3. _____	10. _____	17. _____	24. _____
4. _____	11. _____	18. _____	25. _____
5. _____	12. _____	19. _____	
6. _____	13. _____	20. _____	
7. _____	14. _____	21. _____	

THE VETO

The president of the United States has a very important tool to use: the presidential veto. Veto is defined as the president's power to **nullify** a bill that Congress has passed. If the president does not sign a bill or veto it within ten days after receiving it, it becomes a law. If the president vetoes a bill, the members of Congress can pass the bill over the president's veto if the **majority** is in favor. However, a mere **plurality** of the votes is not enough to override a veto—two-thirds of the Congress must **endorse** the bill in order to override a veto. The **will** of the Congress is then legally in effect, and all of the people, including the president, must **abide by** the new law. Failure to achieve a two-thirds majority over a veto results in the **demise** of the bill as it is written.

Let's imagine that Congress is worried about the **hygienic** conditions of restaurants in America. Its members feel that the **preponderance** of the restaurant owners is too **corrupt** to maintain proper **sanitary** conditions without **directives** from the federal government. The only **remedy,** in their opinion, is to pass a bill requiring federal inspections of all restaurants. The president does not agree at all, however. He feels that the **infinitesimal** details that such a procedure would involve are poorly **delineated.** In addition, he does not want to **allocate** the federal **revenues** necessary to enforce such a law. So, for **financial** as well as procedural reasons, he vetoes the bill. If enough members of Congress strongly favor the bill, they can override the veto. It is also possible for members of Congress to meet with the president in an attempt to **reconcile** their differences. If the bill is finally passed, the Supreme Court must **endorse** the law if it is **challenged** by the people.

Thus we see that the veto is an important tool in this system of government. Laws cannot be **enacted** unless several factions of the government **advocate** their passage. This system minimizes the danger of bloody **uprisings** by dissatisfied citizens, who would have to risk **injury** and even death to achieve their goals.

1. _____	8. _____	15. _____	22. _____
2. _____	9. _____	16. _____	23. _____
3. _____	10. _____	17. _____	24. _____
4. _____	11. _____	18. _____	25. _____
5. _____	12. _____	19. _____	
6. _____	13. _____	20. _____	
7. _____	14. _____	21. _____	

EXERCISE 16

Read the following articles. Do *not* use a dictionary. At least one related word from each of the keyword groups is in these articles. Try to remember the proper keywords as you read.

Prereading Introduction

Even though we are often unaware of it, the government is involved in many details of our everyday life. There are laws designed to protect us from each other, from dishonest companies, from health dangers, and so on. The government also collects money from everyone through various taxes, and then uses that money to finance programs that help us in a number of areas.

This first article examines some of the aspects of our daily lives in which various governmental agencies are involved. The purpose of the article is to make the reader more aware of the wide variety of controls and services that our governmental system provides.

After reading this passage, you should answer the following questions:

1. Why does the author talk about windshield wipers in the first paragraph?
2. Discuss some of the ways in which our government is involved in the food that we eat.

3. What safety devices did the government require in automobiles?
4. Discuss some of the ways that the government affects you while you are a student.
5. Name some of the things that are paid for by taxes.
6. Compare some of the governmental agencies mentioned in this reading with governmental agencies in your country.

THE IMPACT OF GOVERNMENT ON PEOPLE*

Obviously, government can affect the life of students or other citizens by sending them overseas to fight in a war in which they may be killed. Less obvious, perhaps, are the ways in which government pervades most aspects of daily life, sometimes down to minute details. For example, the federal government regulates the amount of windshield[a] that the wipers[b] on a car must cover and even the *speed* of the windshield wipers. (At the fast setting, wipers must go "at least 45 cycles per minute.")[1]

A family sits down to a breakfast of orange juice, bacon and eggs, toast, and coffee. Half a dozen agencies of the federal government have dealt with the food before it arrived at the breakfast table: the orange juice, if the frozen kind, must be manufactured under standards set by the Food and Drug Administration of the Department of Health, Education, and Welfare; the bacon must be inspected by the Department of Agriculture's Consumer and Marketing Service or must meet equivalent state standards; the eggs may have come from a box marked with a Department of Agriculture shield; the toast is made from bread that must by law be produced under sanitary conditions and comply with federal standards; and the coffee arrived in the United States under the eyes of both the Food and Drug Administration and the Bureau of Customs of the Department of the Treasury.

When people drive cars, they are required by law to have a license issued by their state but conforming to federal standards.[c] The cars must meet federal

standards; automobiles manufactured in the United States after 1968 were required to have seat belts, shoulder belts, and head rests to reduce traffic injuries and fatalities. Seat belt buzzers became noisy reminders of the impact of government on our daily lives when federal regulations required 1975 and later model cars to have them.

College students driving to class (perhaps over a highway built largely with federal funds) are expected to observe local traffic regulations. They may have to put a dime in a city parking meter.[d] The classroom in which they sit may have been constructed with a federal grant.[e] Possibly they are attending college with the aid of federal loans or grants made available by the Higher Education Act of 1965. In fiscal 1976,[f] for example, the federal government spent $2.6 billion on loans and grants to more than 4 million college and graduate students.[2]

Clearly government's impact is real and far-reaching. Americans normally must pay three levels of taxes—local, state, and federal. They attend public schools and perhaps public colleges. They draw[g] unemployment insurance,[h] welfare benefits,[i] Medicare,[j] and Social Security.[k] They must either obey the laws or pay the penalty of a fine or imprisonment if they break them and are caught and convicted.[l] Their savings accounts and home mortgages[m] are guaranteed by the federal government. Their taxes support the armed forces, police, fire, health, and sanitation departments. To hunt, fish, marry, drive, fly, or build they must have a government li-

---

[1]Motor Vehicle Safety Standards 104–3 (1969).

[2]Data provided by the Office of Education, Department of Health, Education, and Welfare.

---

*Excerpt from *Democracy under Pressure*, Third Edition, by Milton C. Cummings, Jr., and David Wise, © 1977 by Harcourt Brace Jovanovich, Inc., pp. 9–10. Reprinted by permission of the publisher.

cense. From birth certificate to death certificate, government accompanies individuals along the way. Even after they die, the government is not through with them. Estate taxes[n] must be collected and wills[o] probated[p] in the courts.

In the United States, "government" is extraordinarily complicated. There are federal, state, and local layers of government, metropolitan[q] areas, commissions, authorities, boards and councils, and quasi-governmental bodies. And many of these overlap.

Notes

[a]windshield: glass in a car that keeps the wind from hitting the driver.
[b]wiper: a mechanical device that keeps rainwater off of the windshield.
[c]federal standards: U.S. government (rather than state government) requirements.
[d]put a dime in a city parking meter: place a ten-cent coin in a device that gives the driver a certain amount of time to park for a certain amount of money.
[e]a federal grant: money given by the U.S. government.
[j]fiscal 1976: from September 1975 through August 1976.
[g]draw: receive.
[h]unemployment insurance: money received if one loses his or her job.

[i]welfare benefits: assistance for people who do not make enough money to live on.
[j]medicare: health insurance for older people.
[k]Social Security: money paid to older people who are no longer working.
[l]convicted: found guilty of a crime.
[m]home mortgages: loans made for the purpose of buying houses.
[n]estate taxes: money paid to the government on one's inheritance.
[o]wills: legal statement of one's wishes concerning what to do with one's property after death.
[p]probated: made official, recognized as valid.
[q]metropolitan: city (adjective).

Prereading Introduction

The following article is a discussion of law from several points of view. After giving a brief definition of the word "law," the discussion centers around some of the philosophical and historical considerations that underlie American law. The passage also discusses what types of laws there are and gives examples of some of the processes involved in enforcing the law in the courts.

After reading this passage, you should answer the following questions:

1. According to this article, what is a political definition of law?
2. What is the principle of natural rights?
3. What do you think Dr. Martin Luther King, Jr., did?
4. What is a sociological definition of law? How does it differ from a political definition?
5. What is common law? What is the main common law principle that judges still use today?
6. What was the example using an apple tree supposed to illustrate?
7. What is the difference between civil cases and criminal cases? Give an example of each.
8. What does administrative law deal with?
9. Do you agree with Supreme Court Justice Jackson's views on law?

THE LAW*

In a political sense, law is the body of rules made by government for society, interpreted by the courts, and backed by the power of the state. While this is a simple, dictionary-type definition, there are conflicting theories of law and little agreement on how it should be defined.

If law were limited to what can be established and enforced by the state, then Louis XIV[a] would have been correct in saying, "It is legal because I wish it." The men who founded the American nation were influenced by another tradition, rooted in the philosophy of John Locke and in the principle of natural rights. This tradition was the theory that man, living in a state of nature, possessed certain fundamental rights that he brought with him into organized society. The tradition of natural rights was used by the American revolutionaries of 1776 to justify their revolt against England and, more recently, by Dr. Martin Luther King, Jr.,[b] the civil rights leader, and others who practiced "civil disobedience" against laws they believed to be unjust, unconstitutional, or immoral.

Still another approach to law is sociological. In this view, law is seen as the gradual growth of rules and customs that reconcile conflict among people in societies; it is as much a product of culture, religion, and morality as of politics. There is always a problem of incorporating majority morality into criminal law; if enough people decide to break a law, it becomes difficult to enforce. One example was Prohibition,[c] which was widely ignored and finally repealed; more recently, there have been pressures to legalize marijuana.

Much American law is based on English *common law*. In twelfth-century medieval England, judges began to dispense law, and their cumulative body of decisions, often based on custom and precedent, came to be called common law, or judge-made law (as opposed to written law made by legislatures). In deciding cases, judges have often relied on the principle of *stare decisis,* the Latin phrase meaning "stand by past decisions." In other words, judges generally attempt to find a *precedent* for a decision in an earlier case involving similar principles. Most law that governs the actions of Americans is *statutory law* enacted by Congress, or by state legislatures or local legislative bodies; but many statutes embody principles of English common law.

Laws do not always ensure fairness. If a man discovers that his apple trees are gradually being cut down by a neighbor, he can sue for damages,[d] but the money judgment will not save the trees. Instead, he may, under the legal principle of *equity,* seek an injunction to prevent any further tree chopping. Equity, or fair dealing, may provide preventive measures and legal remedies unavailable under ancient principles of common law.

Cases considered by federal and state courts are either *civil* or *criminal.* Civil cases concern relations between individuals or organizations, such as a divorce action, or a suit for damages arising from an automobile accident or for violation of a business contract. The government is often party to[e] a civil action—when the Justice Department files a civil antitrust suit[f] against a corporation, for example. Criminal cases concern crimes committed against the public order. Most crimes are defined by local, state, and federal statutes, which set forth a range of penalties as well.

A growing body of cases in federal courts concerns questions of *administrative law,* the rules and regulations made and applied by federal regulatory agencies and commissions. Corporations and individuals can go into federal court to challenge the rulings of these agencies.

Supreme Court Justice Robert Jackson once observed that people are governed either by the will of one man, or group of men, or by law. He added, "Law, as the expression of the ultimate will and wisdom of a people, has so far proven the safest guardian of liberty yet devised."[1]

---

[1]Robert H. Jackson, *The Supreme Court in the American System of Government* (Cambridge, Mass.: Harvard University Press, 1955), p. 27.

---

*Excerpt from *Democracy under Pressure,* Third Edition, by Milton C. Cummings, Jr., and David Wise, © 1977 by Harcourt Brace Jovanovich, Inc., pp. 479–80. Reprinted by permission of the publisher.

Notes

^aLouis XIV: king of France from 1643 to 1715.
^bDr. Martin Luther King, Jr.: leader of the movement to get equal rights for blacks in the 1950s and 1960s.
^cProhibition: the period from 1920 to 1933 when it was against the law to possess or sell alcohol.

^dsue for damages: take to court in an attempt to get paid for harm done.
^eparty to: a part of.
^fcivil antitrust suit: legal action to break up a large business which, because of its size, has too much power or control.

EXERCISE 17

Review: This exercise reviews the various word derivations covered in Chapters 2–5. All the words come from Chapter 5.

A. Adjectives

a. strength   b. continuation   c. type   d. give off   e. excite
f. notice   g. find   h. back   i. question   j. spread out

1. arousal ____

2. regressive ____

3. denominational ____

4. The answer is **ascertainable,** but the process will take a long time. ____

5. The child's face was **radiant** after hearing the kind words of the teacher. ____

6. The old man was just as active and **vigorous** as a man half his age. ____

7. The police thought that the man was acting in a very **suspicious** manner. ____

8. The politician was **vehement** in his denial of the charges. ____

9. No one has ever been able to invent a **perpetual** motion machine. ____

10. The outline of the building was barely **discernible** in the fog. ____

B. Nouns

a. different   b. notice   c. irregular   d. join together   e. spread out
f. begin   g. simple   h. false   i. give off

1. distinctness ____

2. inconsistence ____

3. discernment ____

4. The police were able to find most of the "money," but they never could discover who the **counterfeiter** was. ____

5. When the **secretion** from the spider came into contact with air, it hardened almost immediately. _____

6. The two children were twins, but the **dissimilarities** were obvious. _____

7. The cook put all of the ingredients into a **blender.** _____

8. The **initiation** of peace talks finally came after six years of war. _____

9. The scientist studied the **diffusion** of chemicals in various liquids. _____

C. Verbs

    a. false   b. gaslike   c. rightly

1. The criminals attempted to **legitimatize** their activities by giving some of the money they made to the poor. _____

2. The spy was caught when an official noticed that his passport had been **falsified.** _____

3. At a certain temperature, the liquid **vaporizes.** _____

4. Once the liquid has **gasified,** it is extremely poisonous. _____

D. Adverbs

    a. very good   b. similar   c. see-through   d. different   e. false
    f. simple   g. marriage   h. irregular   i. following

    1. incongruously _____

    2. subsequently _____

    3. nuptially _____

    4. The weather this winter was **abnormally** cold. _____

    5. The **crudely** made bomb exploded, killing three people. _____

    6. The child's plan was **transparently** simple. _____

    7. Most tires today are made of **synthetically** produced rubber. _____

    8. The lady **discretely** took some money from her purse and gave it to her son. _____

    9. The dancer was **sensationally** successful. _____

  10. Although the two houses were **comparably** priced, one was much larger. _____

7 Geology

EXERCISE 1

In the following paragraph one word in each sentence is in heavy type. Find the keyword from the list below that is closest in meaning to each of these words and write the keyword in the proper blank underneath the paragraph. Check your answers by looking at Exercise 2.

KEYWORDS

uncovered	**argument**	**break**	**write down**
put out	**opening**	**dirt**	**break into pieces**
introductory	**shaking**	**weak**	**live in**

Let us examine the **initial** events that caused land to be created. The parts of the world which human beings **inhabit** were created millions of years ago. While there are some minor **squabbles** about some of the details, geologists generally agree on the process that produced land. The patterns in rocks **record** what happened. Pressure from inside forced the earth's crust to **split** in places. Melted rock came through the **apertures** in the earth's crust. Time and natural elements combined to **douse** the many fires that developed. Many **barren** mountains, called volcanoes, were thus created. Activities beneath the crust of the earth caused **tremors** to occur. As a result, some places in these volcanoes became relatively **fragile.** Several processes then caused large rocks to **crumble.** In this manner, **soil** was eventually formed.

initial	_____	inhabit	_____
squabbles	_____	record	_____
split	_____	apertures	_____
douse	_____	barren	_____
tremors	_____	fragile	_____
crumble	_____	soil	_____

EXERCISE 2

The first word in each group below is the keyword. All the words under each keyword (the related words) have similar meaning. Read each group and try to remember which related words go with each keyword.

1. **uncovered**
   bare
   naked
   bald
   nude
   barren

2. **to live in**
   reside
   dwell
   occupy
   inhabit
   lodge

3. **shaking**
   vibration
   quake
   quiver
   tremor
   shiver

4. **to put out**
   extinguish
   douse
   smother
   quench
   blow out

5. **to write down**
   document
   transcribe
   record
   log
   chronicle

6. **opening**
   pore
   aperture
   orifice
   incision
   hole

7. **to break**
   fracture
   rupture
   cleave
   shear
   split

8. **introductory**
   preliminary
   initial
   prefatory
   prior
   incipient

9. **argument**
   debate
   quarrel
   row
   polemic
   squabble

10. **to break into pieces**
    shatter
    disintegrate
    crumble
    pulverize
    splinter

11. **weak**
    feeble
    fragile
    puny
    frail
    flimsy

12. **dirt**
    soil
    loam
    ground
    earth
    turf

EXERCISE 3

A. The 12 groups of related words are written below without keywords. Write the correct keyword over each keyword group.

B. Each group of related words has *one* word that does not belong in the group. Find that word, cross it out, and write it under the group to which it belongs.

KEYWORDS

uncovered	**argument**	**break**	**write down**
put out	**opening**	**dirt**	**break into pieces**
introductory	**shaking**	**weak**	**live in**

Dra. Graciela Escalante Olvera
CIRUJANO DENTISTA
U.N.A.M.

CED. PROFESIONAL 486592

REG. S.S.A. 11164

Rx

28 Abril 98

Metafipiren — Forte Tabl.
1 c/ 12 HRS. por 5 dias

(firma)

Sonora # 123-304 esq. Parque España, Col. Condesa, C.P 06140, México, D.F., Tel. 286- 3330, FAX. 589-2097

Neurodelgina Tall adults.
1 c/y HRS. si hay dolor.

1. _____
   bald
   barren
   puny
   nude
   bare
   _____

2. _____
   inhabit
   cleave
   dwell
   reside
   occupy
   _____

3. _____
   quiver
   vibration
   tremor
   quake
   incision
   _____

4. _____
   douse
   smother
   extinguish
   disintegrate
   blow out
   _____

5. _____
   quench
   transcribe
   chronicle
   record
   document
   _____

6. _____
   aperture
   pore
   orifice
   loam
   hole
   _____

7. _____
   rupture
   split
   fracture
   shear
   lodge
   _____

8. _____
   prior
   initial
   naked
   preliminary
   prefatory
   _____

9. _____
   quarrel
   shiver
   row
   debate
   squabble
   _____

10. _____
    crumble
    pulverize
    log
    shatter
    splinter
    _____

11. _____
    feeble
    frail
    fragile
    flimsy
    incipient
    _____

12. _____
    polemic
    ground
    soil
    turf
    earth
    _____

EXERCISE 4

Each sentence below contains one keyword, which is in heavy type.

A. Find the word below each sentence that is *not* a related word for the keyword. Circle that word. (The keyword numbers from Exercise 2 are in parentheses. These will help you if you need to look back.)

B. After completing instruction A, write each circled word under the keyword in the sentence to which it belongs.

1. The forest fire burned out of control until a thunderstorm **put it out.**

   a. doused it   b. extinguished it   c. ruptured it   (4)

2. **Shakings** beneath the earth's surface cause bands of energy to go out from the source.

   a. Tremors   b. Orifices   c. Vibrations   d. Quivers   (3)

3. The rocks rolled down the hill, **breaking into pieces** buildings that were in their path.

   a. disintegrating   b. pulverizing   c. crumbling   d. smothering   (10)

4. The speaker made a few **introductory** remarks about his subject.

   a. flimsy   b. preliminary   c. initial   (8)

5. The geologists very carefully removed the **dirt** from around the crystal structure.

   a. earth   b. row   c. soil   d. loam   (12)

6. People who **live in** the area near the center of an earthquake are in great danger.

   a. occupy   b. inhabit   c. dwell in   d. chronicle   (2)

7. The underground water came to the top through a small **opening** in the rock.

   a. hole   b. aperture   c. quake   (6)

8. An **argument** developed in scientific circles about the origin and cause of the earthquake.

   a. (A) debate   b. (A) ground   c. (A) quarrel   d. (A) polemic   (9)

9. Geological events of prehistoric time are **written down** in the rock formations of the area.

   a. transcribed   b. recorded   c. documented   d. shattered   (5)

10. Mountains that are very high are always **uncovered.**

    a. prefatory   b. bare   c. barren   (1)

11. The tent proved to be **weak** protection against the storm.

    a. puny   b. feeble   c. bald   d. frail   (11)

12. The earthquake caused many of the water pipes to **break.**

    a. shear   b. reside   c. split   (7)

EXERCISE 5

In the following paragraph at least one word in each sentence is in heavy type. Find the keyword from the list below that is closest in meaning to each of these words, and write it in the proper blank underneath the paragraph. Check your answers by looking at Exercise 6.

KEYWORDS

main	division	raise	become smaller
rock	flow slowly	strong	cause to move
wet	enough	growth	period of time

One of the **principal** concepts in modern geology deals with how changes occur on the earth's surface. Water can cause considerable change, even if it is just **trickling.** As the land near the water becomes **soaked,** certain changes occur. For example, **stones** that are supported by this land are **dislodged** as the soil is washed away. As **epochs** pass, the changes caused by water can be tremendous. Volcanic activity is another example of a **potent** force of nature. If there is **sufficient** pressure from beneath the earth's crust, great changes can take place quickly. Huge amounts of material can be suddenly **elevated.** This process causes a **swelling** of material that can later become a mountain. As the material cools, it **contracts.** As a result, **crevices** form in the sides of the new mountain that allow natural forces to modify its shape even further.

principal	_____	trickling	_____
soaked	_____	stones	_____
dislodged	_____	epochs	_____
potent	_____	sufficient	_____
elevated	_____	swelling	_____
contracts	_____	crevices	_____

EXERCISE 6

The first word in each group below is the keyword. All the words under each keyword (the related words) have similar meaning. Read each group and try to remember which related words go with each keyword.

13. **wet**	14. **rock**	15. **period of time**	16. **to raise**
moist	stone	duration	heave
damp	pebble	cycle	lift
soaked	boulder	phase	hoist
drenched	gravel	era	elevate
soggy	concretion	epoch	boost

17. **main**	18. **enough**	19. **to flow slowly**	20. **division**
principal	sufficient	trickle	crevice
foremost	adequate	dribble	fissure
predominant	ample	ooze	crack
prevailing	plenty	percolate	cleft
paramount	sufficing	drip	rift

21. **to become smaller**	22. **strong**	23. **to cause to move**	24. **growth**
contract	violent	dislodge	expansion
subside	mighty	displace	augmentation
wither	powerful	eject	escalation
recede	potent	propel	heightening
shrivel	intense	uproot	swelling

EXERCISE 7

A. The 12 groups of related words are written below without keywords. Write the correct keyword over each keyword group.

B. Each group of related words has *one* word that does not belong in the group. Find that word, cross it out, and write it under the group to which it belongs.

KEYWORDS

main	division	raise	become smaller
rock	flow slowly	strong	cause to move
wet	enough	growth	period of time

13. _____   14. _____   15. _____   16. _____

damp	boulder	epoch	displace
soggy	stone	cycle	elevate
moist	escalation	phase	lift
mighty	gravel	era	boost
soaked	concretion	fissure	heave

_____   _____   _____   _____

17. _____   18. _____   19. _____   20. _____

principal	sufficient	ooze	crevice
paramount	predominant	percolate	rift
foremost	plenty	trickle	duration
adequate	sufficing	drip	cleft
prevailing	ample	shrivel	crack

_____   _____   _____   _____

21. _____   22. _____   23. _____   24. _____

wither	drenched	dislodge	expansion
contract	powerful	eject	pebble
recede	intense	uproot	heightening
dribble	violent	propel	augmentation
subside	potent	hoist	swelling

_____   _____   _____   _____

EXERCISE 8

Each sentence below contains one keyword, which is in heavy type.

A. Find the word below each sentence that is *not* a related word for the keyword. Circle that word. (The keyword numbers from Exercise 6 are in parentheses. These will help you if you need to look back.)

B. After completing instruction A, write each circled word under the keyword in the sentence to which it belongs.

1. The chemical composition and physical arrangement of rocks help geologists reconstruct events that took place in **periods of time** before human beings existed.

    a. concretions   b. epochs   c. phases   d. cycles (15)

2. Rock formations inside caves are caused by mineral deposits from water that **flowed slowly** for thousands of years.

    a. dribbled   b. trickled   c. percolated   d. heaved (19)

3. The force of the volcanic explosion **raised** tons of rock into the air.

    a. boosted   b. dripped   c. lifted   d. hoisted (16)

4. Dr. Smith was the **main** authority in the world on geothermal energy.

    a. prevailing   b. predominant   c. intense   d. principal (17)

5. The area was of no value to farmers because it was covered with **rocks.**

    a. boulders   b. augmentations   c. stones   d. pebbles (14)

6. Sometimes oil is **caused to move** to the surface by pressure from natural gas.

    a. ejected   b. withered   c. displaced (23)

7. As the snow melted, the entire area became **wet.**

    a. damp   b. drenched   c. soaked   d. foremost (13)

8. The sun shone brightly through a **division** in the rock.

    a. crack   b. rift   c. crevice   d. (an) era (20)

9. The long period of dry heat seemed to make the entire area **become smaller.**

    a. shrivel   b. propel   c. contract (21)

10. A **strong** storm hit the mainland, causing death and injury.

    a. powerful   b. potent   c. plenty (of)   d. violent (22)

11. There was **enough** rainfall in the area to allow vegetation to grow.

    a. adequate   b. ample   c. soggy   d. sufficient (18)

12. The **growth** in food production was made possible by the quality of the soil and the availability of water.

    a. escalation   b. cleft   c. expansion (24)

EXERCISE 9

In the following paragraph some of the words are in heavy type. Find the keyword from the list below that is closest in meaning to each of these words, and write the keyword in the proper blank underneath the paragraph. Check your answers by looking at Exercises 10.

KEYWORDS

fast	**unusual**	**very hot**	**force into a**
air	**area**	**originating**	**smaller space**
harm	**wavy**	**outer**	**very carefully**
			not enough

Geologists have **painstakingly** studied the effect of sunlight on the earth. They know that heat and light **emanating** from the sun travel in an **oscillating** pattern through space. This sunlight strikes different parts of the world at different angles. The **compressed,** cool air in the atmosphere is warmed according to its angle from the sun. As a result, different **zones** of the world have different climates. Some parts of the earth are **blistering** because sunlight strikes them at a straight angle. Other parts of the world never warm up, since the sunlight that strikes them is **insufficient** because of the angle of approach. For the temperature to rise above freezing is **rare** in some places. If all the sun's heat reached the **exterior** portion of the earth, however, it would cause tremendous **devastation.** The gentlest **breeze** would become deadly. There would be a **speedy** disappearance of life as we know it.

painstakingly	_____	emanating	_____
oscillating	_____	compressed	_____
zones	_____	blistering	_____
insufficient	_____	rare	_____
exterior	_____	devastation	_____
breeze	_____	speedy	_____

EXERCISE 10

The first word in each group below is the keyword. All the words under each keyword (the related words) have similar meaning. Read each group and try to remember which related words go with each keyword.

25. to force into a **26. area** **27. outer** **28. unusual**
    smaller space

consolidate	zone	exterior	extraordinary
compress	region	outside	rare
condense	district	external	unique
concentrate	territory	surface	atypical
compact	locality	extrinsic	exceptional

29. wavy **30. air** **31. not enough** **32. harm**

swaying	atmosphere	deficient	devastation
oscillating	breeze	inconclusive	impairment

pulsating	draft	inadequate	vandalism
undulatory	gust	insufficient	detriment
ripply	wind	meager	damage

33. **fast**	34. **very carefully**	35. **originating**	36. **very hot**
rapid	meticulously	generated	sizzling
swift	painstakingly	derived	molten
speedy	in detail	emanating	scalding
hasty	scrupulously	springing	scorching
expeditious	minutely	arising	blistering

EXERCISE 11

A. The 12 groups of related words are written below without keywords. Write the correct keyword over each keyword group.

B. Each group of related words has *one* word that does not belong in the group. Find that word, cross it out, and write it under the group to which it belongs.

KEYWORDS

fast	**unusual**	**very hot**	**force into a**
air	**area**	**originating**	** smaller space**
harm	**wavy**	**outer**	**very carefully**
			not enough

25. _____	26. _____	27. _____	28. _____
compress	zone	exterior	rare
consolidate	detriment	extrinsic	extraordinary
generated	locality	surface	exceptional
compact	territory	scalding	unique
concentrate	district	outside	swift
_____	_____	_____	_____

29. _____	30. _____	31. _____	32. _____
pulsating	region	deficient	vandalism
swaying	atmosphere	atypical	impairment
oscillating	wind	insufficient	damage
ripply	breeze	inadequate	draft
meticulously	gust	inconclusive	devastation
_____	_____	_____	_____

33. _____	34. _____	35. _____	36. _____
hasty	minutely	derived	scorching
expeditious	painstakingly	condense	molten
external	in detail	emanating	sizzling

rapid	scrupulously	arising	meager
speedy	undulatory	springing	blistering

_____   _____   _____   _____

EXERCISE 12

Each sentence below contains one keyword, which is in heavy type.

A. Find the word below each sentence that is *not* a related word for the keyword. Circle that word. (The keyword numbers from Exercise 10 are in parentheses. These will help you if you need to look back.)

B. After completing instruction A, write each circled word under the keyword in the sentence to which it belongs.

1. Energy from earthquakes moves in a circular, **wavy** pattern.

   a. oscillating   b. extraordinary   c. undulatory (29)

2. In March 1964, an earthquake of **unusual** strength hit southern Alaska.

   a. exceptional   b. rare   c. extrinsic (28)

3. The scientists wanted to prove their theory, but the evidence they gathered was **not enough.**

   a. inadequate   b. deficient   c. insufficient   d. scrupulously (31)

4. The chemical composition of soil sometimes allows geologists to identify the **area** from which it was taken.

   a. territory   b. zone   c. gust   d. region (26)

5. Tiny pieces of rock are **forced into a smaller space** by natural pressures.

   a. compacted   b. scorching   c. compressed (25)

6. One of the problems caused by earthquakes in populated areas is **harm** to electrical and water systems.

   a. damage   b. devastation (of)   c. locality (32)

7. When the climate changed, dinosaurs, which dominated the area, made a relatively **fast** departure.

   a. inconclusive   b. swift   c. rapid   d. speedy (33)

8. In the desert, **very hot** temperatures make life difficult.

   a. sizzling   b. blistering   c. springing (36)

9. The geologist **very carefully** avoided making mistakes as she conducted her research.

   a. ripply   b. meticulously   c. painstakingly (34)

10. The water **originating** from the ground was clean enough to drink.

    a. emanating   b. arising   c. consolidating (35)

11. The **outer** appearance of a rock seldom reveals the intricate operations of the natural forces which formed it.

    a. exterior   b. surface   c. external   d. hasty (27)

12. I knew a window was open someplace because I kept feeling **air.**

    a. impairment   b. wind   c. a breeze (30)

EXERCISE 13

In each blank write the keyword that corresponds to the word(s) in heavy type in the sentence. The number in parentheses can be used to check your answer.

1. There are several types of **soil** in the world. _____ (12)

2. **Preliminary** investigations indicated that the type of dirt was dependent upon the type of rock from which it was **derived.** _____ (8) _____ (35)

3. For example, soil that came from rocks that were formed by the cooling down of **molten** material would all be of one type. _____ (36)

4. Rocks formed from tiny pieces of material that have been **compacted** would produce a different type of soil. _____ (25)

5. There is **ample** evidence to show that other factors contribute to soil formation. _____ (18)

6. Geologists have **documented** that climate plays a major role. _____ (5)

7. The type of vegetation that grows in a **district** also influences the development of soil. _____ (26)

8. In addition, soil that is newly developed is different from soil that developed in a distant **epoch.** _____ (15)

9. So, although geologists have studied soil **in detail,** they have been unable to predict soil formation very accurately. _____ (34)

10. Whatever the final product, the **paramount** factor in the creation of all soils is weathering. _____ (17)

11. Weathering is the process whereby natural forces **pulverize** rocks. _____ (10)

12. All rocks, even large **boulders,** will eventually be reduced to soil if they are exposed to nature. _____ (14)

13. All rocks have **cracks** and **holes** in them. _____ (20) _____ (6)

14. Water **percolates** into these openings. _____ (19)

15. Streams and rivers also **uproot** rocks. _____ (23)

16. This action causes the rocks to **fracture.** _____ (7)

17. **Bare** rocks are also exposed to the **wind.** _____ (1) _____ (30)

18. This causes the **surface** layers to be worn away. _____ (27)

19. While the force of wind against a rock may appear to be **feeble,** the effect over millions of years can be **powerful.** _____ (11) _____ (22)

20. Also, in some areas, **vibrations** caused by movements deep beneath the earth can cause **rapid** changes in the rocks above. _____ (3) _____ (33)

21. This shaking of the earth (earthquakes) can cause serious **damage** to areas where people **dwell.** _____ (32) _____ (2)

22. The **swaying** motion of earthquakes can knock down buildings and cause fires that must be **extinguished.** _____ (29) _____ (4)

23. However, it is not at all **exceptional** for the same forces that create soil to destroy it. _____ (28)

24. If there is **inadequate** rainfall to keep the dirt **moist,** the same wind that makes dirt can blow it away. _____ (31) _____ (13)

25. Streams and rivers can cause the shore to **recede,** washing away tons of soil in the process. _____ (21)

26. Thus the forces of nature cause both an **expansion** and a decrease of available soil. _____ (24)

27. But, whenever soil is washed or blown away, new rocks are **lifted** to the surface to be transformed eventually into soil. _____ (16)

28. There is no **debate** about the fact that the forces of nature, creative and destructive, combine to keep things in proper balance. _____ (9)

EXERCISE 14

Solve the puzzle by writing the correct keyword for each of the words given below. The numbers in parentheses can be used to check your answers, but try to complete the puzzle without using them.

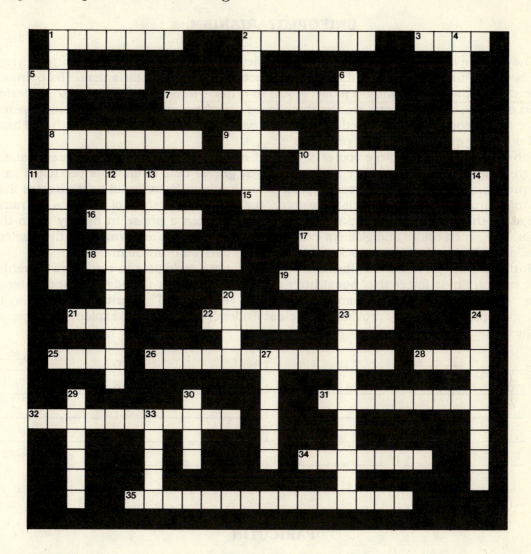

ACROSS

1. sizzling (36)
2. atypical (28)
3. region (26)
5. escalation (24)
7. prior (8)
8. quarrel (9)
9. puny (11)
10. fracture (7)
11. cycle (15)
15. turf (12)
16. inhabit (2)
17. dribble (19)
18. rift (20)
19. eject (23)
21. damp (13)
22. hoist (16)
23. breeze (30)
25. predominant (17)
26. subside (21)
28. expeditious (33)
31. log (5)
32. uproot (23)
34. tremor (3)
35. splinter (10)

DOWN

1. meticulously (34)
2. nude (1)
4. sufficing (18)
6. compress (25)
12. generated (35)
13. orifice (6)
14. pulsating (29)
20. vandalism (32)
24. deficient (31)
27. mighty (22)
29. blow out (4)
30. pebble (14)
33. external (27)

EXERCISE 15

Some of the words in the following reading passages are in heavy type. Read the passages and write the keywords for each in the blanks below.

UNIFORMITARIANISM

The science of geology was born in 1785 when a Scottish man, James Hutton, wrote the basis for future geological theories: the doctrine of uniformitarianism. His opinion, which is the **prevailing** opinion today, states that those forces which change the **exterior** crust of the world we **occupy** are the same forces that have operated for millions of years. Since this theory was established, geologists have **minutely** examined the earth and have had no major **quarrel** with this principle.

For example, glaciers (large bodies of ice that move slowly) **disintegrate stones** that are caught under them. When they melt, the **moist gravel** that remains is scratched in a **unique** manner. Rocks with these **atypical** scratches have been found in **territories** that are too warm for glaciers to exist. However, the geological history of the area is **transcribed** by the marks in the rocks. There must have been a **phase** in history when the areas were much colder and glaciers existed there. As the climate warmed up, the glaciers **receded,** leaving behind **bare** rocks with scratches **derived** from them.

Hutton's concept of uniformitarianism allowed early geologists to reconstruct prehistoric events. Those forces that **boost** huge masses to the top or **dislodge surface** material today operated in the same manner millions of years ago. This **initial** explanation of geological phenomena has provided **sufficient** evidence to allow us to explain the physical shape of the world today.

1. _____	7. _____	13. _____	19. _____
2. _____	8. _____	14. _____	20. _____
3. _____	9. _____	15. _____	21. _____
4. _____	10. _____	16. _____	22. _____
5. _____	11. _____	17. _____	
6. _____	12. _____	18. _____	

PARICUTIN

On February 20, 1943, a farmer was working in his cornfield about 320 kilometers west of Mexico City. He noticed some smoke coming up through **pores** in the **earth** nearby. He was witnessing the birth of a volcano, which was later to be named Paricutin. Four hours later, **violent** explosions were sending up clouds of ashes into the **atmosphere.** Two days later, **molten** rock (lava) was **oozing** out of a **fissure.** This lava had been **concentrated** under the crust of the earth for untold centuries, waiting for the bedrock above to **shear.**

Swift changes took place in the area. The **heightening** of the cone continued for several years. **Quivers** caused by the explosions caused new **rifts** to appear in the **frail** covering above the lava. Since few people **resided** in the area, the **damage** was minimal. However, the **undulatory** flow of the lava changed the entire area.

After nine years, the pressure under the earth was **insufficient** to allow the volcano to remain active. The fires started by the lava were **extinguished,** and the area calmed down. However, the changes made by Paricutin will remain for future geologists to study thousands of years from now.

1. _____	6. _____	11. _____	16. _____
2. _____	7. _____	12. _____	17. _____
3. _____	8. _____	13. _____	18. _____
4. _____	9. _____	14. _____	19. _____
5. _____	10. _____	15. _____	

EXERCISE 16

Read the following articles. Do *not* use a dictionary. At least one related word from each of the keyword groups is in these articles. Try to remember the proper keywords as you read.

Prereading Introduction

The following article is an explanation of the three categories into which geologists have divided all rocks. After the introductory paragraph, each paragraph explains the origin of the name of one of the categories and tells how rocks in that category are formed.

After reading this article, you should answer the following questions:

1. How did igneous rocks get their name?
2. How were igneous rocks formed?
3. Why can we see igneous rocks that cooled down beneath the surface of the earth's crust?
4. What are sedimentary rocks made from?
5. What are some of the forces that contribute to the creation of sedimentary rocks?
6. How did metamorphic rocks get their name?
7. What natural forces are involved in the creation of metamorphic rock?

THE THREE ROCK FAMILIES*

Observations, then, have led geologists to divide the earth's rocks into three main groups based on mode of origin: **igneous, sedimentary,** and **metamorphic.** Later on, we shall discuss each type in detail, but here is a short explanation of all three.

Igneous rocks, the ancestors of all other rocks, take their name from the Latin120/

---

*L. Don Leet, Sheldon Judson, and Marvin E. Kauffman, *Physical Geology*, Fifth Edition, © 1978, pp. 5, 7. Reprinted by permission of Prentice-Hall, Inc., Englewood Cliffs, N.J.

ignis, "fire." These "fire-formed" rocks were once a hot, molten mass known as **magma,** which subsequently cooled into firm, hard rock. Thus the lava[a] flowing across the earth's surface from an erupting[b] volcano soon cools and hardens into an igneous rock. There are other igneous rocks exposed at the surface that actually cooled some distance beneath it. We see such rocks today only because erosion[c] has stripped away the rocks that covered them during their formation.

Most sedimentary (Latin *sedimentum,* "settling") rocks are made up of particles derived from the breakdown of preexisting rocks. Usually these particles are transported by gravity, water, wind, or ice to new locations where they are deposited in new arrangements. For example, waves beating against a rocky shore may provide the sand grains and pebbles for a nearby beach. If these beach deposits were to be hardened, we should have sedimentary rock. One of the most characteristic features of sedimentary rocks is the layering of the deposits[d] that go to make them up.

Metamorphic rocks compose the third large family of rocks. Metamorphic (from the Greek words *meta,* "change," and *morphē,* "form") refers to the fact that the original rock has been changed from its primary form to a new form. Earth pressures, heat, and chemically active fluids beneath the surface may all be involved in changing an originally sedimentary or igneous rock into a metamorphic rock.

Notes

[a]lava: melted rock.
[b]erupting: violently active.
[c]erosion: slow wearing away or removal of the earth's crust.

[d]layering of the deposits: material being placed in rows, one on top of the other.

Prereading Introduction

The earth's crust is constantly changing as a result of natural forces that operate upon it. While we may not be able to see the changes in a lifetime, or even in several lifetimes, changes over the centuries can be spectacular.

The following article examines one type of natural force that slowly alters the earth's crust: mechanical weathering. Weathering refers to processes of change that are usually related in some way to the weather.

Two types of mechanical weathering are discussed: expansion/contraction and frost action. The first type concerns changes that occur to rocks as they heat up or cool down; the second type concerns changes that occur because of the freezing and melting of water that collects in cracks and crevices.

After reading this article, you should answer the following questions:

1. What is mechanical weathering? What other type(s) of weathering can you think of?
2. Why do changes in temperature cause weathering?
3. What effect do changes in temperature from day to night or summer to winter have? What evidence is there to support your answer?
4. Describe the weathering process that occurs when water freezes.
5. What is meant by the term "frost heaving"? How does it explain some of the damage that occurs to highways during the winter?
6. How active a force is frost heaving where you are living now? Where you grew up? Explain.

MECHANICAL WEATHERING*

Mechanical weathering, which is also referred to as **disintegration,** is the process by which rock is broken down into smaller and smaller fragments as the result of energy developed by physical forces. For example, when water freezes in a fractured rock, sufficient energy may develop from the pressure caused by expansion of the frozen water to split off pieces of the rock. Or a boulder moved by gravity down a rocky slope may be shattered into smaller fragments.

Expansion and contraction. Changes in temperature, if they are rapid enough and great enough, may bring about the mechanical weathering of rock. In areas where bare rock is exposed at the surface and is unprotected by a cloak of soil, forest or brush fires can generate heat adequate to break up the rock. The rapid and violent heating of the exterior zone of the rock causes it to expand and if the expansion is sufficiently great, flakes and larger fragments of the rock are split off. Lightning often starts such fires and, in rare instances, may even shatter exposed rock by means of a direct strike.

The debate continues concerning whether variations in temperature from day to night or from summer to winter are enough to cause mechanical weathering. Theoretically, such variations cause disintegration. For instance, we know that the different minerals forming a granite expand and contract at different rates as they react to rising and falling temperatures. We expect that even minor expansion and contraction of adjacent minerals would, over long periods of time, weaken the bonds between mineral grains and that it would thus be possible for disintegration to occur along these boundaries. In deserts we may find fragments of a single stone lying close beside one another. Obviously, the stone has split. But how? Many think the cause lies in expansion and contraction caused by heating and cooling.

But laboratory evidence to support these speculations is inconclusive. In one laboratory experiment coarse-grained granite was subjected to temperatures ranging from 14.5 to 135.5°C every 15 min. This alternate heating and cooling eventually simulated 244 years of daily heating and cooling; yet the granite showed no signs of disintegration. Perhaps experiments extended over longer periods of time would produce observable effects. In any event, we are still uncertain of the mechanical effect of daily or seasonal temperature changes; if these fluctuations bring about the disintegration of rock, they must do so very slowly.

Frost action. Frost is much more effective than heat in producing mechanical weathering. When water trickles down into the cracks, crevices, and pores of a rock mass and then freezes, its volume increases about 9 percent. This expansion of water as it passes from the liquid to the solid state sets up pressures that are directed outward from the inside of the rock. These pressures can dislodge fragments from the rock's surface.

The dislodged fragments of mechanically weathered rock are angular, and their size depends largely on the nature of the bedrock from which they have been displaced. Usually the fragments are only a few centimeters in maximum dimension, but in some places—along the cliffs bordering Devil's Lake, Wisconsin, for instance—they reach sizes of up to 3 m.

A second type of mechanical weathering produced by freezing water is **frost heaving.** This action usually occurs in fine-grained, unconsolidated deposits rather than in solid rock. Much of the water that falls as rain or snow soaks into the ground, where it freezes during the winter months. If conditions are right, more and more ice accumulates in the zone of freezing as water is added from the atmosphere above and drawn upward from the unfrozen ground below, much as a blotter soaks up moisture. In time, lens-shaped masses of it

*L. Don Leet, Sheldon Judson, and Marvin E. Kauffman, *Physical Geology,* Fifth Edition, © 1978, pp. 72–73. Reprinted by permission of Prentice-Hall, Inc., Englewood Cliffs, N.J.

are built up, and the soil above them is heaved upward. Frost heaving of this sort is common on poorly constructed roads, and lawns and gardens are often soft and spongy in the springtime as a result of the soil's heaving up during the winter.

Certain conditions must exist before either type of frost action can take place: There must be an adequate supply of moisture; the moisture must be able to enter the rock or soil; and temperatures must move back and forth across the freezing line. As we might expect, frost action is more pronounced in high mountains and in moist regions where temperatures fluctuate across the freezing line, either daily or seasonally.

Prereading Introduction

Earthquakes are natural phenomena that produce a combination of fear and fascination in the minds of most people. Geologists have studied them for many years and are still unable to predict them accurately or prevent them.

The following account of an earthquake in Japan is unique because it was provided by a trained geologist who took notes as he experienced the quake firsthand.

After reading this article, you should answer the following questions:

1. What are some of the geological effects that a very strong earthquake can have?
2. How many earthquakes a year can be classified as dangerous?
3. Which earthquake does this article describe? Why is it different from most other earthquakes of similar force?
4. What did Professor Imamura do when he felt the first movements of the earthquake?
5. Describe what happened during the first 12 seconds.
6. How long did the most violent vibrations continue?
7. Describe what happened to the building according to Professor Imamura.
8. When was the building finally safe?
9. The article ends by stating that four of the scientists in the building lost their homes and property to fire. In your opinion, why is fire such a danger after earthquakes?

EFFECTS OF EARTHQUAKES*

Earthquakes are interesting to most people because of their effects on human beings and structures. Their geological effects may also be profound. However, of all the earthquakes that occur every year, only one or two are likely to produce spectacular geological effects such as landslides or the elevation or depression of large landmasses. A hundred or so may be strong enough near their sources to destroy human life and property. The rest are too small to have serious effects. One of the best-known damaging earthquakes was that of 1923 in Japan.

At 11:58.5 A.M. on September 1, 1923, there occurred an earthquake whose center was under Sagami Bay, 80 km from Yokohama and 110 km from Tokyo. The vibrations spread outward with such energy that they caused serious destruction

*L. Don Leet, Sheldon Judson, and Marvin E. Kauffman, *Physical Geology*, Fifth Edition, © 1978, p. 132. Reprinted by permission of Prentice-Hall, Inc., Englewood Cliffs, N.J.

along the Japanese coast over an area 150 km long and 100 km wide. When the earthquake began, Professor Akitsune Imamura was sitting in his office at the Seismological Institute of Tokyo Imperial University, and his account is one of the few accurate eyewitness reports of an earthquake from within a zone of heavy damage, carefully documented by a knowledgeable observer.

At first, the movement was rather slow and feeble, so I did not take it to be the forerunner of so big a shock. As usual, I began to estimate the duration of the preliminary tremors, and determined, if possible, to ascertain the direction of the principal movements. Soon the vibration became large, and after 3 or 4 seconds from the commencement, I felt the shock to be very strong indeed. Seven or 8 seconds passed and the building was shaking to an extraordinary extent, but I considered these movements not yet to be the principal portion. At the 12th second from the start, according to my calculation, came a very big vibration, which I took at once to be the beginning of the principal portion. Now the motion, instead of becoming less and less as usual, went on increasing in intensity very quickly, and after 4 or 5 seconds I felt it to have reached its strongest. During this epoch the tiles were showering down from the roof making a loud noise, and I wondered whether the building could stand or not. I was able accurately to ascertain the directions of the principal movements and found them to have been about NW or SE. During the following 10 seconds the motion, though still violent, became somewhat less severe, and its character gradually changed, the vibrations becoming slower but bigger. For the next few minutes we felt an undulatory movement like that which we experience on a boat in windy weather, and we were now and then threatened by severe aftershocks. After 5 minutes from the beginning, I stood up and went over to see the instruments. . . . Soon after the first shock, fire broke out at two places in the University, and within one and a half hours our Institute was enveloped in raging smoke and heat; the shingles now exposed to the open air as the tiles had fallen down due to the shock, began to smoke and eventually took fire three times. . . . It was 10 o'clock at night before I found our Institute and Observatory quite safe. . . . We all, 10 in number, did our best, partly in continuing earthquake observations and partly in extinguishing the fire, taking no food or drink till midnight, while four of us who were residing in the lower part of the town lost our houses and property by fire.

EXERCISE 17

The following exercises show how different word forms are derived in English. Try to remember the endings and what parts of speech they indicate.

A. Words ending in -ic are often adjectives.

Example: cycle → cyclic

Put the letter of the correct keyword in the blank after each derived word. Some keywords are used more than one time:

a. cruelty   b. mystery   c. make peace   d. unreality
e. environment

1. atmosphere → atmospheric _____

2. In view of his background and environment, his behavior was **enigmatic.** _____

3. The treatment of the prisoners could only be called **barbaric.** ____

4. The transfer of the soldiers to another part of the country had a **pacific** effect in the area. ____

5. The author became famous for his **fantastic** stories about events in the future. ____

6. The man's **sadistic** crimes made the police believe that he was insane. ____

B. Words ending in *-ful* are usually adjectives.

Example: power → powerful

a. laughter   b. question   c. anger   d. fright

1. fear → fearful ____

2. Some people believe in a **wrathful** god, but others do not. ____

3. The child soon learned to be **distrustful** of everyone she met. ____

4. Walking home alone late at night was a **dreadful** experience. ____

5. Many teenagers are **resentful** of their parents' attempts to help them. ____

6. The **mirthful** mood of the children soon changed to disappointment. ____

C. There are several things that can be added to the beginning of an adjective to change its meaning to the opposite. One example is *in-*.

Examples: sufficient → insufficient (*not* sufficient)
                 adequate → inadequate (*not* adequate)

a. obvious   b. equal   c. kind   d. real   e. possible   f. safe
g. large   h. open to question

1. considerate → inconsiderate ____

2. distinct → indistinct ____

3. It was **inconceivable** that the team would lose the championship so quickly. ____

4. The evidence against the man was **indisputable.** ____

5. The law was designed to prevent anyone from receiving **inequitable** treatment from any government official. ____

6. The closeness of the war made everyone in the area feel **insecure.** ____

7. The additional cost of the new equipment proved to be **insubstantial.** ____

8. The passport was **invalid** because it did not have the necessary stamp from the government. ____

In summary:

1. We saw two more endings that usually make words into adjectives. What are they? _____ and _____

2. We added _____ to the beginning of a word to change its meaning. What change in meaning does this addition create? _____

_____

8 Sociology

EXERCISE 1

In the following paragraph one word in each sentence is in heavy type. Find the keyword from the list below that is closest in meaning to each of these words, and write the keyword in the proper blank underneath the paragraph. Check your answers by looking at Exercise 2.

KEYWORDS

promise	average	always the same	make a part of oneself
power	understood	faithfulness	put into one's head
assign	especially	not allowed	throw out from a group

Every society has behavior that is **forbidden.** Some acts are not allowed by law, but other rules are not written out; in other words, there are **implicit** rules that govern the behavior of a group. As a child grows up in a group, these unwritten rules are **inculcated** by parents, peers, and school. By adulthood, these rules are so thoroughly **absorbed** that members of the group follow them without knowing it. These unwritten laws define behavior that is considered to be **par** for the group. Of course there is no **oath** taken by any member of a society to follow these rules. What, then, gives a group **authority** over individual members? **Loyalty** to the group is demonstrated by one's behavior. Because members of the group follow these unwritten rules, many of their actions are **uniform.** If, however, one fails to follow these rules, he or she may be **expelled.** Thus group membership is often determined by judgments of behavior that are **ascribed** to an individual. Since most people need to and want to belong to a group, membership can be a **particularly** powerful weapon for a group to use.

forbidden	_____	implicit	_____
inculcated	_____	absorbed	_____
par	_____	oath	_____
authority	_____	Loyalty	_____
uniform	_____	expelled	_____
ascribed	_____	particularly	_____

EXERCISE 2

The first word in each group below is the keyword. All the words under each keyword (the related words) have similar meaning. Read each group and try to remember which related words go with each keyword.

1. **to put into one's head**
   instill
   propagandize
   brainwash
   inculcate
   indoctrinate

2. **always the same**
   immutable
   invariable
   uniform
   homogeneous
   consistent

3. **to throw out from a group**
   expel
   cast out
   ostracize
   banish
   exile

4. **power**
   hegemony
   authority
   jurisdiction
   dominion
   sovereignty

5. **average**
   mean
   norm
   medium
   par
   middle point

6. **understood**
   tacit
   implied
   implicit
   unspoken
   inferred

7. **not allowed**
   banned
   taboo
   forbidden
   prohibited
   barred

8. **especially**
   particularly
   notably
   singularly
   eminently
   supremely

9. **promise**
   pledge
   oath
   vow
   commitment
   one's word

10. **faithfulness**
    allegiance
    loyalty
    fidelity
    fealty
    devotion

11. **to assign**
    ascribe
    credit
    impute
    accredit
    attribute

12. **to make a part of oneself**
    soak up
    assimilate
    digest
    internalize
    absorb

EXERCISE 3

A. The 12 groups of related words are written below without keywords. Write the correct keyword over each keyword group.

B. Each group of related words has *one* word that does not belong in the group. Find that word, cross it out, and write it under the group to which it belongs.

KEYWORDS

promise	average	always the same	make a part of oneself
power	understood	faithfulness	put into one's head
assign	especially	not allowed	throw out from a group

1. _____

inculcate
instill
propagandize
assimilate
indoctrinate

_____

2. _____

invariable
uniform
consistent
homogeneous
inferred

_____

3. _____

impute
banish
ostracize
expel
exile

_____

4. _____

hegemony
sovereignty
jurisdiction
fealty
authority

_____

5. _____

par
one's word
norm
mean
middle point

_____

6. _____

implied
tacit
singularly
implicit
unspoken

_____

7. _____

banned
taboo
medium
prohibited
forbidden

_____

8. _____

supremely
notably
eminently
immutable
particularly

_____

9. _____

oath
dominion
vow
commitment
pledge

_____

10. _____

allegiance
fidelity
loyalty
barred
devotion

_____

11. _____

attribute
accredit
cast out
ascribe
credit

_____

12. _____

absorb
digest
soak up
internalize
brainwash

_____

EXERCISE 4

Each sentence below contains one keyword, which is in heavy type.

A. Find the word below each sentence that is *not* a related word for the keyword. Circle that word. (The keyword numbers from Exercise 2 are in parentheses. These will help you if you need to look back.)

B. After completing instruction A, write each circled word under the keyword in the sentence to which it belongs.

1. Before one becomes a citizen, he or she has to make a **promise.**

   a. (an) oath   b. (an) allegiance   c. pledge   d. commitment (9)

2. The purpose of this vow is to give one's **faithfulness** to the new country of citizenship.

   a. loyalty   b. fidelity   c. sovereignty   d. fealty (10)

3. There is an **understood** rule in most societies that one never marries one's close relative.

   a. (a) consistent   b. unspoken   c. implicit (6)

4. Even though respect for the law is **put** deeply **into one's head,** many people may feel sorry for the lawbreaker, depending, of course, on which law is broken.

   a. indoctrinated   b. inculcated   c. credited (1)

5. Violation of a society's customs is certainly **not allowed.**

   a. taboo   b. tacit   c. forbidden (7)

6. The war was fought because nobody could agree on who had **power** in the area.

   a. hegemony   b. authority   c. jurisdiction   d. vow (4)

7. As a punishment for his work, the author was **thrown out (from a group).**

   a. expelled   b. banished   c. ostracized   d. soaked up (3)

8. The behavior of individuals within a group is not **always the same.**

   a. homogeneous   b. eminently   c. invariable   d. uniform (2)

9. The professor was an **especially** well-qualified researcher.

   a. (a) mean   b. (a) supremely   c. (a) particularly   d. (a) notably (8)

10. The student spent a year in Mexico **making** the language and culture **a part of himself.**

   a. assimilating   b. absorbing   c. internalizing   d. exiling (12)

11. Scholars usually **assign** to Auguste Comte the establishment of sociology as a science.

   a. attribute   b. instill   c. ascribe (11)

12. A score of 500 on the TOEFL was the **average** for all of the students who finished the program.

   a. prohibited   b. norm   c. middle point (5)

EXERCISE 5

In the following paragraph at least one word in each sentence is in heavy type. Find the keyword from the list below that is closest in meaning to each of these words, and write it in the proper blank underneath the paragraph. Check your answers by looking at Exercise 6.

KEYWORDS

tradition	job	accidental	be responsible for
connection	to end	watchful eye	place in society
purpose	to expect	organized	purposeful

A university is an example of a **regimented** society with each individual having his or her **standing** within the organization. This standing helps to establish the **bonds** that exist between various members of the community. Each place in society ("status" in sociological terms) has several **roles.** The roles attached to a particular status are not **coincidental.** For example, being a college professor, which is a status, involves several **duties,** each of which requires a different role. A professor **is charged with** teaching, research, advising, publishing, and so on. In comparison, students are at a university making a **deliberate** effort to achieve a certain status. They **foresee** having a better future as a result. Their role is very different: they work under the **tutelage** of a variety of professors. Years of hard work for them is **culminated** by graduation. The graduation **ceremony** itself symbolizes society since each person's status is marked by the clothing he or she wears.

regimented	_____	standing	_____
bonds	_____	roles	_____
coincidental	_____	duties	_____
is charged with	_____	deliberate	_____
foresee	_____	tutelage	_____
culminated	_____	ceremony	_____

EXERCISE 6

The first word in each group below is the keyword. All the words under each keyword (the related words) have similar meaning. Read each group and try to remember which related words go with each keyword.

13. **to be responsible for**	14. **purposeful**	15. **place in society**	16. **job**
be charged with	premeditated	status	assignment
be accountable	willful	rank	chore
be answerable	intentional	station	duty
be liable	conscious	footing	obligation
be obligated (to)	deliberate	standing	task

17. **organized**	18. **accidental**	19. **purpose**	20. **to expect**
regimented	unintentional	utility	anticipate
regulated	coincidental	function	look forward to
structured	unintended	role	have a hunch
ordered	chance (adj.)	objective	reckon on
systematic	inadvertent	use	foresee

21. **watchful eye**	22. **tradition**	23. **to end**	24. **connection**
supervision	ritual	climax	link
guidance	rite	culminate	tie
administration	ceremony	conclude	bond
tutelage	custom	come to a head	affinity
auspices	formality	cap	relation

EXERCISE 7

A. The 12 groups of related words are written below without keywords. Write the correct keyword over each keyword group.

B. Each group of related words has *one* word that does not belong in the group. Find that word, cross it out, and write it under the group to which it belongs.

KEYWORDS

tradition	job	accidental	be responsible for
connection	to end	watchful eye	place in society
purpose	to expect	organized	purposeful

13. _____	14. _____	15. _____	16. _____
be accountable	premeditated	station	task
have a hunch	deliberate	status	chore
be answerable	intentional	rank	relation
be charged with	regulated	standing	assignment
be obligated	conscious	objective	duty
_____	_____	_____	_____

17. _____	18. _____	19. _____	20. _____
systematic	inadvertent	role	foresee
regimented	unintended	formality	anticipate
ordered	willful	use	look forward to
structured	coincidental	function	come to a head
chance	unintentional	utility	reckon on
_____	_____	_____	_____

21. _____	22. _____	23. _____	24. _____
guidance	rite	culminate	tie
auspices	custom	be liable	link
supervision	obligation	climax	bond
tutelage	ritual	conclude	administration
footing	ceremony	cap	affinity
_____	_____	_____	_____

EXERCISE 8

Each sentence below contains one keyword, which is in heavy type.

A. Find the word below each sentence that is *not* a related word for the keyword. Circle that word. (The keyword numbers from Exercise 6 are in parentheses. These will help you if you need to look back.)

B. After completing instruction A, write each circled word under the keyword in the sentence to which it belongs.

1. The schedule of the school was so **organized** that it was often compared to the army.

   a. regulated   b. regimented   c. premeditated   d. structured (17)

2. If someone violates a custom, even though the action may be **accidental,** every member of that society rises up in opposition.

   a. inadvertent   b. unintentional   c. systematic (18)

3. Everyone **is responsible for** his or her social behavior.

   a. is climaxed by   b. is accountable for   c. is liable for (13)

4. In many societies, a child's future depends on the **place in society** of the family into which he or she is born.

   a. station   b. standing   c. status   d. affinity (15)

5. In the Western world, the seriousness of a crime is partially determined by whether or not the act was **purposeful.**

   a. willful   b. unintended   c. deliberate   d. conscious (14)

6. Nobody **expected** the large number of voters that turned out for the election.

   a. reckoned on   b. foresaw   c. was answerable for (20)

7. The **job** of cleaning up after the storm seemed endless.

   a. assignment   b. ritual   c. chore   d. duty (16)

8. Many people believe that there is a special **connection** between opposite personality types.

   a. rank   b. relation   c. link   d. bond (24)

9. Marriage **traditions** vary from country to country and culture to culture.

   a. ceremonies   b. customs   c. rites   d. supervision (22)

10. A week of hard work and long study was **ended** by a party for all of the participants.

    a. concluded   b. capped   c. anticipated   d. culminated (23)

11. A soldier is trained to obey orders whether or not he understands their **purpose.**

    a. objective   b. task   c. function   d. utility (19)

12. New doctors must spend several years under the **watchful eye** of experienced physicians.

   a. guidance   b. tutelage   c. use   (21)

EXERCISE 9

In the following paragraph one word in each sentence is in heavy type. Find the keyword from the list below that is closest in meaning to each of these words and write the keyword in the proper blank underneath the paragraph. Check your answers by looking at Exercise 10.

KEYWORDS

buyer	**language**	**likely to**	**to decide the value**
friend	**to measure**	**quick look**	**helpful to each other**
absolute	**subject**	**unchanging**	**following of (the rule, etc.)**

Many societies believe that a group of people is **liable to** make better decisions than an individual. Just a **glimpse** at this idea will help us see if it is always true. Let's imagine that you are a **purchaser** who is about to make a very big buying decision. It would be **out-and-out** foolishness to make such a decision quickly and thoughtlessly. You must **evaluate** the product you are considering buying and compare it with the price being asked for the product. You ask several **companions** for their advice. Products, as well as their prices, are not **fixed,** so your friends' experiences can be helpful. This example shows that, if a decision is complex and requires special knowledge or experience, two or more people (a group) can make efforts that are **collaborative.** Also, if the problem has only one correct solution, the group does better. In the **jargon** of sociology, these types of problems are called "determinate." At times, however, the **topic** under consideration is such that the problem has no one correct solution. The solution to this type of problem, which is known as "indeterminate," does not necessarily depend on special experience or **obedience** to a set of rules. In this type of problem-solving situation, sociologists have not been able to **gauge** the superiority of a group over an individual.

liable to	_____	glimpse	_____
purchaser	_____	out-and-out	_____
evaluate	_____	companions	_____
fixed	_____	collaborative	_____
jargon	_____	topic	_____
obedience	_____	gauge	_____

EXERCISE 10

The first word in each group below is the keyword. All the words under each keyword (the related words) have similar meaning. Read each group and try to remember which related words go with each keyword.

25. unchanging

stable
fixed
steadfast
steady
adamant

26. quick look

glimpse
peek
glance
scan
peep

27. following of (the rule, etc.)

adherence
obedience
compliance
observance
minding

28. friend

companion
ally
close
acquaintance
crony
confidant

29. to measure

gauge
calibrate
survey
quantify
scale

30. likely to

apt to
prone to
inclined to
liable to
given to

31. absolute

outright
utter
out-and-out
sheer
unmitigated

32. buyer

consumer
purchaser
client
customer
patron

33. to decide the value

evaluate
estimate
assess
appraise
assay

34. language

jargon
tongue
dialect
vernacular
parlance

35. subject

topic
theme
thesis
matter
issue

36. helpful to each other

complementary
collaborative
cooperative
symbiotic
reciprocal

EXERCISE 11

A. The 12 groups of related words are written below without keywords. Write the correct keyword over each keyword group.

B. Each group of related words has *one* word that does not belong in the group. Find that word, cross it out, and write it under the group to which it belongs.

KEYWORDS

buyer **friend** **absolute**	**language** **to measure** **subject**	**likely to** **quick look** **unchanging**	**to decide the** **value** **helpful to each** **other** **following of** **(the rule, etc.)**

25. _____ 26. _____ 27. _____ 28. _____

adamant	glimpse	compliance	ally
stable	peep	adherence	patron
symbiotic	glance	vernacular	crony
fixed	peek	observance	companion
steady	matter	obedience	close
			acquaintance

_____   _____   _____   _____

29. _____ 30. _____ 31. _____ 32. _____

calibrate	prone to	utter	scan
gauge	apt to	outright	consumer
quantify	liable to	sheer	client
assay	inclined to	given to	purchaser
scale	steadfast	out-and-out	customer

_____   _____   _____   _____

33. _____ 34. _____ 35. _____ 36. _____

assess	parlance	issue	reciprocal
estimate	jargon	minding	collaborative
survey	dialect	topic	complementary
appraise	confidant	thesis	cooperative
evaluate	tongue	theme	unmitigated

_____   _____   _____   _____

EXERCISE 12

Each sentence below contains one keyword, which is in heavy type.

A. Find the word below each sentence that is *not* a related word for the keyword. Circle that word. (The keyword numbers from Exercise 10 are in parentheses. These will help you if you need to look back.)

B. After completing instruction A, write each circled word under the keyword in the sentence to which it belongs.

1. People have always wished for a magical machine that would give them a **quick look** into the future.

   a. glimpse   b. crony   c. glance   (26)

2. Strict **following of** the rules was expected of every student who attended there.

   a. adherence to   b. observance of   c. obedience to   d. apt to   (27)

3. The **subject** of the paper was that social customs were stronger forces than laws.

   a. thesis   b. tongue   c. topic   (35)

4. Everyone agrees, of course, that it is very difficult to **decide the value of** various types of service.

   a. calibrate   b. assess   c. evaluate   d. appraise   (33)

5. In a complex society, everyone is **likely to** break a law occasionally.

   a. liable to   b. inclined to   c. compliance with   d. prone to   (30)

6. The two countries signed a trade agreement that was **helpful to each other.**

   a. complementary   b. steady   c. collaborative   d. cooperative   (36)

7. The theory that one race of people is superior to another is **absolute** stupidity.

   a. unmitigated   b. out-and-out   c. utter   d. reciprocal   (31)

8. The store has had several very famous **buyers** over the past 20 years.

   a. clients   b. patrons   c. themes   (32)

9. The general and several of his **friends** took control of the government.

   a. customers   b. allies   c. companions   d. close acquaintances   (28)

10. An **unchanging** increase in population is a factor which sociologists cannot ignore.

    a. (A) fixed   b. (A) steadfast   c. (A) sheer   d. (A) stable   (25)

11. One cannot hope to understand another culture until one learns the **language** of its people.

    a. vernacular   b. estimate   c. dialect   (34)

12. An experienced architect is able to **measure** distances accurately without using any tools.

    a. gauge   b. scale   c. peek   (29)

EXERCISE 13

In each blank write the keyword that corresponds to the word in heavy type in the sentence. The number in parentheses can be used to check your answer.

1. In preindustrial societies, there was always one **unspoken** rule: have as many children as possible. _____ (6)

2. This was done with a specific **objective** in mind. _____ (19)

3. Making a living was so difficult that it required a **cooperative** effort from every member of the family. _____ (36)

4. The more children one had, the more people there were to do the **chores** that life demanded. _____ (16)

5. The **inadvertent** death of so many infants also gave support to this rule. _____ (18)

6. The **custom,** then, was to have very large families. _____ (22)

7. In many societies, birth control was **taboo.** _____ (7)

8. In 1798, Thomas Malthus wrote a book that dealt with the **issue** of population growth. _____ (35)

9. In this book, he made a **conscious** effort to destroy the tradition of large families by scientific analysis. _____ (14)

10. He maintained that a strict **observance of** the rule to have as many children as possible would result in overpopulation. _____ (27)

11. According to him, while the population could increase rapidly, the amount of food-producing land was **stable.** _____ (25)

12. In anybody's **parlance,** this theory translates into disaster. _____ (34)

13. Humans were periodically **inclined to** reproduce so quickly that the food supply could not keep up. _____ (30)

14. Periods in our history where this occurred always **concluded** in war, disease, or starvation. _____ (23)

15. So, all mankind could **look forward to** as history progressed was hunger and premature death. _____ (20)

16. Many people of his time said that Malthus's ideas were **utter** nonsense. _____ (31)

17. They questioned his **devotion** to God and his fellow man. _____ (10)

18. Malthus was **ostracized** from many social groups as a result of his beliefs. _____ (3)

19. Let's take a **glance** at the situation since Malthus. _____ (26)

20. This will allow us to **assess** how accurate Malthus was. _____ (33)

21. For a while, it seemed that Malthus was wrong because he had failed to **attribute** to humans the ability to make great improvements in agriculture. _____ (11)

22. Rather than remaining **invariable,** food supplies increased. _____ (2)

23. In addition, a decline in the birth rate became the **norm** in industrialized European and American societies. _____ (5)

24. Why did this happen? Certainly not because some individual or group had **dominion** over the birth rate! _____ (4)

25. It happened partly because of the following: as a country becomes more affluent, its citizens desire higher **status.** _____ (15)

26. People become more interested in being promoted at work, in being **consumers** in the marketplace, and in living in more comfort, not in raising a family. _____ (32)

27. Thus it was not political or religious **guidance,** but rather social pressure that caused a decline in the birthrate. _____ (21)

28. Whatever the cause, everyone was **indoctrinated** with the idea that Malthus was in error. _____ (1)

29. However, in the past hundred years, there has been an unexpected population explosion, **notably,** of course, in poorer nations. _____ (8)

30. There is a definite **link** between birthrate and education. _____ (24)

31. In poorer countries, education is not very well **structured.** _____ (17)

32. The more affluent countries make **commitments** to assist poorer countries in educational efforts. _____ (9)

33. But, even though **allies** try to help each other, the results are usually minimal. _____ (28)

34. So the population continues to increase, and nobody **is accountable** for it. _____ (13)

35. Although it is very difficult to **quantify** all of the factors involved, the evidence today indicates that Malthus may have been right. _____ (29)

36. While it is difficult to **internalize** his message, the global food situation today certainly supports it. _____ (12)

EXERCISE 14

Below each puzzle is a list of related words. Write the keyword for each related word in the appropriate squares. After you have written in all of the keywords for one puzzle, read the word in the circles going down. This will be a related word for the first keyword in the *next* puzzle. The numbers in parentheses can be used to check your answers, but try to complete the puzzles without using them.

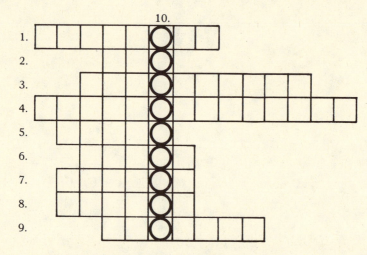

1. dialect (34)	6. client (32)
2. cap (23)	7. close acquaintance (28)
3. adamant (25)	8. reckon on (20)
4. appraise (33)	9. middle point (5)
5. jurisdiction (4)	

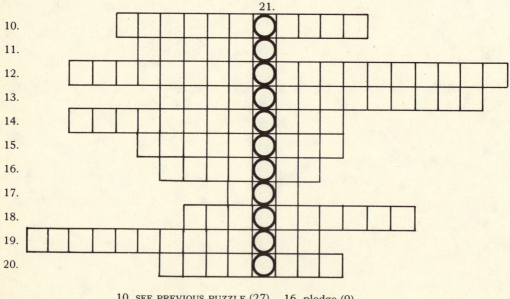

10. SEE PREVIOUS PUZZLE (27)	16. pledge (9)
11. accredit (11)	17. assignment (16)
12. digest (12)	18. tie (24)
13. station (15)	19. homogeneous (2)
14. fidelity (10)	20. outright (31)
15. ceremony (22)	

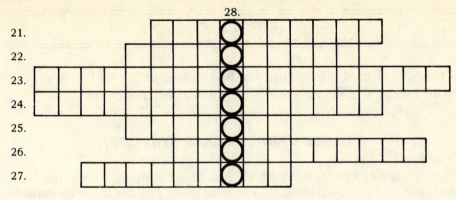

21. SEE PREVIOUS PUZZLE (14)   25. thesis (35)
22. implied (6)   26. auspices (21)
23. complementary (36)   27. peep (26)
24. propagandize (1)

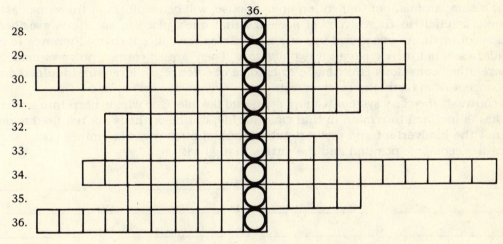

28. SEE PREVIOUS PUZZLE (30)   33. coincidental (18)
29. calibrate (29)   34. banish (3)
30. be charged with (13)   35. banned (7)
31. ordered (17)   36. SEE THIS PUZZLE (8)
32. function (19)

EXERCISE 15

Some of the words in the following reading passages are in heavy type. Read the passages and write the keywords for each in the blanks below.

CASTE VERSUS CLASS SYSTEMS

All societies have categories into which people are grouped. Societies would not be **ordered** without this categorization. In sociolinguistic **jargon,** these **structured** systems that create inequality between groups of people are called stratification systems. Let's take a **glance** at this very interesting **topic.**

In general, there are two types of stratification systems: a caste system and a class system. In a caste system, one's **station** in society is **fixed** by birth. There is nothing to **look forward to** in these types of societies—changing one's social **status** is **forbidden.** All of one's **companions,** not to mention one's spouse, will be members of the same caste. It is, then, **implicit** in these types of societies that one's place in society is **ascribed** by accident of birth. As one grows up, one **assimilates** the concept that **adherence** to class boundaries is not mere custom: it is obligatory. There are, of course, no **vows** made, nor is there other **conscious** effort made to enforce **obedience;** children are **inculcated** with this concept from birth and rarely question it.

In contrast, the class system is more open and flexible. One who is born into a particular class is **inclined to** remain in that class for life, but he or she is not required to do so. It is not the **inadvertent** and unchangeable result of birth that determines social status, but rather economic position and the **duties** that go with it.

1. _____   7. _____   13. _____   19. _____

2. _____   8. _____   14. _____   20. _____

3. _____   9. _____   15. _____   21. _____

4. _____   10. _____   16. _____   22. _____

5. _____   11. _____   17. _____

6. _____   12. _____   18. _____

GROUPS

Muzafer Sharif[1] performed some very interesting experiments with a group of 11-year-old boys to demonstrate group **loyalty.** The boys were fairly **homogeneous** in background and were total strangers to each other at the beginning of the experiment. The boys went to a summer camp under Sharif's **supervision** to take part in the project.

As is the **norm,** the boys quickly formed friendship groups spontaneously. Sharif then randomly divided the boys into two large groups and had them live relatively far from each other. The **objective** was to break the **bonds** the boys had established. The boys soon established new **ties** within the new groups. Sharif then had the groups compete against each other in sports and games. The boys were **cooperative** within their groups and hostile to the other group, which included, of course, some of their former friends. To **culminate** the experiment, Sharif created an emergency situation: the cutting off of the

[1]Muzafer Sharif, "Experiments in Group Conflict," *Scientific American,* Vol. 195 (1956): 54–58.

water supply. The groups were **obligated** to work together, and the situation was **particularly** successful in making the boys forget their recently acquired hatred for each other. Boys who were **banished** from a group were suddenly welcomed by it.

Sharif's experiment gave him the opportunity to **assess** the **dominion** of situation over other elements which may also contribute to the formation of group boundaries. While it is impossible to **quantify** its influence, it would be **utter** stupidity to state that situation has little to do with group dynamics.

1. _____   5. _____   9. _____   13. _____
2. _____   6. _____   10. _____   14. _____
3. _____   7. _____   11. _____   15. _____
4. _____   8. _____   12. _____   16. _____

EXERCISE 16

Read the following article. Do *not* use a dictionary. At least one related word from each of the keyword groups is in this article. Try to remember the proper keywords as you read.

Prereading Introduction

As humans develop from children to adults, one of the very important processes that occur is training to make them fit into society. While some of this training is done at the conscious level, most of it occurs at a level below consciousness. There are many factors in the environment that contribute to the training process. The following article examines four of the most important ones: the family, the school, the peer group, and the mass media (television, newspapers, magazines, etc.). The roles of each facet, both intentional and unintentional, are examined. The article concludes with a brief examination of other agencies that also make contributions to the overall process of socialization.

After reading this article, you should answer the following questions:

1. Why are agencies of socialization so important during one's early years?
2. What are some of the ways in which a family socializes children?
3. Compare or contrast the family socialization process in the United States with that in your country.
4. How does the phrase *by accident of birth* relate to the socialization process according to this passage?
5. The author mentions another very important social function of schools besides educating children. What is it?
6. What are some of the values that children learn in school?
7. What types of socialization do peers provide that neither family nor school give a child?
8. Does the author's description of the role of peers in this society sound similar to the role of peers in your background?

9. What sorts of socializing information can one get from the mass media?
10. Is it necessary for the government to control the types of advertising that are permitted in mass media? Why or why not?
11. The author lists several other agencies of socialization in the United States. What other agencies of socialization can you name from your own experience? Are they positive or negative sources?

AGENCIES OF SOCIALIZATION*

The socialization process involves many different influences that affect the individual throughout life. The most important of these influences are *agencies of socialization,* institutions or other structured situations in which socialization takes place, particularly in the early years of life. Four agencies of socialization are especially important in modern societies, for they affect almost everyone in a powerful and lasting way. These agencies are the family, the school, the peer group, and the mass media.

The Family

The family is without doubt the most important single agency of socialization in all societies. One reason for the importance of the family is that it has the main responsibility for socializing children in the crucial early years of life. The family is where children establish their first close emotional ties, learn language, and begin to internalize cultural norms and values. To young children the family is all-encompassing. They have little social experience beyond its boundaries and therefore lack any basis for comparing and evaluating what is learned from family members. A great deal of the socialization that takes place in the family is conscious and deliberate, but much of it is quite unintentional. The patterns of social interaction within the family, for example, may provide unintended models for the later behavior and personality traits of the children.

A second reason for the importance of the family is that the family is located somewhere in the social structure. From the moment of birth, therefore, the children have an ascribed status in a subculture of race, class, ethnicity,[a] religion, or region—all of which may strongly influence the nature of later social interaction and socialization. For example, the values and expectations that are learned by children depend very much on the social class of the parents. To appreciate the significance of family background for socialization and personality, we need only consider the likely differences between the experiences of, say, a child born into a poor family of fundamentalist Baptists[b] living in rural Alabama and a child born into a wealthy professional family living in the exclusive suburbs of Los Angeles.

The School

The school is an agency formally charged by society with the task of socializing the young in particular skills and values. We usually think of the school as being mainly concerned with teaching skills and knowledge, and this is certainly one of its major functions. But the schools in every society also engage in outright indoctrination in values. We may find this fact more readily apparent in societies other than our own—until we consider the content of civics classes[c] or the daily ritual of the pledge of allegiance. The school socializes not only through its formal academic curriculum but also through the "hidden curriculum" implicit in the content of school activities, ranging from regimented classroom schedules to organized sports. Children learn that they must be neat and punctual.[d] They learn to sit still, keep quiet, wait their turn, and not be distracted from their work. They learn to respect and obey without question the commands of those who have social authority over them.

In the school, children come for the first

---

*Ian Robertson, *Sociology* (New York: Worth Publishers, 1977), pp. 108–10.

time under the direct supervision of people who are not relatives. The children learn to obey other people not because they offer love and protection but because a social system requires uniform adherence to rules. The individual child is no longer considered somebody special; he or she is now one of a crowd, subject to[e] the same regulations and expectations that everyone else is subject to. Personal behavior and academic achievements or failures become part of a permanent official record, and the children learn to evaluate themselves by the same standards that others apply to them. Participation in the life of the school also lessens the children's dependence on the family and creates new links to the wider society beyond.

The Peer Group

As children grow older they spend more and more time in the company of their peers, children of roughly the same age and usually of similar background and interests. As the influence of the peer group increases, that of the parents diminishes. In the United States young people of school-going age spend on average twice as much time with peers as with parents, and most of them prefer to spend their time this way.

Membership in a peer group places children for the first time in a context where most socialization is carried out unintentionally and without any deliberate design. Individuals are able at last to choose their own companions and friends and to interact with other people on a basis of equality. Unlike the family or school, the peer group is entirely centered on its own concerns and interests. Its members can explore relationships and topics that are tabooed in the family and the school, and they can thus learn to break away from the influence of these two agencies and establish separate (and often disapproved) roles and identities. In modern industrial societies, the generations are often highly compartmentalized[f] with the youthful peer group claiming the primary loyalty of its members and often demanding that they reject the values and authority of parents and teachers. The influence of the peer group climaxes in adolescence,[g] when young people are apt to form a distinctive subculture with its own tastes, dress, jargon, symbols, values, and heroes. By rewarding members for conformity to peer-group norms and by criticizing or ostracizing them for nonconformity, the group exerts a very strong influence on their social behavior and personality.

The Mass Media

The mass media are the various forms of communication that reach a large audience without any personal contact between the senders and the receivers of the messages: newspapers, magazines, books, television, radio, movies, and records. The mass media are unquestionably a powerful socializing influence, although their precise impact is difficult to gauge. The most influential medium[h] is probably television. There is a TV set in 95 percent of American homes, and the average American between the ages of three and sixteen spends more time in front of the TV set than in school.

The media provide instant coverage of social events and social changes, ranging from news and opinions to fads[i] and fashions. They offer role models and glimpses of life-styles that people might otherwise never have access to. Through the media, children can learn about courtroom lawyers, cowboys, police detectives, or even such improbable characters as Batman.[j] These images are not necessarily very realistic, but this failing need not lessen their influence. Through media advertising, too, the young learn about their future roles as consumers in the marketplace, and about the high value our society places on youth, success, beauty, and materialism. Changing social norms and values are quickly reflected in the media and may be just as quickly adopted by people who might not otherwise be exposed to them. The rapid spread of youth culture in the sixties, for example, depended very heavily on such media as records, FM radio, and underground newspapers and comics.

Other Agencies

The individual may be influenced by many other agencies of socialization—religious groups, Boy Scouts and Girl Scouts, youth organizations, and, later in life, by such agencies as the military, corporations or other employment settings, and by voluntary associations such as clubs, political movements, and retirement homes. It is obvious that the influences of the various agencies are not always complementary and can often be in outright conflict. The church, for example, may hold quite different values from the military, the peer group quite different values from the school. It is also obvious that people do not always learn what they are supposed to learn. The socialization process may fail in certain respects, and people may come to behave in ways that were never anticipated or intended. Personality and behavior are never entirely stable; they change under the influence of socialization experiences throughout the life cycle.

Notes

^{a}ethnicity: the qualities that distinguish a particular culture.

^{b}Fundamentalist Baptists: members of a particular church which is noted for its conservative ideas and attitudes.

^{c}civics classes: school courses that deal with public affairs and one's duties and rights as citizens.

^{d}punctual: always on time.

^{e}subject to: under the control of; required to follow.

^{f}compartmentalized: divided into separate groups or parts.

^{g}adolescence: that period of time between childhood and adulthood.

^{h}medium: singular of "media."

^{i}fads: customs, styles, etc., that are popular for a short time.

^{j}Batman: an imaginary children's hero from comic books who fights criminals.

EXERCISE 17

The following exercises show how different word forms are derived in English. Try to remember the endings and what parts of speech they indicate.

A. Words that end in *-ate* are usually verbs:

Examples: cooperative → cooperate
assimilation → assimilate

Put the letter of the correct keyword in the blank after each derived word. Some keywords are used more than one time:

a. law   b. wavy   c. unreality   d. main   e. push
f. originating   g. physical harm

1. stimulus → stimulate _____

2. laceration → lacerate _____

3. The motion of the ocean caused the vegetation to **undulate** constantly. _____

4. The police were called to investigate because of the strange noises **emanating** from the house. _____

5. The city decided to install traffic signals at the intersection in an effort to **regulate** the flow of traffic. _____

6. The drug that the person took caused him to **hallucinate.** _____

7. Many people were opposed to the new law, but the will of the majority **predominated.** _____

8. The physicists were studying how sound waves **oscillate.** _____

B. *Non-* added to the beginning of a word usually changes the meaning to not + word:

Examples: deliberate → nondeliberate
compliance → noncompliance

a. exact   b. neighboring   c. angry   d. total   e. strong
f. wealth   g. economic   h. bother

1. cumulative → noncumulative _____

2. specific → nonspecific _____

3. This is obviously the **nonaffluent** section of the city. _____

4. The basketball team was placed in several **nonadjacent** rooms in the hotel. _____

5. The storm was **nonviolent,** much to the relief of the inhabitants. _____

6. The man was careful to act in a very **nonantagonistic** manner because his success depended upon the support of his colleagues. _____

7. The politician tried to disagree in a **nonirritating** manner because she needed every vote. _____

8. Although money was not plentiful, it was the **nonbudgetary** aspects of the plan that caused its ultimate failure. _____

C. Another way to change an adjective into its opposite is by adding *un-* to its beginning:

Examples: intentional → unintentional
regulated → unregulated

a. skillful   b. usual   c. smart   d. serious   e. clean   f. kind
g. possible

1. thoughtful → unthoughtful _____

2. adroit → unadroit _____

3. The government closed the restaurant because of the **unsanitary** conditions. _____

4. It was **unimaginable** that my friend could act in such an insensitive manner. ____

5. It was very **unlikely** that anybody would ever be able to solve the problem. ____

6. After thinking about it for a few minutes, I realized how **unintelligent** my answer had been. ____

7. I could not understand why the committee was taking so much time with such an **unimportant** decision. ____

8. She always looked attractive although she dressed in a very **unordinary** manner. ____

In summary:

1. We saw two ways to change words as follows: word → not + word. What are they? _____

2. A word ending in -*ate* is probably a _____.

CHAPTER 9 Economics

In the following paragraph one word in each sentence is in heavy type. Find the keyword from the list below that is closest in meaning to each of these words, and write it in the proper blank underneath the paragraph. Check your answers by looking at Exercise 2.

KEYWORDS

pay	**backward**	**according to**	**unable to operate normally**
usable	**fairness**	**do without**	**what one owes**
collect	**succeed**	**rising quickly**	**money received**

Hyperinflation is defined as an economic condition during which there is a **steep** increase in prices. **In accordance with** the laws of economics, three factors combine to create this condition. First, demand must be much greater than the supply of **available** goods. Second, the country must continuously create and thereby **build up** an ever-increasing supply of money. Third, the governmental processes that are used to collect taxes must be **crippled.** Let's imagine a country where production is barely **accomplishing** its goal: to keep up with demand. When this happens, the government should decrease the **salaries** of the workers by raising taxes. But the government is powerless to collect the taxes, so it prints more money to **compensate** for the goods it must purchase. This new money goes to the workers who produced the goods; as a result, the people are not forced to **give up** certain things for a while—they actually become richer. While this might appear to be a positive step, it is actually **regressive.** Every month the government is forced to print more and more money, thereby increasing its **liabilities** until it is destroyed. The only way to prevent total economic collapse in such a situation is for the government to increase taxes in a manner that is characterized by **impartiality** to everyone involved.

steep	_____	In accordance with	_____
available	_____	build up	_____
crippled	_____	accomplishing	_____
salaries	_____	compensate	_____

give up	_____	regressive	_____
liabilities	_____	impartiality	_____

EXERCISE 2

The first word in each group below is the keyword. All the words under each keyword (the related words) have similar meaning. Read each group and try to remember which related words go with each keyword.

1. **usable**
   available
   disposable
   accessible
   at one's
     disposal
   on/at hand

2. **to collect**
   accumulate
   accrue
   assemble
   compile
   build up

3. **according to**
   in keeping with
   in proportion to
   in accordance with
   in consonance with
   in line with

4. **money received**
   income
   wage
   salary
   dividend
   pension

5. **to pay**
   defray
   compensate
   remunerate
   reimburse
   reward

6. **to succeed**
   manage to
   accomplish
   achieve
   prevail
   triumph

7. **backward**
   regressive
   reverse
   retro-
   atavistic
   astern

8. **to do without**
   forgo
   sacrifice
   give up
   relinquish
   part with

9. **what one owes**
   debit
   indebtedness
   deficit
   liability
   debt

10. **fairness**
    justice
    impartiality
    evenhandedness
    equity
    objectivity

11. **rising quickly**
    steep
    precipitous
    sheer
    sharp
    uphill

12. **unable to operate normally**
    disabled
    crippled
    handicapped
    incapacitated
    immobilized

EXERCISE 3

A. The 12 groups of related words are written below without keywords. Write the correct keyword over each keyword group.

B. Each group of related words has *one* word that does not belong in the group. Find that word, cross it out, and write it under the group to which it belongs.

KEYWORDS

pay	backward	according to	unable to operate normally
usable	fairness	do without	what one owes
collect	succeed	rising quickly	money received

1. _____

at one's disposal
available
incapacitated
accessible
on/at hand

_____

2. _____

accrue
compile
accumulated
build up
forgo

_____

3. _____

in accordance with
disposable
in keeping with
in proportion to
in consonance with

_____

4. _____

wage
salary
income
dividend
debit

_____

5. _____

remunerate
compensate
reimburse
defray
assemble

_____

6. _____

achieve
manage to
reward
triumph
accomplish

_____

7. _____

astern
sharp
regressive
atavistic
reverse

_____

8. _____

relinquish
prevail
give up
part with
sacrifice

_____

9. _____

debt
liability
deficit
equity
indebtedness

_____

10. _____

pension
impartiality
objectivity
justice
evenhandedness

_____

11. _____

precipitous
steep
retro-
sheer
uphill

_____

12. _____

handicapped
crippled
immobilized
disabled
in line with

_____

EXERCISE 4

Each sentence below contains one keyword, which is in heavy type.

A. Find the word below each sentence that is *not* a related word for the keyword. Circle that word. (The keyword numbers from Exercise 2 are in parentheses. These will help you if you need to look back.)

B. After completing instruction A, write each circled word under the keyword in the sentence to which it belongs.

1. In a free enterprise system, a hardworking person usually **succeeds** over a lazy person.

   a. prevails   b. relinquishes   c. achieves (6)

2. All businesses try to keep a good supply of material that is **usable** whenever needed.

   a. at their disposal   b. available   c. accessible   d. atavistic (1)

3. Transportation was **unable to operate normally** because of the severe winter weather.

   a. crippled   b. disabled   c. in keeping with (12)

4. Federal laws require **fairness** by all employers when making decisions concerning employees.

   a. wages   b. evenhandedness   c. impartiality (10)

5. It was very difficult to put a railroad through the area because of the number of **quickly rising** mountains that were there.

   a. steep   b. precipitous   c. immobilized (11)

6. The book company added two dollars to each order to **pay** the costs of shipping and handling.

   a. compensate for   b. compile (5)

7. **Money received** both influences and is influenced by inflation.

   a. Salaries   b. Income   c. Dividends   d. Deficits (4)

8. The company **collected** a tremendous amount of marketing information before deciding to produce the new merchandise.

   a. assembled   b. accumulated   c. defrayed (2)

9. In our technically advanced society, war remains as a favorite, although **backward** activity between nations.

   a. regressive   b. sheer (7)

10. The company was able to get through a very difficult period because the employees **did without** part of their salaries for six months.

    a. triumphed   b. relinquished   c. forwent   d. sacrificed (8)

11. **What the company owed** was so large that it had almost no chance of recovering.

    The company's:

    a. debt   b. liability   c. indebtedness   d. objectivity (9)

12. The cost of a house varies **according to** the interest rate.

    a. in accordance with   b. deficit   c. in proportion to (3)

EXERCISE 5

In the following paragraph one word in each sentence is in heavy type. Find the keyword from the list below that is closest in meaning to each of these words, and write it in the proper blank underneath the paragraph. Check your answers by looking at Exercise 6.

KEYWORDS

be like	be more than	using up	money paid to government
be with	loss	demand	economic assistance
used up	money after costs	located	change directions (of)

One of the functions of a government is to **divert** money from the richer segment of the population. It does this by collecting various types of **tariffs.** One of the decisions that always **accompanies** this process is deciding how much money to collect. The amount collected must never **surpass** what the people can afford to pay. So the rate of collecting money—that is, taxation—must **mirror** the citizens' ability to pay. At the same time, however, the government must collect enough money so that its economic resources are never totally **exhausted.** Another problem involves the **expending** of money by the government. The government must decide what kind of financial **encumbrances** it should make on its money for various segments of the population. For example, what kind of **subsidy** should the government make available for education? A third problem concerns how to avoid a **deterioration** in the value of the money the government has collected. The government must invest in those activities which provide the highest **profit.** The various offices that deal with the problems mentioned above are **housed** in the Treasury Department.

divert	_____	tariffs	_____
accompanies	_____	surpass	_____
mirror	_____	exhausted	_____
expending	_____	encumbrances	_____
subsidy	_____	deterioration	_____
profit	_____	housed	_____

EXERCISE 6

The first word in each group below is the keyword. All the words under each keyword (the related words) have similar meaning. Read each group and try to remember which related words go with each keyword.

13. **to change directions (of)**	14. **using up**	15. **money paid to government**	16. **economic assistance**
sidetrack	consumption	tax	subsidy
divert	utilization	excise	grant
veer	depletion	duty	stipend
deflect	expending	tariff	scholarship
swerve	drain	toll	donation

17. **to be like**	18. **used up**	19. **money after costs**	20. **to be more than**
correspond	worn out	profit	exceed
match	depleted	return	surpass
resemble	exhausted	proceeds	transcend
parallel	consumed	take	better
mirror	drained	markup	outdo

21. **located**	22. **loss**	23. **demand**	24. **to be with**
situated	depreciation	claim	accompany
housed	decline	declaration	escort
stationed	deterioration	requisition	usher
deposited	minus	encumbrance	chaperon
lodged	degeneration	lien	go hand in hand

EXERCISE 7

A. The 12 groups of related words are written below without keywords. Write the correct keyword over each keyword group.

B. Each group of related words has *one* word that does not belong in the group. Find that word, cross it out, and write it under the group to which it belongs.

KEYWORDS

be like	be more than	using up	money paid to government
be with	loss	demand	economic assistance
used up	money after costs	located	change directions (of)

13. _____	14. _____	15. _____	16. _____
swerve	utilization	excise	grant
veer	expending	drain	subsidy
deflect	markup	toll	donation
divert	consumption	tax	degeneration
parallel	depletion	tariff	stipend

17. _____   18. _____   19. _____   20. _____

surpass	exhausted	proceeds	transcend
correspond	drained	scholarship	outdo
mirror	deposited	profit	exceed
match	worn out	take	accompany
resemble	consumed	return	better

_____   _____   _____   _____

21. _____   22. _____   23. _____   24. _____

lodged	minus	lien	escort
situated	decline	claim	sidetrack
depleted	depreciation	encumbrance	chaperon
housed	deterioration	declaration	go hand in hand
stationed	requisition	duty	usher

_____   _____   _____   _____

EXERCISE 8

Each sentence below contains one keyword, which is in heavy type.

A. Find the word below each sentence that is *not* a related word for the keyword. Circle that word. (The keyword numbers from Exercise 6 are in parentheses. These will help you if you need to look back.)

B. After completing instruction A, write each circled word under the keyword in the sentence to which it belongs.

1. The state collected **money paid to the government** from the drivers to pay for the highway.

   a. tax   b. lien   c. tariff (15)

2. The **money after costs** from the sale went to support cancer research.

   a. returns   b. take   c. profit   d. depletion (19)

3. The company received federal **economic assistance** to do research on their new engine.

   a. stipends   b. depreciations   c. subsidies (16)

4. The truck **changed directions** suddenly and struck a car.

   a. swerved   b. escorted (13)

5. When determining costs, businesses must be sure to include **loss** of property in their calculations.

   a. deterioration   b. proceeds (22)

6. The president ordered the return of all soldiers who were **located** in the area.

   a. worn out   b. lodged   c. situated   d. housed   (21)

7. Sales this year **were more than** last year's by 10 percent.

   a. bettered   b. surpassed   c. exceeded   d. resembled   (20)

8. The **using up** of available oil supplies is a serious problem.

   a. consumption   b. drain   c. grant   d. utilization   (14)

9. Before purchasing property, one must be sure that there are no **demands** against it.

   a. tolls   b. claims   c. encumbrances   (23)

10. I had been working for so long that I was completely **used up.**

    a. exhausted   b. drained   c. outdone   (18)

11. The secretary **was with** the young lady as she entered the office.

    a. accompanied   b. stationed   (24)

12. The economy of this country **is like** the economy of France 200 years ago.

    a. parallels   b. corresponds to   c. mirrors   d. veers   (17)

EXERCISE 9

In the following paragraph one word in each sentence is in heavy type. Find the keyword from the list below that is closest in meaning to each of these words, and write the keyword in the proper blank underneath the paragraph. Check your answers by looking at Exercise 10.

KEYWORDS

price	long-lasting	unmistakable	provide money for
business	not active	subtract (from)	business agreement
payment	worker	fighting	give a job to

The problem of unemployment is connected to various types of jobs in a very **straightforward** way. Less skilled **laborers** are unemployed the most. These workers, the so-called blue-collar workers, are often **employed** seasonally or during those periods when demand is high. When the season changes or demand drops, these workers often experience a period of time during which they are **idle.** In contrast, some highly trained workers are protected from unemployment because their **firms** cannot operate at all if they do not work. Some businesses continue to employ certain highly skilled workers even when the market does not **fund** their employment. This is because they fear they will be unable to find workers with such skills when **competitive** companies are also looking for them.

Thus these workers are employed regardless of the **outlay** to the business. These companies feel that they will receive their **compensation** when demand is high and the workers are immediately available. In other words, even after the companies **deduct** from their income what it costs them to keep these people employed, they will still make money. Other skilled workers are protected from unemployment by special **deals** between labor unions and management. Therefore, highly skilled workers usually have more **durable** jobs than less skilled workers.

straightforward	_____	laborers	_____
employed	_____	idle	_____
firms	_____	fund	_____
competitive	_____	outlay	_____
compensation	_____	deduct	_____
deals	_____	durable	_____

EXERCISE 10

The first word in each group below is the keyword. All the words under each keyword (the related words) have similar meaning. Read each group and try to remember which related words go with each keyword.

25. fighting
competitive
rival
opposing
competing
contending

26. unmistakable
explicit
definite
straightforward
plain
sure

27. price
value
worth
outlay
expenditure
charge

28. worker
laborer
employee
hired hand
breadwinner
wage earner

29. to subtract (from)
deduct
decrease
debit
take (away) from
remove

30. long-lasting
durable
enduring
sturdy
imperishable
perennial

31. to provide money for
finance
subsidize
underwrite
fund
endow

32. to give a job to
employ
hire
enlist
appoint
commission

33. payment
reimbursement
contribution
restitution
remittance
compensation

34. business
corporation
company
establishment
enterprise
firm

35. not active
idle
inert
unemployed
loafing
passive

36. business agreement
transaction
deal
contract
settlement
arrangement

EXERCISE 11

A. The 12 groups of related words are written below without keywords. Write the correct keyword over each keyword group.

B. Each group of related words has *one* word that does not belong in the group. Find that word, cross it out, and write it under the group to which it belongs.

KEYWORDS

price	long-lasting	unmistakable	provide money
business	not active	subtract (from)	for
payment	worker	fighting	business
			agreement
			give a job to

25. _____

contending
loafing
competitive
opposing
competing

_____

26. _____

straightforward
plain
explicit
rival
definite

_____

27. _____

worth
charge
settlement
value
outlay

_____

28. _____

hired hand
laborer
breadwinner
employee
expenditure

_____

29. _____

decrease
subsidize
take (away) from
deduct
remove

_____

30. _____

sturdy
enduring
perennial
sure
durable

_____

31. _____

fund
finance
underwrite
endow
hire

_____

32. _____

debit
enlist
appoint
employ
commission

_____

33. _____

restitution
compensation
remittance
contribution
enterprise

_____

34. _____

firm
establishment
reimbursement
corporation
company

_____

35. _____

inert
imperishable
idle
passive
unemployed

_____

36. _____

contract
transaction
arrangement
deal
wage earner

_____

EXERCISE 12

Each sentence below contains one keyword, which is in heavy type.

A. Find the word below each sentence that is *not* a related word for the keyword. Circle that word. (The keyword numbers from Exercise 10 are in parentheses. These will help you if you need to look back.)

B. After completing instruction A, write each circled word under the keyword in the sentence to which it belongs.

1. Businesses often **provide money for** programs on public television.

   a. subsidize   b. fund   c. take from   d. finance (31)

2. The business **gave a job to** an artist to create a new symbol.

   a. underwrote   b. hired   c. appointed   d. employed (32)

3. The company wanted the instructions to be written in **unmistakable** language.

   a. explicit   b. straightforward   c. contending (26)

4. When video tape recorders first came out, there were very few **fighting** companies in the market.

   a. rival   b. competitive   c. competing   d. perennial (25)

5. The **price** for services is often higher than the price for material.

   a. expenditure   b. contract   c. outlay (27)

6. The government must control large **businesses** to insure that they do not gain control over a marketing area.

   a. companies   b. enterprises   c. firms   d. remittances (34)

7. Most businesses require **payment** before they will ship their goods.

   a. compensation   b. breadwinners   c. reimbursement (33)

8. Because of sound management policies, the company enjoyed **long-lasting** success.

   a. enduring   b. unemployed (30)

9. It is much more common for both the husband and wife to be **workers** today than it was 20 years ago.

   a. employees   b. wage earners   c. corporations (28)

10. **Not active** citizens are a problem in every society.

    a. Plain   b. Loafing   c. Idle (35)

11. Federal income tax is **subtracted** from everybody's salary.

    a. deducted   b. commissioned   c. removed (29)

12. According to the **business agreement,** construction was to be completed in two years.

    a. arrangement   b. deal   c. settlement   d. charge (36)

EXERCISE 13

In each blank write the keyword that corresponds to the word(s) in heavy type in the sentence. The number in parentheses can be used to check your answer.

1. Markets have a **definite** influence in controlling the economic systems of any area. _____ (26)

2. A group of **companies** supply products to the marketplace.
   _____ (34)

3. Information about what is needed is provided to the producers by the rate of **consumption.** _____ (14)

4. The **value** of a particular product is increased if demand for that product increases. _____ (27)

5. So, producers increase their output **in proportion to** the market demand for the commodity. _____ (3)

6. On the other hand, a low demand **decreases** the price of a product.
   _____ (29)

7. Production is then **deflected** into other, more valuable areas.
   _____ (13)

8. Thus **competing** businesses are always adjusting according to market demand. _____ (25)

9. If the supply **exceeds** demand in some markets, production changes quickly. _____ (20)

10. Businesses are no longer properly **remunerated.** _____ (5)

11. The **return** for their investments is not as high as it should be.
    _____ (19)

12. As a result, they have their **employees** work in other areas to produce more profitable products. _____ (28)

13. Long-term **declines** in production are not good for businesses or governments. _____ (22)

14. **Income** for businesses and workers goes down. _____ (4)

15. The government suffers because it is **financed** by the **taxes** it collects.
    _____ (31) _____ (15)

16. A decline in income and a decline in taxes **go hand in hand.**
    _____ (24)

17. Because the market is so complicated, businesses often **enlist** marketing specialists who study the situation and make predictions.
_____ (32)

18. If these specialists **manage to** foresee directions accurately, businesses can make a lot of money very quickly. _____ (6)

19. There is considerable debate over whether such an economic system operates with **evenhandedness** insofar as individuals are concerned.
_____ (10)

20. Let's take as an example a person who is **situated** on a farm that produces potatoes. _____ (21)

21. The amount of work he does one year **matches** the amount of work he does the next. _____ (17)

22. Let's say that the market one year climbs **precipitously** and the farmer makes a lot of money. _____ (11)

23. The market for potatoes then changes in the **reverse** direction.
_____ (7)

24. This change proves to be more **enduring** than anyone expects.
_____ (30)

25. The farmer uses the savings that he **accumulated** during the good year until they are **drained.** _____ (2) _____ (18)

26. He begins to **sacrifice** in his personal life in order to save money.
_____ (8)

27. One day he finds that he has used up all of the money **at his disposal.**
_____ (1)

28. The market for potatoes, in the meanwhile, remains **inert.**
_____ (35)

29. His **debts** begin to rise. _____ (9)

30. He reaches a point where he cannot make **restitution** for the **claims** against him. _____ (33) _____ (23)

31. Because he lacks the funds necessary to make the required **transactions,** his farming operation is **disabled.** _____ (36)
_____ (12)

32. He may be able to recover by obtaining federal **subsidies** until the market changes, but he also might be forced to go out of business even though he has worked very hard. _____ (16)

EXERCISE 14

Below each puzzle is a list of related words. Write the keyword for each related word in the appropriate squares. After you have written in all of the keywords for one puzzle, read the word in the circles going down. This will be a related word for the first keyword in the *next* puzzle. The numbers in parentheses can be used to check your answers, but try to complete the puzzle without them.

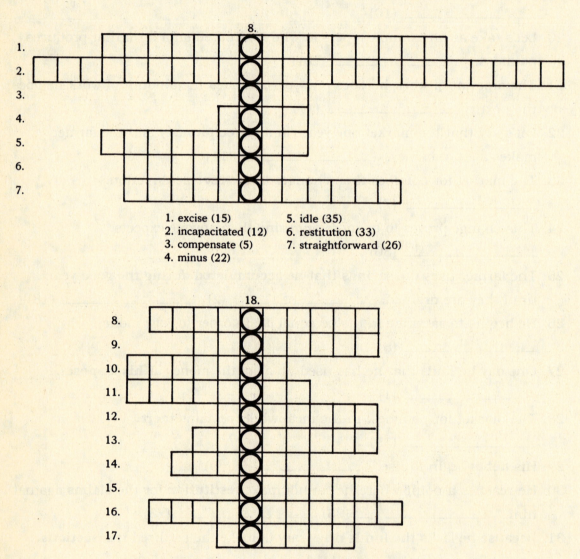

1. excise (15)
2. incapacitated (12)
3. compensate (5)
4. minus (22)
5. idle (35)
6. restitution (33)
7. straightforward (26)

8. SEE PREVIOUS PUZZLE (32)
9. astern (7)
10. accumulate (2)
11. justice (10)
12. utilization (14)
13. establishment (34)
14. mirror (17)
15. escort (24)
16. sturdy (30)
17. declaration (23)

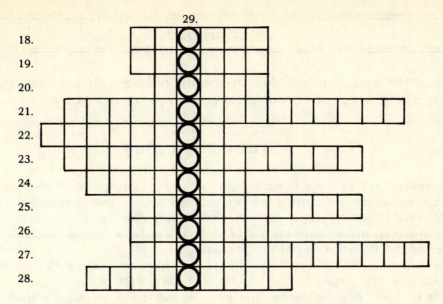

18. SEE PREVIOUS PUZZLE (1)   24. achieve (6)
19. laborer (28)   25. better (20)
20. outlay (27)   26. consumed (18)
21. take (19)   27. dividend (4)
22. opposing (25)   28. give up (8)
23. uphill (11)

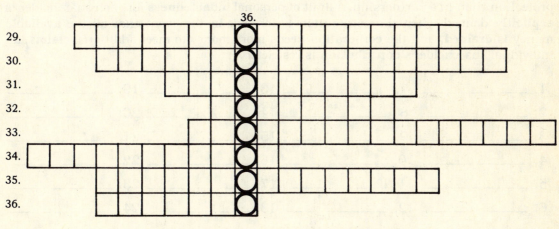

29. SEE PREVIOUS PUZZLE (36)   33. swerve (13)
30. scholarship (16)   34. in line with (3)
31. debt (9)   35. endow (31)
32. remove (29)   36. SEE THIS PUZZLE (21)

EXERCISE 15

Some of the words in the following reading passages are in heavy type. Read the passages and write the keywords for each in the blanks below.

THE CORPORATION

A corporation is one type of **enterprise** that allows many people to combine their wealth into a single area. The corporation is created by a state document called a charter. This charter establishes the corporation as a legal "person" separate from its owners. The **firm** itself, then, can make **contracts** and other business **deals** without involving the individuals personally. It also must pay its own **taxes.**

The owners receive shares of the corporation **in consonance with** their investment in the business. They then receive a portion of the **profits** of the corporation that **corresponds** to the number of shares they own. So the size of an owner's **dividend** each year depends upon how many shares that person owns and how much the **company's income surpassed** its expenses.

The **value** of the shares themselves can also change. If the corporation is successful, the shares can **accrue** in value very quickly; if, on the other hand, there is a **sharp decline** in a corporation's business, the value of the shares will also be **decreased.**

Since a corporation is a "person," the people who **underwrite** it are able to have more protection than in a partnership. A limit of personal **indebtedness** for each shareholder is **explicitly** defined when the corporation is formed. In the event that all the **available** money is **drained,** and the corporation needs more money to meet additional **claims,** an individual shareholder's **contribution** is restricted.

1. _____   7. _____   13. _____   19. _____

2. _____   8. _____   14. _____   20. _____

3. _____   9. _____   15. _____   21. _____

4. _____   10. _____   16. _____   22. _____

5. _____   11. _____   17. _____   23. _____

6. _____   12. _____   18. _____   24. _____

ECONOMIC DECISIONS IN BUSINESS

Productive capacity is the amount of production possible when a factory **manages to** operate at maximum efficiency. Operating rate is the ratio between actual output and productive capacity. These two figures are very important when deciding future investments.

Let's imagine a factory that is **lodged** in an old building in the northern United States. The buyer's reactions to this factory's products were **passive** for several years, and the economy, rather than improving, went in the **reverse** direction. Suddenly this factory begins to make a very **durable** product that becomes extremely popular. Management **employs** more **hired hands,** but it soon becomes obvious that the factory's productive capacity cannot keep up with demand.

Management must make a difficult decision. Should they **divert** the necessary funds to purchase new machinery? Is it wise to **part with** the money at this time? Will the factory's operation be **handicapped** if they do not buy the machinery? Will **rival** companies get a large share of the market if productive capacity is not increased? Will the increase in productive capacity **reimburse** the company for the cost of the new machinery? Will the operating rate remain high? If not, then **expending** the funds would be foolish.

All of these questions, and many others, must be answered with thoroughness and **impartiality** if management wishes to make a wise decision. Since private companies in the United States cannot depend on public **donations** or federal **stipends,** management must analyze every aspect carefully. Such analyses often **usher** in long-range success for a company. Failure to perform such analyses may very easily result in disaster.

1. _____   6. _____   10. _____   14. _____
2. _____   7. _____   11. _____   15. _____
3. _____   8. _____   12. _____   16. _____
4. _____   9. _____   13. _____   17. _____
5. _____

EXERCISE 16

Read the following articles. Do *not* use a dictionary. At least one related word from each of the keyword groups is in these articles. Try to remember the proper keywords as you read.

Prereading Introduction

Every government of every country has ways to receive the funds necessary for its operation. Many countries in the world collect money through taxation. The process of taxation raises several questions, however, including how to tax all portions of the population fairly.

The following article deals with the question of fairness of taxes. The article discusses approaches based on two main philosophies: taxation according to usage of government services and taxation according to how much one earns. The article concludes with a discussion of whether taxes should be a constant percentage of one's income or whether the percentage should increase as income increases.

After reading the article, you should answer the following questions:

1. What are the two aspects that comprise fairness in taxation, according to this article?
2. In this country, some taxes are collected mainly from those who receive the government services. An excise tax on gasoline is an example of this type of taxation. Explain why this is true.
3. Can you think of another example, in the United States or any other country, that the author does not mention?

4. Why is it not possible to base all taxes on the benefit principle?

5. Explain what the author means in the following sentence: "The more income a family receives, the lower the priority of items it would have to sacrifice in paying taxes."

6. What are "progressive taxes"?

7. Which do you think is fairer—a proportional tax or a progressive tax? What are the advantages of each?

8. Is a regressive tax fair? Where does it exist in the United States? Could the system be changed to make all taxes progressive?

9. While most people agree with the concept of progressive taxation, there is widespread disagreement about the rate of progression. What is the danger (from an economic point of view) of taxes that rise too steeply?

FAIRNESS OF TAXES*

Our ideas about what makes a tax "fair" or "just" extend in two different directions. On the one hand, we feel that when certain people obtain specific benefits from government service, they should pay in proportion to the benefits received. On the other hand, we also feel that the burden of community-wide services should be shouldered according to ability to pay.

Taxation on the Benefit Principle. The *benefit principle* implies that taxes should be so assigned that those who benefit most from government service pay the most taxes. This principle represents a logical extension of the idea of market price to government services. That is, when benefits to particular people can be identified, those people should be compelled to pay, just as they would in a private transaction. Since the biggest users of highways buy the most gasoline, financing highway maintenance by an excise tax on gasoline agrees with the benefit principle, as does the application of a property tax to defray the cost of fire protection.

Taxation in Proportion to Ability to Pay. There are, however, obvious limitations to the benefit principle as a general basis for taxation. The benefits of some governmental services are so broadly diffused that it is impossible to measure how much accrues to any particular person. Moreover, even when they are identifiable and measureable, substantial benefits often accrue to people unable to afford them. This is most clearly the case of transfers and welfare services for the poor. Indeed, the very purpose of hot-lunch programs in schools, welfare payments to the disabled, and social welfare agencies is to provide income and services to people who could not obtain them otherwise.

An alternative to taxation on the basis of benefit received is that each taxpayer be required to contribute in proportion to his ability to pay. The more income a family receives, the lower the priority of the items it would have to sacrifice in paying taxes. Poor families who need all their income for high-priority essentials can often afford only an inadequate diet, and the cost of taxation for them would be greater hunger. Rich families, on the other hand, pay their taxes with income that might otherwise be spent to satisfy trivial whims.[a]

It follows that people with higher incomes should pay more taxes than similarly situated people with lower income, but the important question is *how much* more? If a total of $3,000 in taxes is to be collected from two families, one with income of $10,000, the other with $20,000, how should the tax be apportioned? Should the low-income family pay $1,200 and the other $1,800? Should the tax be divided $1,000–$2,000, or $800–$2,200, or how?

---

*From pp. 218–19 in *Principles of Economics* by Daniel B. Suits. Copyright © 1970 by Daniel B. Suits. Reprinted by permission of Harper & Row, Publishers, Inc.

The Need for Progressive Taxes. To help analyze this problem, taxes are classified according to the ratio of tax liability to income. A *proportional tax* is one for which the ratio is the same at all levels of income. In the example above, the tax that would divide the liability $1,000–$2,000 would represent a proportional tax, because it would take 10 percent of the income of both families. Under a *regressive tax* the ratio of tax liability to income is smaller for higher than it is for lower incomes, and although families with lower incomes usually pay less total tax than those with higher incomes, the tax represents a larger fraction of their income. In the example above, the tax that would collect $1,200 from the $10,000 income and $1,800 from the $20,000 income would be a regressive tax. The liability of the low-income family would be $1,200/$10,000, or 12 percent of its income, while the higher income family would pay only $1,800/$20,000, or 9 percent.

A retail sales tax on food is regressive because the proportion of family income spent on food tends to decline as income rises. Since the average food budget is about one-third of a $3,000 family income but only about 20 percent of a $10,000 income, a 4 percent tax on food purchases takes 1.33 percent of the lower but only 0.8 percent of the higher income.

A *progressive tax* is one for which the ratio of tax liability to income rises with income. Not only do lower-income families pay less tax, but the tax liability is a smaller fraction of their income than it is for higher-income families. The $800–$2,200 division of liability would represent a progressive tax, since the liability would be $800/$10,000, or 8 percent of the lower income, but $2,200/$20,000, or 11 percent of the higher.

Since families with higher incomes have more than proportionally greater ability to pay, it is generally agreed that a fair tax system should be progressive, but it is not clear how steeply progressive it should be. A progressive tax that collects 10 percent of a $10,000 income must collect more than 10 percent from an income of $20,000. But should it collect 11 percent, 40 percent or how much? There is no simple answer to this question, although there is clearly an upper limit. Taxes should never be so steeply progressive that their payment leaves a higher-income family with less disposable income than a similar family that started with a lower income before taxes. Put another way, a family that manages to raise its own income must always be permitted to keep some of the additional receipts. This is not only justice, but is also an important economic incentive.

Note

[a]whims: temporary desires; things that are wanted for a short period of time.

Prereading Introduction

Usually when we think of the word "rent," we think of money that we pay a landlord for an apartment or money we pay a store to use furniture or other equipment temporarily. In economic terms, however, the term "rent" takes on a broader meaning.

The following article discusses rent from an economic point of view. The author explains what rent means and how it affects economics, to include its role in determining income.

After reading this article, you should answer the following questions:

1. In economic philosophy, are we truly renting when we rent a car? An apartment? Why or why not?
2. What single factor determines whether or not rent is a part of a person's income?

3. Give an example of rent in economic terminology.
4. How do economists determine the amount of rent?
5. Do you agree that this concept of rent should be added to a person's income? Discuss.

THE SOURCE OF RENT*

Rent as a Component of Income. Like so many words, the term "rent" has several different meanings. In ordinary popular usage, it means payment for the temporary use of anything that one does not own himself. A family "rents" an apartment, a vacationer "rents" an automobile, a farmer "rents" a field. In technical economics, the term is narrower in one sense and broader in another. Economic usage is narrower in that the term "rent" is restricted to income derived from the services of land and other natural resources whose supply is naturally fixed. In this sense, the farmer's payment for a field is an example of economic rent. The land was put there by nature and will remain, regardless of human needs. It will not increase or decrease in response to demand for it. The economic question is purely how to use it. We can plant it, erect a building on it, build a road over it, or even leave it idle, but we have no control over how much there is of it.

Payment for the use of houses is rent only to the extent that it covers the services of the lots they stand on. No economic rent at all is involved in hiring an automobile. Houses and automobiles are not fixed in amount. The economic question is not only who will get the use of the existing units, but how many new units to make and how large a stock to maintain.[1]

Rent appears as an explicit payment when a landowner rents or leases the services of his land to somebody else, but since most land is used by the owner in his own business, most rent is received as an implicit part of the owner's residual income. For example, part of the income of a farmer who cultivates his own land is attributable to rent. Likewise the "profits" of an oil or coal producer consist very largely of rent from the ownership of wells or mines. Under these circumstances the rent of a piece of land is defined as the annual amount that a would-be user would pay for its services on a competitive market. In other words, the part of a farmer's income that can be attributed to rent is the amount his own land would cost him annually if he rented or leased it from somebody else at competitive prices.

---

[1] Since it takes time to alter the stocks of buildings or durable equipment, these are virtually fixed within any short period. For this reason, the short-run behavior of returns for their services has many of the properties of economic rent, and is often called "quasi rent."

Prereading Introduction

On the surface, it seems like a fairly simple problem to analyze a nation's income: one must simply calculate how much each person makes and total it all up. However, there are many complex questions that must be answered and terms that must be defined before national income can be determined. The following article is a discussion of some of the issues relating to this surprisingly complicated process.

After reading this article, you should answer the following questions:

1. What are some of the ways that income gets passed around from person to person?

2. What is the national income of a country? Why is it never the same as the total amount produced by a country (the gross national product)?
3. What is depreciation? Why is it subtracted from gross national product?
4. What is the purpose of taxes on businesses?
5. What was used to exemplify subsidies that must be deducted from gross national products? Can you think of another example?
6. Give some examples of what this author calls business transfer payments.

THE STRUCTURE OF INCOME*

An analysis of the distribution of income must take into account the fact that a given dollar of income sometimes passes through several different hands before it reaches a final recipient who can spend it. For example, when corporate profits are passed on to individual business owners as dividends, the owners are required to turn over a share of them to the government in the form of income taxes. Or as another example, social security contributions deducted from the paycheck of an employed worker are transferred by the government to a retired worker as a social security pension.

National Income.   National income is the total compensation paid for the services of labor and productive property employed in turning out the gross national product. It includes all receipts of wages and salaries, rents, interest, incomes of proprietors and professionals, and corporate profits before any of these are subdivided with the government by payment of personal taxes or taxes on corporate income.

The difference between national income and the total value of the gross national product consists of four types of claims against output that do not correspond to income payments for currently supplied productive services.

1. *Depreciation* or *capital consumption allowances*, as we have already seen, are not income, but represent compensation of owners for the value of property worn out in the process of production.

2. *Indirect business taxes* are legal claims asserted in the form of sales taxes and similar charges to divert revenue to the government. They are not accompanied by any corresponding productive service, but merely raise the market prices of final products above the cost of production.

3. *Subsidies less surpluses of government enterprises* are, in a sense, the opposite of indirect business taxes. When a government enterprise like the post office sells its services to the public at a loss, payments for the services of mail carriers and others exceed value added. Therefore, the subsidy needed to cover the loss must be added to the value of the output to arrive at national income.

4. *Business transfer payments* consist of pensions, sick pay, and similar payments made by business firms to employees who were not on the job. Also included are such items as prizes paid to customers who win advertising games and contests, scholarships, donations, and similar contributions unconnected with current production.

*From pp. 447–48 in *Principles of Economics* by Daniel B. Suits. Copyright © 1970 by Daniel B. Suits. Reprinted by permission of Harper & Row, Publishers, Inc.

EXERCISE 17

The following exercises show how different word forms are derived in English. Try to remember the endings and what parts of speech they indicate.

A. Words that end in *-ory* are usually adjectives:

> **Example:**   compensate → compensatory

Put the letter of the correct keyword in the blank after each derived word. Some keywords are used more than one time:

a. unreality   b. expect   c. make peace   d. order

1. anticipate → anticipatory ____
2. The belief that he could become president soon proved to be **illusory.** ____
3. After the war had continued for more than two years, one of the countries removed some of its soldiers in a **conciliatory** move. ____
4. Eating certain mushrooms produces a **hallucinatory** effect. ____
5. I didn't want to take any mathematics, but the course was **mandatory.** ____

B. *Dis-* added to the beginning of a word usually changes the meaning to its opposite:

> **Example:**   assemble → disassemble (opposite of assemble—to take apart)

a. following the rules   b. likely to   c. declare   d. faithfulness
e. join

1. unite → disunite ____
2. The man **disavowed** having any connection with the people who had robbed the bank. ____
3. Because of the child's **disobedience,** the mother had to go to school and talk with his teachers. ____
4. Since it was hot outside, I was **disinclined to** work in the yard. ____
5. In some countries, people are shot if they are suspected of **disloyalty.** ____

C. *Mis-* added to the beginning of a word usually means "in error," or *mis*take:

> **Example:**   justice → misjustice (mistake in justice)

a. declare   b. be like   c. make clear   d. control

1. interpret → misinterpret ____
2. The business failed because the president **mismanaged** the funds. ____

3. The ambassador **misstated** his country's position on the sensitive issue. ____

4. The husband and wife were obviously **mismatched:** they fought constantly. ____

5. Because the president **misgoverned** the country, it suffered economic collapse. ____

In summary:

1. *Dis-* added to the beginning of a word changes its meaning to _____.

2. *Mis-* added to the beginning of a word changes its meaning to _____.

3. Words that end in *-ory* are usually _____.

D. *Review*. Listed below are the beginnings and endings of words that we have
studied. Put each one in its proper category.

un-	-ize	in-	dis-	-ful
-ory	-ly	-(i/u)al	-ant/-ent	-ive
-ity	-ness	-tion/-sion	-(i)ous	mis-
non-	-ment	-ic	-ate	
-er/-or	-ify	-ance/-ence	-able	

Noun	*Verb*	*Adjective*	*Opposite*	*Adverb*
____	____	____	____	____
____	____	____	____	
____	____	____	____	
____		____	____	
____		____	____	
		____		
		____		

E. *Review*. Put the letter of the correct keyword in the blank after each sentence.
All the derivations in this exercise come from Chapter 9.

a. fairness   b. rising quickly   c. economic assistance   d. succeed
e. unmistakable   f. change directions (of)   g. be with
h. money after costs

1. The effectiveness of a company is usually measured by how **profitable** it
is. ____

2. After the long and difficult strike, the **triumphant** workers returned to their
jobs. ____

3. The accident was caused by a **deflection** of the sun's rays off a mirror into the eyes of the driver. ____

4. The road went up so **steeply** that heavy trucks were advised to take an alternate route to the city. ____

5. The soldiers paraded through the street to the **accompaniment** of music played over loudspeakers. ____

6. The children were told **explicitly** not to play near the pool. ____

7. In a court of law, the judge must be absolutely **impartial.** ____

8. In order to provide more equal opportunity, the federal government decided to **subsidize** education in each state. ____

a. loss   b. not active   c. be like   d. business agreement
e. subtract (from)   f. do without   g. unmistakable   h. give a job to

1. The **contractual** arrangements took several months to complete. ____

2. Most insurance policies specify a certain amount of money that is **deductible** from the amount the company is to pay. ____

3. Tourists are not allowed into the area for an **indefinite** amount of time because of the volcanic activity. ____

4. The people in the neighborhood were opposed to the construction of apartments nearby because they feared that these buildings would have a **depreciatory** effect on the value of their land. ____

5. **Employers** must be careful not to create an environment that is dangerous or unhealthy. ____

6. It is certainly wrong to assume that a person is a **loafer** just because he or she does not have a job. ____

7. The police assumed that the same person had committed both crimes because of the close **resemblance** between them. ____

8. The **sacrificial** lamb was very carefully selected. ____

Keyword Index

Keywords are listed in heavy type. The first number is the chapter number; the second number is the keyword number.